Architecture & Sensuality

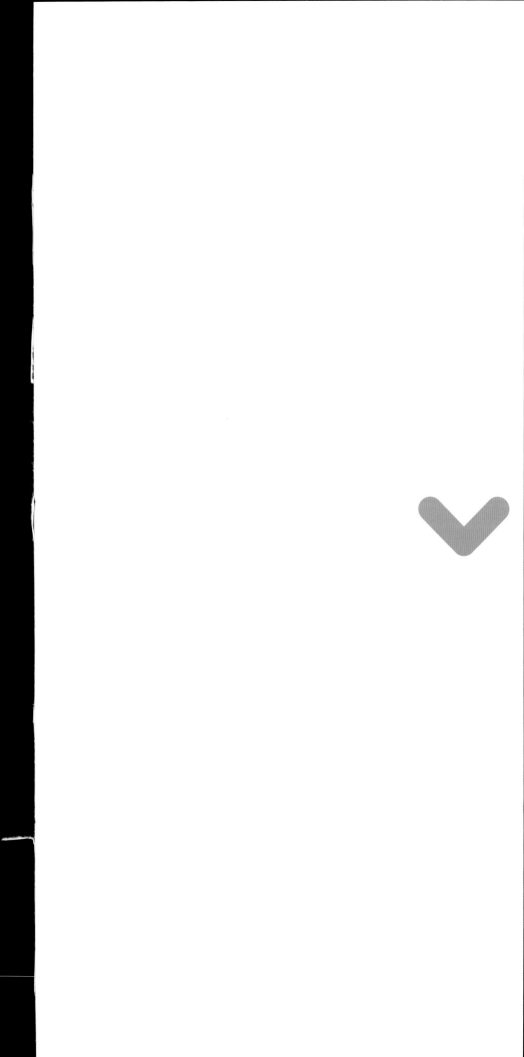

# Architecture & Sensuality

Andrew Bromberg of Aedas Recent Works

Text by:

Foreword **Larry Rouch**
Essay **Rodolphe el-Khoury**
Interview with **Michael Speaks**

ORO *editions*

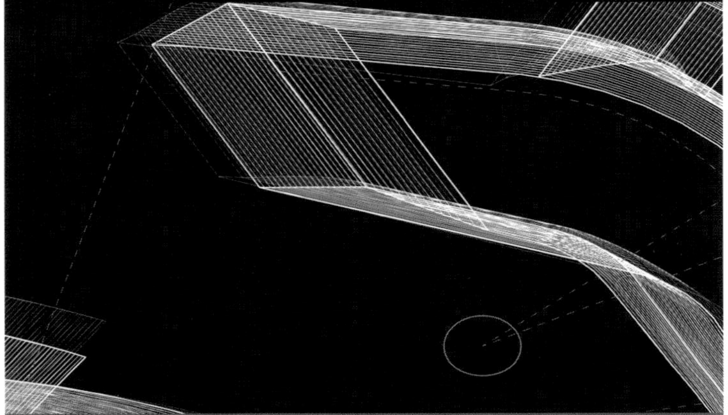



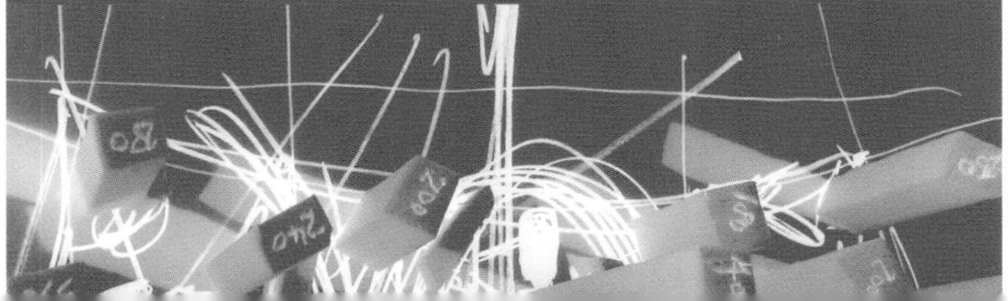

# Contents

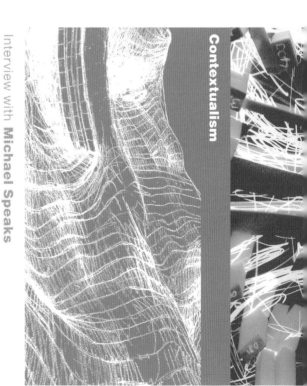

800

Foreword
**Larry Rouch**

Foreword
**Larry Rouch**

Sketches for West Kowloon Cultural District

This monograph presents many of the fantastical projects that Andrew Bromberg has recently designed in areas of the world ranging from the Persian Gulf to the Yellow Sea. As the reader will see, the scope, scale, and geographic distribution of the projects are astonishing, though it's the pace of their development that's unprecedented. To meet demand, the gestation of many of these projects occurred over days or weeks rather than months.

In the past four years, Andrew's projects have included the award-winning finalist submission for the West Kowloon Cultural District Competition (US$5B, pending) and several high-rise residential and office towers in the United Arab Emirates, including one that will be 618 meters high. Eleven of his projects are under construction or are scheduled to be under construction in the near future. In the aggregate, his projects account for millions of square meters of development, including some of the tallest and largest projects that have ever been commissioned.

Work of this magnitude could only have occurred in contemporary Asia, where several economies recently leapt from pre-modern to post-modern status through strategically leveraging their manufacturing, petroleum, or intellectual resources in global markets. The rampant cumulative growth of these economies has tilted the world's economic center of gravity to the East.

Within these economies, including the People's Republic of China, an entrepreneurial class has emerged that has accumulated massive fortunes unimaginably quickly. The economic strength and capitalistic vigor of these entrepreneurs have accelerated the development of purpose-built and speculative buildings at a rate and scale that would be inconceivable in the West. The truck farmer who once sold sunglasses in a Beijing alley with the tacit blessing of Deng-Xiaoping may be the same man who advanced to produce a significant percentage of the designer sunglasses manufactured worldwide. In turn, his offspring are likely to have leveraged their filial wealth into enterprises that extend well beyond labor-based manufacturing.

In 2008, Beijing will host the Summer Olympics, marking China's formal debut on the world stage. In the deserts of Abu Dhabi and Dubai, 21st-century cities have erupted where mud-brick huts were recently common. We are witnessing the long anticipated ascension of the wild, wild East.

This maelstrom of development has seduced legions of architects, engineers, construction managers, contractors, and laborers into decamping to this new frontier. Andrew Bromberg's employer, Aedas, positioned itself to play a prime role there. With 1,600 architectural employees in 26 offices on 3 continents, Aedas has become a top player in architectural services globally, but especially in Asia. Over half of the staff of Aedas is in Asia, with two-thirds of that total in the Hong

Kong office. Andrew Bromberg found employment in the Hong Kong office in 2002, but soon thereafter was promoted to Executive Director, in charge of all of the firm's design in Asia and the Middle East.

I've known Andrew since he entered my graduate design studio at the University of Washington in Seattle, in 1992. What distinguished him from other students was his relentless appetite for criticism. Like an untempered blade, Andrew sought the fire and the hammer ceaselessly. Although he was more ambitious than any student I've ever encountered, his ambitions were indisputably and sincerely centered on refining his architecture rather than on aggrandizing his career. He was and is an unusual but endearing mixture of hubris and humility.

It's easy to imagine that Andrew's move to Hong Kong was kismet, although I know that it was motivated by a quest for adventure as much as it was by a desire for opportunity. His arrival at Aedas may have been fated, because in order for Aedas to compete in Asia as a premier design firm, they needed a prodigiously talented and fearless lead designer; and in order for Andrew to be effective there to the level of his expectations, he needed a supportive and broadly capable professional sponsor, which Aedas willingly became.

The initial results of the collaboration between Aedas and Andrew Bromberg are chronicled in this book. The work is comprehensively

As attested in this monograph, Andrew's work for Aedas has been widely awarded and acclaimed. More importantly, clients of the firm have commissioned the work with enthusiasm. To date, though, the projects illustrated here exist only as prospectuses, although renderings and plans are in the process of becoming buildings. In order for Andrew to mature as a designer, he must see these projects through the gauntlet of practical obstacles that threaten to strip any architectural work of its most salient attributes. Andrew and I share the opinion that architecture can only be judged in situ. To be persuaded that Andrew has finally mastered his architecture, I'll need to see these buildings artfully sustaining the rhythms of their inhabitants and enhancing the mundane routines of the cities that they were designed for.

It's clear that Andrew has become extremely adept at responding to sites and programs that might be deemed unfeasible or at least impractical for development elsewhere. He credits much of his facility for successfully "challenging conventions" to the ace structural, mechanical, and curtain-wall engineers and other consultants that Aedas mobilizes to help resolve the work. In order for Andrew to perform at his level, these experts are critical to the development of the work. They deserve acknowledgement. If the skin of "The Legs" in Abu Dhabi can be made to work as conceived and rendered, the engineers responsible will be acclaimed as geniuses. Who are they?

presented. In addition, Michael Speaks' interview of Andrew in Hong Kong afforded Andrew the opportunity to comment personally about the work that he and Aedas have produced in the phantasmagoric world where they work. In another essay, Rodolphe el-Khoury has assessed the projects and the circumstances of their development with wit, imagination and keen insight. For my part, I'd like to make a few observations from the vantage point of being Andy's friend and occasional didactic counselor for the past 15 years.

First, it's nearly impossible to comprehend the level of emotional and physical stamina that's been required to produce the work chronicled here. It seems to me that few architects would subject themselves to the withering demands of this work, and fewer still would persevere in the face of it and thrive. Despite having a game and dedicated staff that can avail itself of the substantial resources of the larger Hong Kong office, Andrew inevitably carries the burden of the work. Combined with the dizzying travel requirements of his position, Andrew risks becoming one of those pan-zonal professionals who calls a business-class seat and a Blackberry home. For example, via Blackberry Andrew recently described making a midnight presentation in Kazakhstan so that he could catch a 3:00 AM flight to Hong Kong! This kind of pace can't be sustained without the work and its author eventually being diminished. I wonder how Andrew and Aedas might parlay today's collaborative momentum into long-term viability?

The projects that intrigue me most are those that have tectonic, civic, or cultural attributes at their core, in addition to being formally inventive. With the resources that designers have at their disposal these days, any form can be conceived—and with a sufficient budget, it can also be built—so the temptation to vary building form is common. In my view, though, architects who design principally on the basis of formal invention debase their buildings by encouraging them to be assessed as objects about which one may simply say, "I like them" or "I don't." This stretches the Vitruvian dictum of delight to a farcical and counterproductive level. Many architects feel the need to do this because their commissions often have no intrinsic content other than their responsibility to perform well as commodities in a market economy.

Andrew has steadfastly tried to avoid this by working beyond the rudiments of the programs for his projects. I know that he acutely feels the need to find or create added value, especially in his speculative residential and office projects. This is a dilemma that Andrew and Aedas have faced numerous times. They yearn to be engaged in architecture that more frequently transcends the exigencies of competitive markets. They've succeeded in projects such as the aforementioned "Legs," where structural, sensual, and tectonic expressions are artfully merged, thus strongly distinguishing this project from others in which relatively standard aluminum and glass curtain walls are employed. The West Kowloon Cultural District Competition program was so heavily

imbued with civic and urban objectives that it begged for a response substantially outside the norm. Andrew's proposal vertiginously entwines the program elements into what would be an enthrallingly urbane respite from Hong Kong's chaotic density. Site planning for the Xian Residential Project is lyrical. Traces of an abandoned munitions depot and the rail lines that served it are intertwined with new low-rise housing. Finally, the Arabian Performance Venue may be the best summation of Andrew's current abilities and aspirations. Attributes that appear in other projects—the sinuous "stems," the vast open-air promenades, the cultural facilities, the elevated domains, and the porosity—are in this project in concert. This is the project that Andrew should strive to construct most of all.

Aedas is an unabashedly commercial architecture practice, although the actual scope of the firm's work is broader. Andrew's projects emanate from the most vigorously speculative arena of building development that the world has ever witnessed. How may they secure more work that lends itself to substantive design and interpretation? One hopes they'll find a way, if only because the formidable capabilities of these partners deserve to be tested on a more fundamental basis. Andrew will need it to remain engaged in the game. In the meantime he will surely continue to search for all that can possibly be right and good about his work and its role in the personal, social, and civic lives of the people that his projects house and the cities that they inhabit.

It's been a pleasure to engage Andrew for the past 15 years while he's evolved from grad student to "power" practitioner. I'm honored that Andrew occasionally seeks my counsel. I'll put the fire and hammer to his work as long as he relishes it, but he's certainly no longer an untempered blade. He has the talent and aptitude to take on any architectural commission conceivable.

Biography

**LARRY ROUCH** (MArch Univ. of Washington, Seattle) established Larry Rouch Co. in Seattle after producing large commercial and public projects for other firms. The firm has designed notable residences and commercial and interior projects throughout the Western United States, including the 55,000 square foot San Francisco exhibition: "Toshimitsu Imäi -- Ka Cho Fu Getsu." Larry Rouch Company projects have been featured in publications including: *Architectural Record, Progressive Architecture, ID Annual Design Review, Interiors, Ottagono* (Italy) and *Worldspace Design* (Japan). Larry also has taught graduate design at the University of Washington and SCI-ARC, and has been a guest instructor or critic at Otis College of Art & Design, the University of British Columbia, Tulane University, Columbia University, California College of Arts and Crafts, Washington State University, the University of Idaho and the University of Oregon.

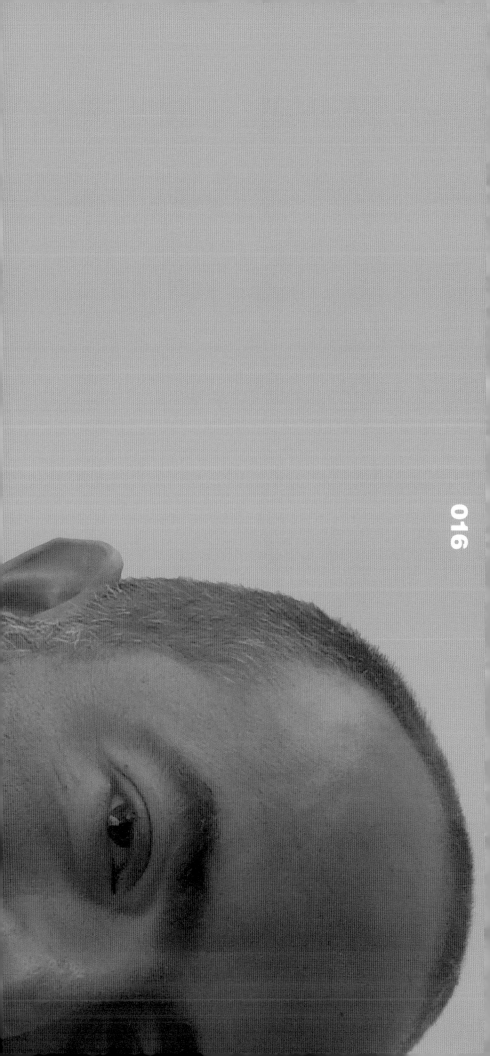

016

# Rodolphe el-Khoury

# Smart Figure/Sensible Ground
The Architecture of Andrew Bromberg

## Rodolphe el-Khoury

Andrew Bromberg's West Kowloon development, as a case study of his work, is an urban environment with multiple levels of commercial and public facilities that only metropolitan urban cores like Hong Kong's could sustain with the vertical density and consistent intensity suggested in the renderings. The dominant architectural element is a colossal modular canopy supported on tree-like pillars and extended repetitively over 40 hectares. It shelters a densely packed cityscape arranged in an intricate pattern of interlocking building blocks and spaces. This urban scenario is presented among more or less familiar features: an archipelago of suspended gardens with unobstructed views of the city; a network of public walkways and shops stacked on several levels above a complex of performance venues; and, towering above the layered landscape, a collection of high-rise buildings of varying sizes and shapes.

From a bird's-eye view the whole development stands out as a distinct, branded artifact against the competing patterns of adjacent districts. The strong identity is due to a unique formal language that is consistent in plan and elevation. It would be instantly recognizable in the Hong Kong skyline, as easily as in the satellite imaging of a GoogleEarth search. In the close-up views we see a media-saturated environment with activities staged on every level. Throughout the project and at all scales the plans call for extraordinary architectural means to orchestrate shopping, entertainment, and leisure into a spectacle of urban life designed to stimulate the senses as much as commerce.

This is a photogenic architecture that is very much attuned to the demands of the market. The economics and spatial logic of retail, entertainment, and real-estate development have been assimilated into the design intelligence that guides every move. Ostensibly free-flowing lines and whimsically shaped volumes are informed by pro-forms, market analyses, and demographic studies. They are engineered for optimal views, optimal exposure, optimal accessibility, optimal capacity, and optimal variety.

The mercantile framework also accounts for the bold formal moves that seem to elude any overt utilitarian logic. They are valued for their capacity to reinforce the brand with distinctive features. Even the atmospherics are subjected to the demands of the market: colors, mood, and ambiance are mobilized in delivering the memorable experience that would give this development a competitive edge in the new economy.

Bromberg's architecture is conditioned under enormous financial pressure by market imperatives. But what sets it apart from the overwhelming majority of commercial-building projects is its unrelenting capacity to escape the commonplace. At every opportunity it reaches into the unknown with unprecedented propositions in lieu of the tried and tested solution that risk-avoiding speculation continues to favor.

And with every risky move comes a great deal of innovation and ingenuity. The new architectural forms are thrilling. But equally inventive—and rewarding—are the means, techniques, and processes that the architects devise to translate the bold new vision into a buildable and viable proposition.

Bromberg's is a commercial architecture that is motivated by private interests. It is, nevertheless, setting a new standard for what is possible in the field. Not only is it pushing the envelope in terms of form and building technology—it is also reshaping the public realm with a civic ambition that had been primarily reserved for buildings with more overt public mandates and institutional sponsorship.

For a critical establishment in architecture that is accustomed to valorizing artisanally crafted and highly customized buildings for high-profile clients and institutions, the notion that commercial architecture like Aedas' should be leading the field in design innovation may be a difficult, if not surprising, proposition. But few would doubt the innovative resourcefulness of market-driven practices in other fields. Compare, for instance, a consumer product such as a Ducati motorcycle to a masterfully customized chopper. I can safely assume that anyone who is remotely invested in design would favor the Ducati—we are not comparing performance, where the crushing superiority of a Ducati would be an objective and quantifiable fact. However seductive

Ducati Monster Motorcycle

**072**
**Abu Dhabi Dancing Towers**

in attracting increasingly sophisticated Wallpaper magazine-trained buyers. If there was one single critical quality that distinguished Bromberg among other talented designers in rival commercial offices, it would have to be the knack for nailing down the extraordinary form that never fails to sell his signature buildings.

His staple forms are vaguely figurative but not literal. They are strangely evocative of familiar yet unknown things. Occasionally, they approximate anthropomorphic or zoomorphic shapes while remaining somehow abstract. They are never reducible to a single reading, leaving the viewer guessing as to the intended meaning or references. Some acquire monikers that unfortunately tend to narrow down the interpretive options, fixing the semantic fluidity perhaps too prematurely.

Anthropomorphic references are common in journalistic accounts of Bromberg's architecture. The interplay of masses in Dancing Towers, a commercial development in Abu Dhabi featuring two high-rise buildings, is, for instance, inevitably likened to the notion of a ballet. The slabs in question are strictly non-figurative. The ballet connotation is entirely due to the complexity of the composition, to an intricacy in the interplay of actions and reactions between two responsive forms. The sense of responsiveness is what facilitates or even encourages the anthropocentric projection of effect. In Dancing Tower's form we see

the originality of style, the artistry of construction, the impeccable finishes, and the exquisite craftsmanship, the chopper will be found lacking in the rigor and discipline that a precisely calibrated consumer product demonstrates. Granted, in the context of industrial design, the comparison is rather unfair given disciplinary prejudice in favor of mass-produced products. But the analogy is relevant insofar as it exposes architecture's own prejudice. The fact that architectural critics tend to privilege the precisely tailored, thoroughly customized, exquisitely detailed, and lavishly produced one-off designs over the streamlined commercial products is a reality that begs further critical scrutiny. It is bound to reveal a reactionary, hard core within the architecture discipline.

## Complex Beings

The search for the iconic form that would sell the project in a highly competitive global market is perhaps the most potent force that drives Bromberg's architecture. In a place like Dubai, where every building stridently proclaims its unique identity, superlatives—tallest building, largest units, highest ceilings—were all it took only a few years ago, to sell property. Far more extraordinary attributes are now required

a dancer's posture; in another twin-tower proposal we see legs and even a hint of eroticism.

How do Bromberg's strange forms provoke such empathy, allowing us to imagine a gesture or an embrace in place of objects in space? How does abstract geometry become virtually figurative? Bromberg states that he "looks for soul", this remark has to be taken more literally beyond the cliché that attributes a spiritual character to architectural essences. The soul, or animus, is what animates objects—that breathes life, so to speak, into form.

Bromberg doesn't shape his buildings freely, as if from readily malleable clay. The masses he works with are always already buildings, complex organizational and material propositions that he works into new configuration by means of design. Every move he makes is considered with respect to the repercussions it would have on program, structure, material, and building cost. When he bends a line on the elevation, he is also devising ingenious ways to deform the curtain wall at no additional cost and anticipating how stacked building systems will be impacted. So when you look at the twisting geometry of Dancing Towers, you can actually see, literally, in the hinged deformation of the curtain wall, how the orthogonal steel frame has been engineered into a new form. The transformative process that pushed against the norm is laid bare for you to comprehend and appreciate, beyond the formal interest of the sculpted envelope.

Bromberg wrestles with the "stuff" of architecture to produce his forms. Commentators have called him an "artist" to account for the sculptural character of his architecture. But this is an artist who is heavily invested in the particulars of his medium, in what is unique about its material and craft, in the discipline and practice of architecture.

When we look at his buildings we see artfully sculpted form, but we also recognize how objects with complex constitutions and internal organizations have been reworked into these sculptural contours. It is the capacity to intuit the organizational and structural complexity that lie just beneath the surface, in the continuously adjusting trajectory of a studied curve that imparts intelligence, a soul, to Bromberg's architecture.

The curve is one of the persistent features in Bromberg's high-rise designs. It is pervasive in plan as much as in section, imparting the distinct kinetic quality that characterizes much of his work. The curve is not only about styling, although it is quite effective in branding the work with a characteristic figure. Beyond the gestural effect, it liberates the building from the normative orthogonal framework, providing opportunities for a more fluid and diversified occupation of the floor plates. In contradistinction to conventional high-rises, where a single extruded plan basically generates the entire building, Bromberg's curvilinear forms differentiate each floor, providing for slightly different

and clear views higher above. But the unprecedented architecture it serves to generate far exceeds the brute economics of the market-conscious strategy. The building is unlike any other; it is made possible by means of considerable technical innovation, and a great deal of imagination. Once again it illustrates how Bromberg's designs elevate necessity into art and fashion, and transform banal objects to remarkable ones.

## Social Objects

The affirmation of the object in Bromberg's work must be read in light of a market logic that privileges or even demands individuality and imageability over the polite anonymity of contextually integrated buildings. The same logic drives the tendency for rapidly developing cities such as Dubai to sprawl into a collection of discrete objects, all gesticulating for attention in an undifferentiated metropolitan field.

Bromberg's objects are very much prone to such gesticulation. But the gestures, as I earlier stated, are of a sophisticated kind. Their language is clearly distinguishable from the more common variety. The temptation is to attribute the je ne sais quoi that sets them apart to the ineffable

unit layouts on each level. Curvature also helps in optimizing views for a maximum number of units so as to significantly enhance their value. For instance, in Ocean Heights One, the entire structure torques so as to expose all sides to a greater variety of views.

The curving geometry is not a superficial treatment. It permeates the whole building to occasionally even refashion the structural frame and liberate the plan from the "orthopedic" restrictions of the vertical core. Empire Tower is a remarkable example of this structural tour de force. In this 230-meter-tall tower, the concrete piers gradually bend as the building mass splays wide open toward the base to maximize the occupancy of the lot. Unlike most other instances where curvilinear inflections are limited to the building envelope, the entire structure here is bent. Even at the scale of the individual unit, the eccentricity of the structure is made palpable in the slight but dramatic deviation of the load-bearing walls from the expected vertical. This organic relationship between the individual dwelling and the overall shape is furthermore articulated on the striated elevations. Vertical recesses here objectify the stacked housing units in distinct stripes. Their varying curvature exacerbates the deformation of the building shaft, translating the building's organizational diagram into an expressive form. The diagram aims for the most efficient exploitation of the site by means of a smooth transition from a large base to a slender tower, from maximum coverage and exposure at street level to maximum distance from property lines

**056**
Dubai **Ocean Heights One**

**064**
Abu Dhabi **Empire Tower**

**196**
Dubai **Pentominium**

workings of a design intuition. There is a more tangible explanation: Bromberg's forms are not superficial effects that are gratuitously overplayed on indifferent structures. His bulges, twists, and sweeps are precisely and painstakingly negotiated with a building's normative constitution. They rub against the set of material, typological, and cultural predispositions that cosmetics treatment would leave unperturbed and that Bromberg chooses to engage in depth with the transformative power of form. In Bromberg's strangely shaped buildings, each curve manifests the outcome of an intellectual and material struggle through which type and structure are transformed by design.

In addition to the inner organizational turmoil, the object's contours also register the complex rapport they have with their surroundings. These are discrete objects but they are not entirely autonomous. They may stand as separate entities, but they have a keen sense of the context. Theirs is a complex personality that has a capacity for a nuanced and responsive attitude to the surroundings. They converse with their environment. They are urbane subjects.

Consider, for instance, Pentominium, one of the highest towers currently planned for Dubai. On the side facing an unusually close tall building, the building mass is clustered into a set of discrete five-storey pods cantilevered from the core and separated by generously proportioned gardens. The crenellated side creates a memorable silhouette; it also

serves to mitigate the proximity of the neighboring tower. It is an object with a very distinct image, but one that was fashioned in response to context. Pentominium's distinct figure against the adjacent building and the sky framed in between radicalizes a more or less latent tendency in Bromberg's design: the propensity for shaping space as much as the objects they inhabit.

This explains, perhaps, why Bromberg is particularly successful with building ensembles in which two or several structures are caught in a complex web of reciprocal influences. Dancing Towers is the prime example of a charged relationship between two objects, fraternal twins whose individual characteristics are heightened by mutual responsiveness. But what is also unique and equally effective is the way the two towers shape the surrounding space. In Dancing Towers, much like in most of Bromberg's ensemble compositions, positive building masses and negative residual spaces share a common pattern language, so much so that figure and ground become reversible, in a manner reminiscent of some of M.C. Escher's puzzles, where one pattern gradually morphs into another while figure and ground are reversed in their respective roles.

Let us translate Escher's Sky and Water One 1938 woodcut into an architectural language. Imagine the dark bottom of the picture to be a Nolli Plan-like diagram, with the fish representing a space that is shaped

Sky and Water Wood Cut M.C. Escher

The design still features a dispersed field of atomized masses, the quasi-universal attribute of commercial developments. But there is no residual space in this field. The public realm is shaped with the same deliberate strokes that have fashioned the building blocks. The strategy allows for buildings to be individuated and tailored for optimal views and exposure, to effectively compete in the marketplace with subtle but effective inflections. It also provides for civic conformity, and a capacity for integration in a larger whole and with a common purpose.

The bird's-eye view is very telling, almost emblematic of Bromberg's urban sensibility: it shows his strange objects in a swarm-like pattern, as if locked in a synchronized movement. Each object has its own character, implicit in a distinct bend or a kink. This character is mindful of others, though. It betrays a social aptitude in the virtual flocking behavior. It is unmistakably urban.

Perhaps the greatest virtue of Bromberg's strange objects is their not-so-strange relation to the ground. The Dancing Towers' eloquent ballet is very effective in selling the development with compelling images of graceful building silhouettes. It is also tremendously convincing in shaping and animating the surrounding urban field into an inviting public space.

The commitment to the city's public realm is most forcibly stated in the

by the poché of building mass. In this analogy the duck on top would be a modern object-building freestanding in an open field. Space is figured below and residual at the top. It would be typical of traditional urban form below and of modern cities above.

In this diagram Bromberg's architecture would occupy the central band, where figure and ground are reversible, and where both fish and duck sustain their legibility in an interplay of mutually defining contours. In most urban projects designed by Bromberg, buildings consistently define the surrounding space as much as space shapes the enveloping buildings. Take a look at the North Star development, or Union Square: are the public corridors residual, leftover spaces between figured slabs? Or is the other way around? Are the buildings shaped by the figure of the public realm?

This ambiguity is one of the defining features of Bromberg's urbanism. It is evident, for instance, in the design for a residential district in historic Xian. The site is a former ammunitions-storage area that is crisscrossed with disused rail tracks. Bromberg here deploys an array of housing slabs in a pattern that negotiates the traces of the obsolete infrastructure as well as the city's orthogonal grid. The reversible figure ground—as well as the concomitant spatial ambiguity—is here applied persistently.

Union Square development for Dubai. This is a project that is primarily dedicated to the deliberate shaping of urban space and to fashioning a rich and sustainable urban realm. Much like in Bromberg's larger urban plans, the buildings here are discrete objects as much as containers, figures as much as ground. They maintain their status as independent objects but they are still coordinated in their primary dedication: shaping the space in between. We recognize Bromberg's staple urban strategy, but there is a new twist in this particular scenario. Beyond a figurative, symbolic subordination to a civic program, the buildings here also perform as public infrastructure. They provide structural support for a canopy that is designed to enhance the quality and sustainability of the public realm.

## Conclusion

Emerging high-stakes real-estate markets with staggering financial interests invested in building have steadily elevated expectations for quality and innovation in design. They have created a competitive environment in which large corporate offices are able to capitalize on formidable resources to project architecture forward, pushing the envelope of building science and design with every new unprecedented structure. In the last few years, innovation has migrated from academic

The new design vanguard is now busy at work, as Bromberg's buildings clearly suggest, in offices such as Aedas Hong Kong. They now define what is possible and find ways to make it buildable. They give us the Ducatis of architecture when it comes to refinement and technological sophistication. At their best they also do more. Bromberg and his team have the quasi-utopian drive—architecture's defining ethical trait—that delivers socially and environmentally responsible environments for all.

research centers to the professional arena, from studios at Harvard or Columbia to the trenches at SOM, Arup and Fosters.

Biography

**RODOLPHE el-KHOURY (BFA, BArch, SMArchS, MA, Ph.D)** divides his time between design research and scholarship. As a leading academic, he has initiated and directed several programs in **North America. After joining the Faculty of Architecture Landscape and Design at the University of Toronto in 2006, he was appointed to the Canada Research Chair in Architecture and Urban Design** to explore new media and technology and their potential in reshaping the built environment. His publications include: See Through Ledoux: Architecture, Theatre and the Pursuit of Transparency; Monolithic Architecture; Architecture in Fashion; Shaping the City: Studies in Theory, History and Urban Design. el-Khoury conducts project-based research as principal of ReK Productions, a design practice that straddles the academic and professional fields.

# Recent Works

Recent Works

| Page | Project | Program | Site Area | Building Height | Floor Area |
| --- | --- | --- | --- | --- | --- |
| 120 | PRC **Crowne Plaza Hotel** | Hotel | 9,904 sqm | 97 m | 84,237 sqm |
| 126 | Abu Dhabi **Sorouh** | Residential | 29,356 sqm | 185 m | 330,977 sqm |
| 132 | Dubai **Union Square** | Mixed Use | 43,000 sqm | 35 m | 139,641 sqm |
| 138 | PRC **Foshan Media Centre** | Media Centre | 63,600 sqm | 81.7 m | 87,696 sqm |
| 140 | PRC **North Star** | Mixed Use | 2,525 sqm | 107 m | 161,780 sqm |
| 148 | Singapore **Civic & Cultural Complex** | Theater/Mixed Use | 19,270 sqm | 60 m | 54,000 sqm |
| **160** | **Contextualism** | | | | |
| 164 | PRC **Xian Residential** | Residential | 2,200 sqm | varies | 2,000,593 sqm |
| 172 | Bangkok **Corporate Towers** | Mixed Use | 54,519 sqm | 428 m | 351,684 sqm |
| 180 | Beirut **Solidere** | Residential | 2,711 sqm | 120 m | 43,987 sqm |
| 182 | Abu Dhabi **Jebel Hafeet** | Hotel | 345,000 sqm | varies | 60,927 sqm |
| 186 | PRC **Luo Xi Residential** | Residential | 32,090 sqm | 45 m | 90,050 sqm |
| 188 | Dubai **Boulevard Plaza** | Hotel | 17,200 sqm | 173.7 m | 60,927 sqm |
| 196 | Dubai **Pentominium** | Residential | 3,500 sqm | 516 m | 111,730 sqm |
| 200 | Asia **Gateway Complex** | Mixed Use | 60,267 sqm | 282 m | 195,803 sqm |

# Challenging
# Conventions

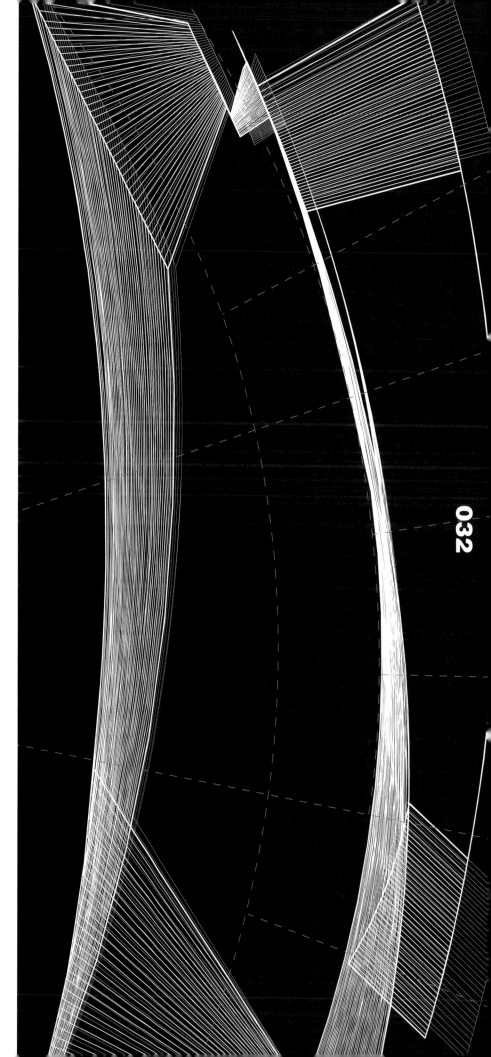

032

# Challenging Conventions

In the pursuit of achieving "meaningful design," staying true to the chosen path in defining the project is often in direct conflict with previous conventional formulas and approaches.

The formula is always changing and moving, shaped by an infinite amount of influences which need to be balanced and prioritized. The purpose of the design and staying true to this vision are where the meaning is achieved. The "challenge of conventions" is a response to reach this goal – not the motive.

The vision may be defined by a specific rationale or an intuitive belief in what is deemed "appropriate." Being critical of the inherent values of what defines this equation is where projects begin to develop meaningfully. There will be economic, time, client, governmental, constructability, marketability and even psychological limitations. Conventions are there because they have been tested and are definable, lending comfort as a response to such limitations.

Arabian **Performance Venue**

036

**046**

If the goal of the design fits within these norms, then there is no reason to go beyond. However, the value that architecture has in the world and its importance in improving the environment in which we live places an enormous pressure on design – often requiring us to push the envelope and transcend conventional limits.

Buildings are required to facilitate their chosen activities and users. This cannot be overlooked – but should be optimized within the context and setting in which the building is being designed for and within.

A simple tower with a traditional, central core, reasonable floor plate depth and high net-area efficiency is a generic developer formula for profitability and a comprehensible equation for the user. This, however, is simplistic without considering the importance of the human spirit who will spend time within the project, as well as the responsibility the project has to the surrounding environment.

Viability of a project is a complex equation with an enormous range of interpretation. For instance, efficiency may be able to be reduced if views are maximized, which may allow rents to increase enough to outweigh the loss of net area. Of course, part of the equation is personal and instinctive – which are important ingredients within the formula. Meaningful design occurs after weighing all these influences

Dubai **Headquarters**

Abu Dhabi **Dancing Towers**

sensitively and critically. Often, a solution will materialize that can even surprise the conceiver. It is the designer's responsibility to understand and critically balance the needs of all parties and, if necessary, push the limits by challenging these conventions – allowing the most optimal and meaningful designs to be fulfilled.

All the projects selected for this book are challenging conventional approaches to architecture. The projects represented in this chapter were chosen because they tended to exemplify distinguishable qualities of this pursuit. They also maintain strong values in the other two chapters dealing with "Civic Approach" and "Contextualism". ■

Program **Performance Venue / Mixed Use** Site Area **320,000 sqm**
Floor Area **650,890 sqm** Building Height **284 m**

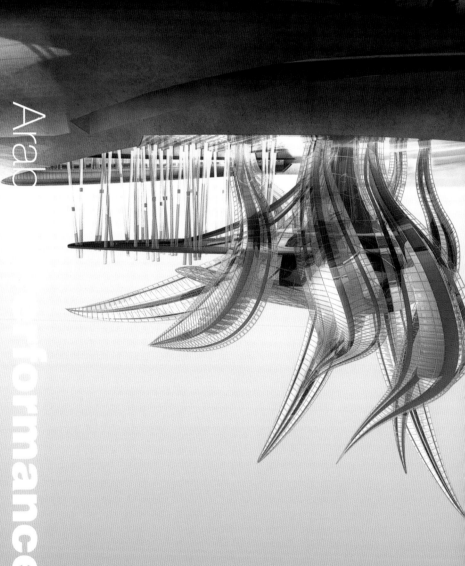

Arab

Performance Venue

## Arabian **Performance Venue**

Surrounded by the desert sands and occupying its own island in the middle of a nature reserve, the Arabian Performance Venue is organically tied to both its context and its use. The venue is experienced through an entry sequence of surprise and discovery.

The island is connected to the mainland via long span bridges for both vehicles and trains. Also approachable by boats, the entrances are cut into the mounded landscape to open into a water-filled cavity. The walls, which contain the water, become the main entry foyer to the complex and a museum/exhibition center. The museum rises in the center and drops on its sides, opening out and focusing on the water, which is filled with people engaged with nature.

Dropping down from the main foyer, the lower concourse opens up and moves underneath the water into a darkened space dappled with reflections from the water above. There are restaurants off to the side and a "black box" performance theatre near the center of the space. Inside this sedated world there are 44 splashes of light from above, which are emitted from glass tubes that house 44 elevators. Entering the elevator, one rises out of the water and above the walls that define this inner space. The walls open up to allow for 360-degree views of the surrounding landscape and waters.

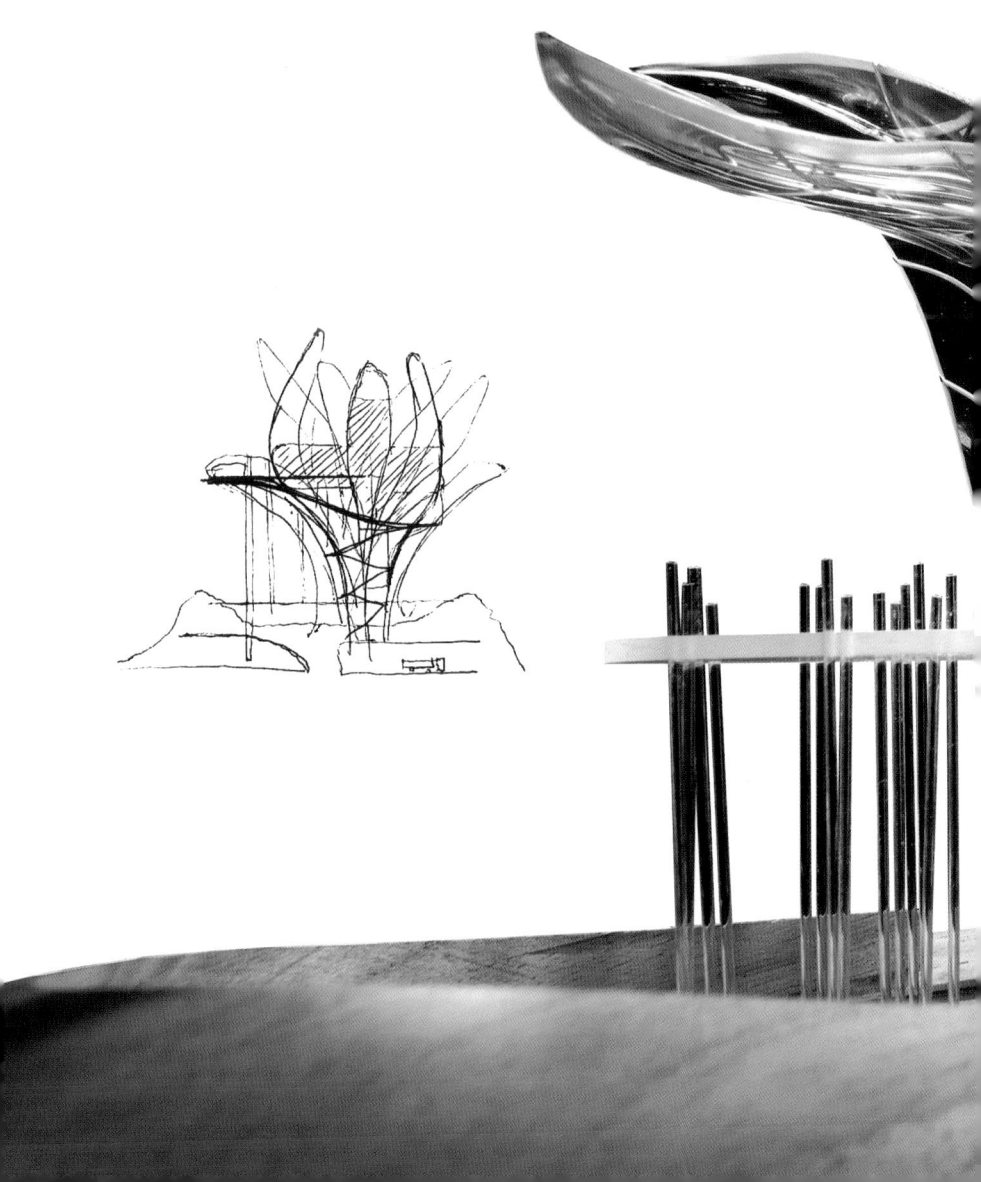

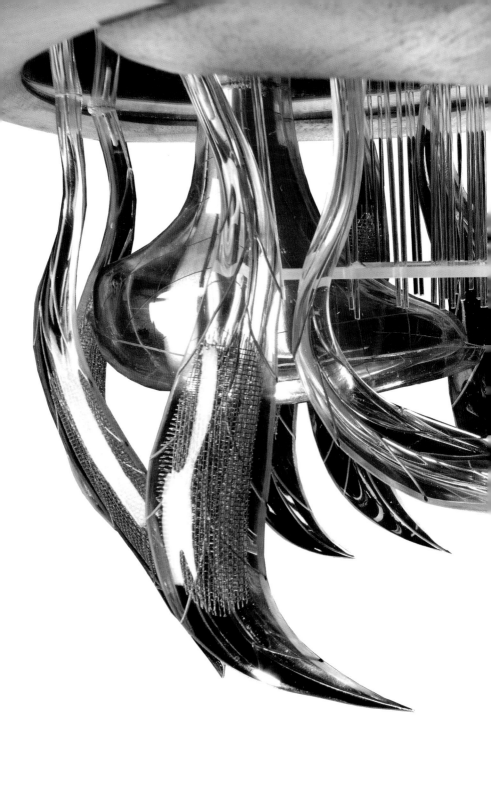

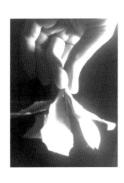
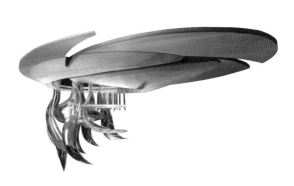

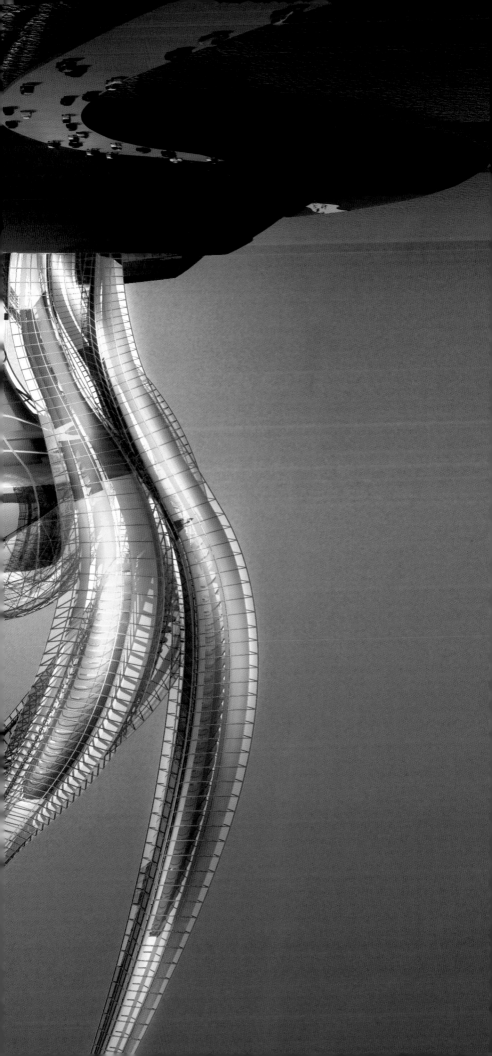

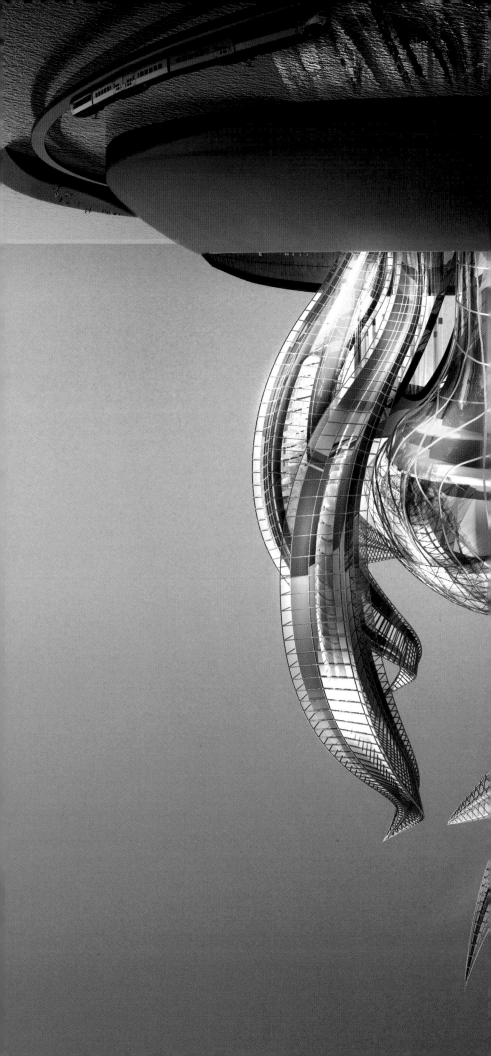

The elevators arrive at a traditional forecourt for the 2,500-seat performance venue 100 meters off the ground. It is surrounded by seven dancing figures that rise high into the sky above. This entry platform also serves as a public observation area, allowing views beyond to the migrating birds which flock to the surrounding waters.

In the center of four dancing figures, filled with different activities, is the solidity of the performance venue, the pearl of the construction. Entrance into the main hall exposes the volume rising from the waters below. The auditorium hall opens up above to the main lobby of the hotel sitting on top of the performance venue, which is enclosed with an outer glass shell. The hotel lobby can be reached with its own express lifts and is flanked by four figures that are reached via sky-bridges. These figures house 300 hotel and service apartment rooms.

The front two figures are filled with public food and beverage stations and provide shade to the forecourt. The back figure contains supporting facilities for the performance venue itself. Overall, the seven dancing figures rise into the sky with the highest one reaching upwards to 284 meters in height ▪

**Vehicular Circulation**

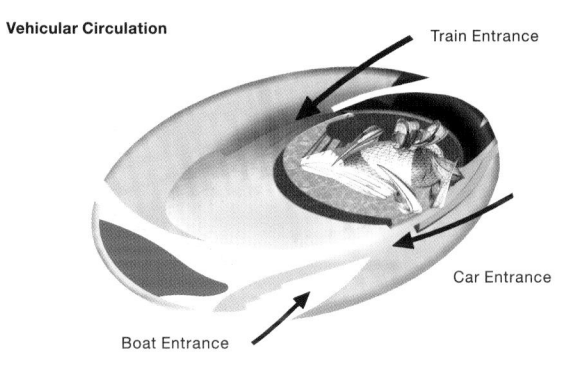

Train Entrance

Car Entrance

Boat Entrance

**Pedestrian Circulation**

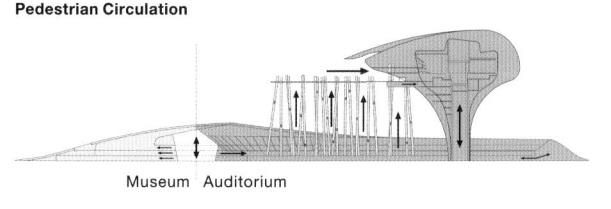

Museum   Auditorium

1. Atrium
2. Temporary Exhibition Space
3. Museum
4. Exterior Viewing Terrace
5. Events Exhibition Hall
6. Parking
7. Valet Services
8. Passenger/Taxi Drop Off
9. Gift Shop
10. Lobby
11. Opera Platform
12. Upper Foyer
13. Opera Lift Lobby
14. Interior Opera House Lift Lobby
15. Performers Drop-Off

16. Drama Theater
17. Opera House Shipping Loading
18. Rehearsal Studios
19. Green Rooms
20. Truck Lift
21. Loading/Storage/Workshop
22. Management/Marketing
23. Dressing Rooms/Rehearsal Rooms
24. Stage/Fly Tower & Orchestra Pit
25. Main Auditorium
26. Staff/Performers Kitchen
27. Bridge
28. Entrance Lobby
29. Hotel Lobby

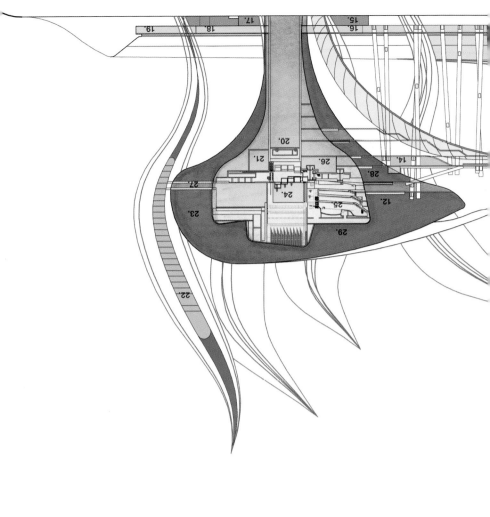

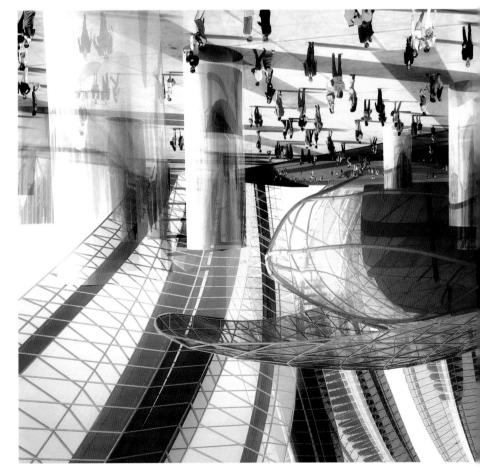

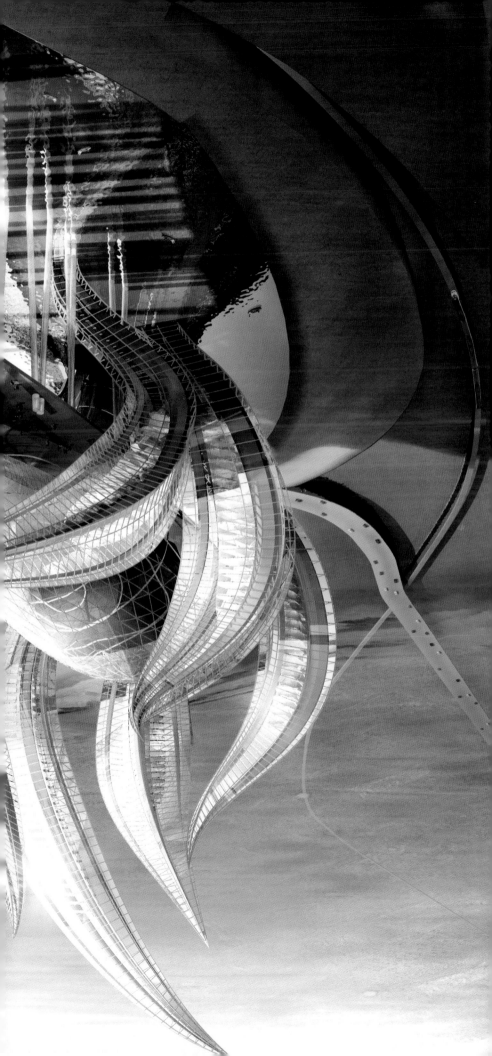

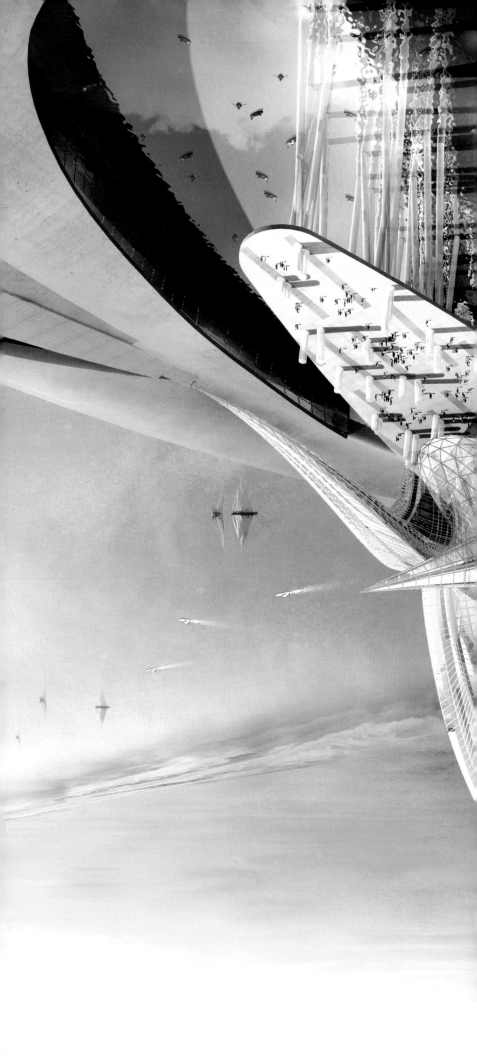

Program **Mixed Use**  Site Area **87,420 sqm**
Floor Area **232,340 sqm**  Building Height **350 m**

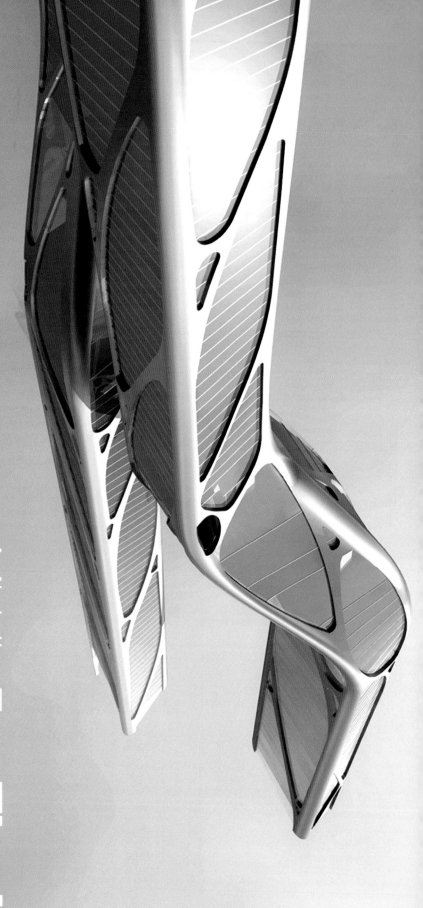

## Middle East **The Legs**

The Legs was conceived to challenge the convention of high-rise construction and structural limitations that have restricted its own evolution.

The project consists of four distinct programs: a five-star hotel, service apartments, residential and offices. The service apartment and hotel both wanted to have the higher floors for views but also can share the lobbies and amenities. The offices and residential components are the financial base for the project, which could occupy the lower floors.

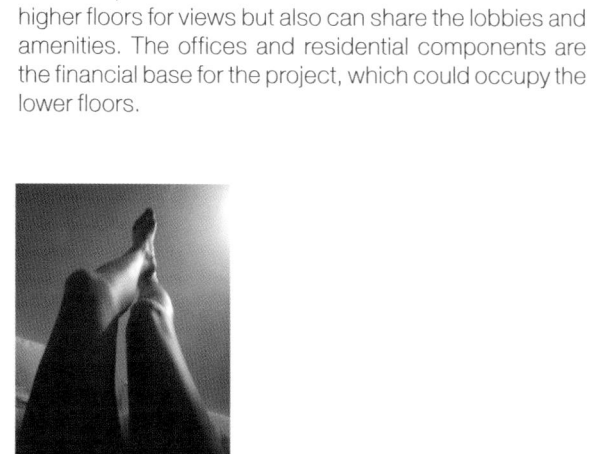

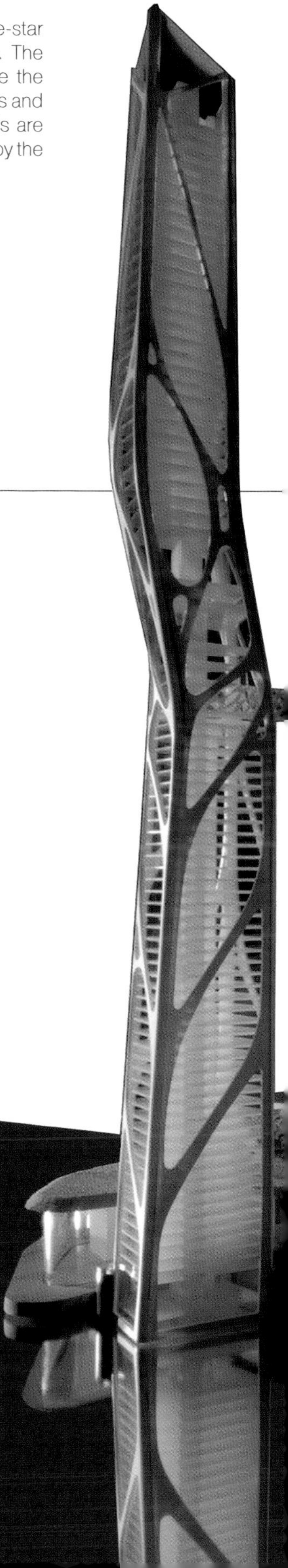

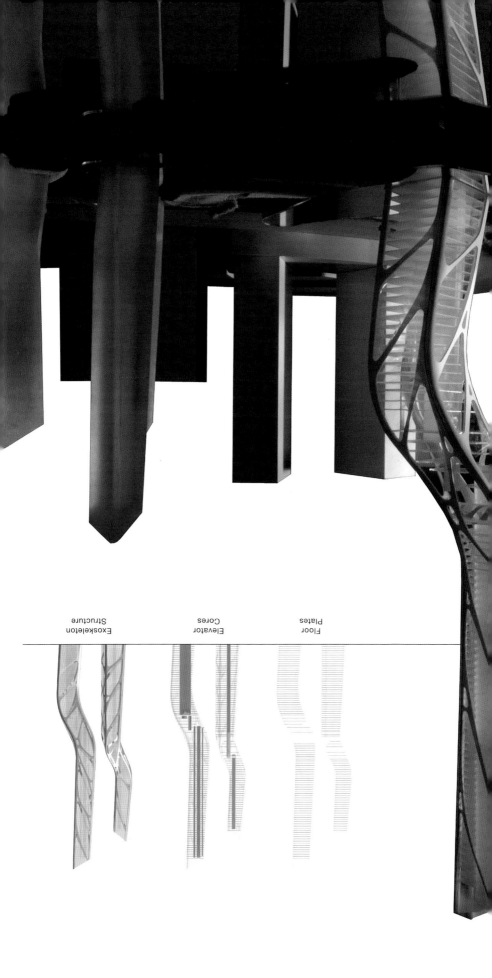

Exoskeleton Structure

Elevator Cores

Floor Plates

It was decided that express elevators could take guests up to a sky lobby system for the upper components and then could transfer to their own cores – a system common today.

If these cores do not stack, another structural system not depending on the cores for support would need to be used. It was decided that another system, also existing today, would be used: an exoskeleton. This structural approach is based on a tube and uses the skin of the building as the structure and is therefore not dependent on the core.

The project pursues these two basic principles to produce two legs which bend and sensually interlock around each other. One leg reaches over 330 meters with the hotel on top. Both legs are organically contained with a structural stocking and linked discreetly in the center with a sky-bridge connecting the upper lobbies as well as aiding the project structurally. The result is two legs that reach into the sky and seem to defy gravity, creating a project that is unique to the entire world ∎

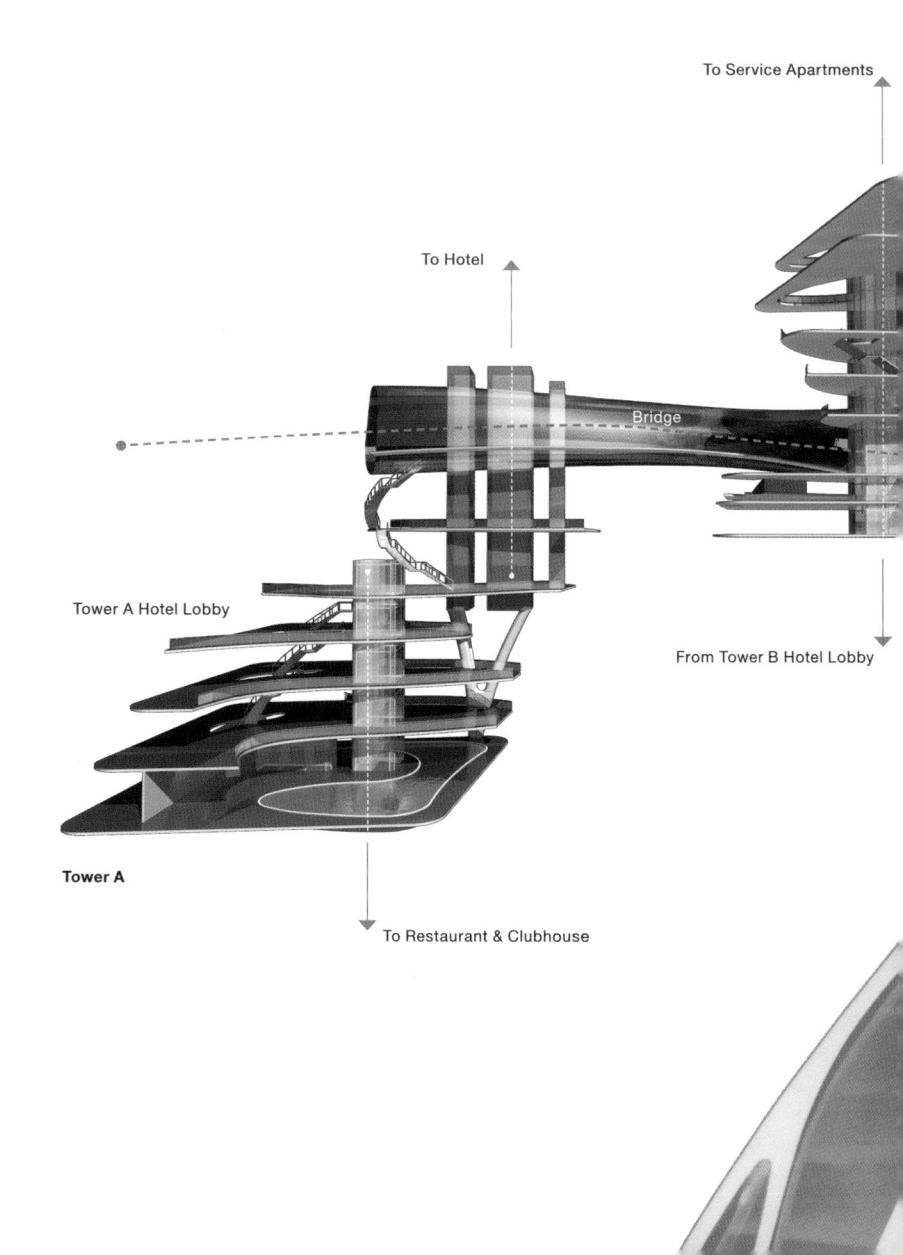

To Service Apartments

To Hotel

Bridge

Tower A Hotel Lobby

From Tower B Hotel Lobby

Tower A

To Restaurant & Clubhouse

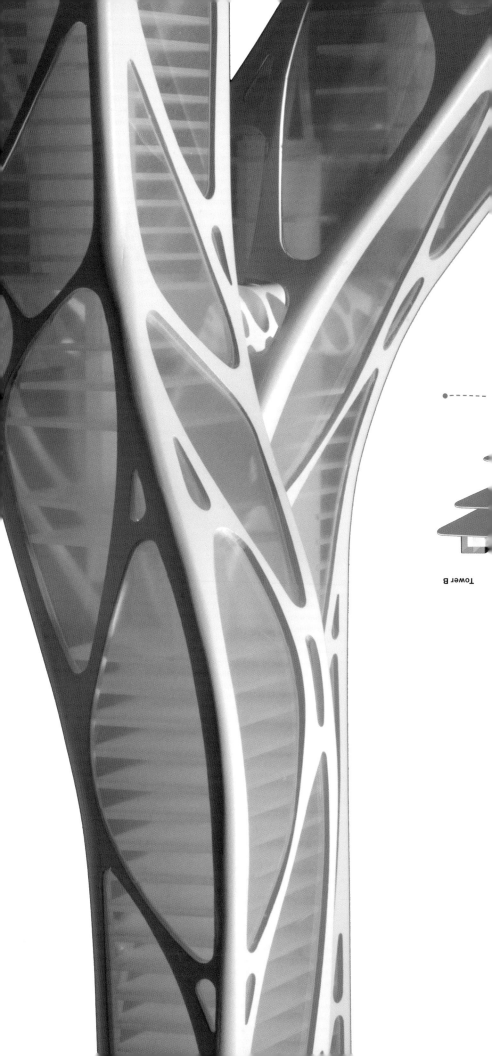

Tower B

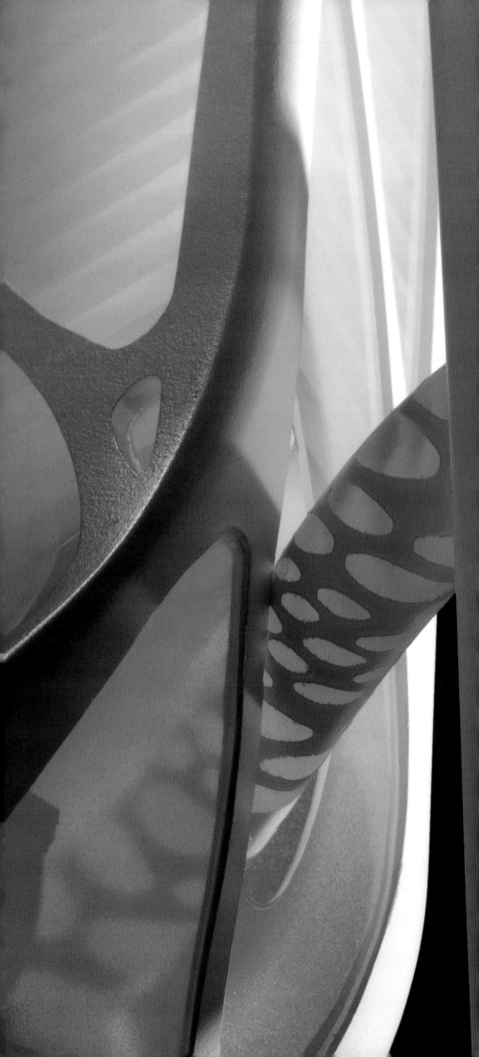

# Dubai **Headquarters**

Headquarters at Media City was an exciting opportunity to design the client's corporate headquarters. With Dubai's impressive Palm Island to the north, the brief asked for a long slender building that would maximize the views out to the water. The outstretched arms play off each other to give both the strength of a unified gesture as well as an ever-changing filigree between them.

The higher arm anchors the corner of the site rising from the elevator core to the chairman's office. The lower arm contains a large rooftop garden and an infinity pool, which opens to the water beyond ▪

■ Headquarters

▥ Core

▨ Club House

▨ Podium

Program **Office** Site Area **10,058 sqm**
Floor Area **37,170 sqm** Building Height **194 m**

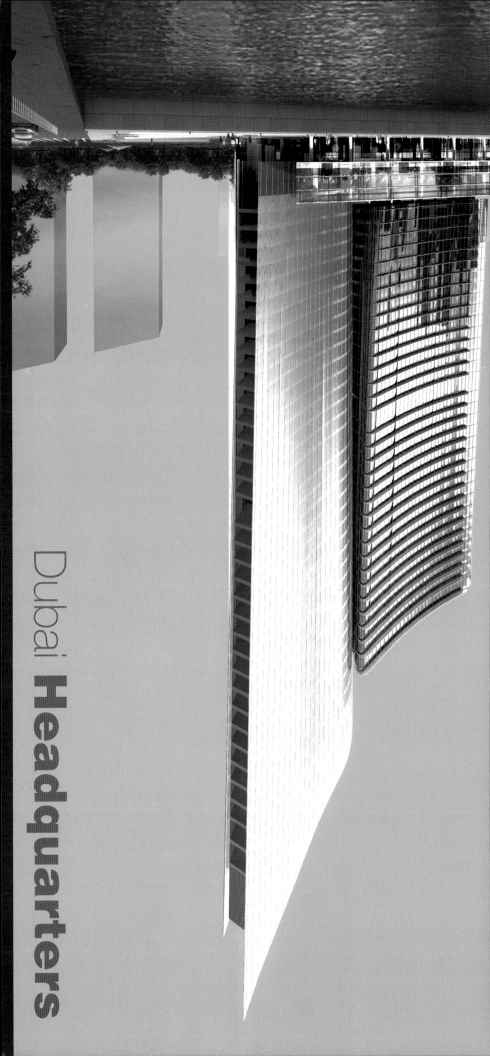

Dubai **Headquarters**

Program **Residential**  Site Area **3,746 sqm**
**Floor Area 858,655 sqm**  Building Height **310 m**

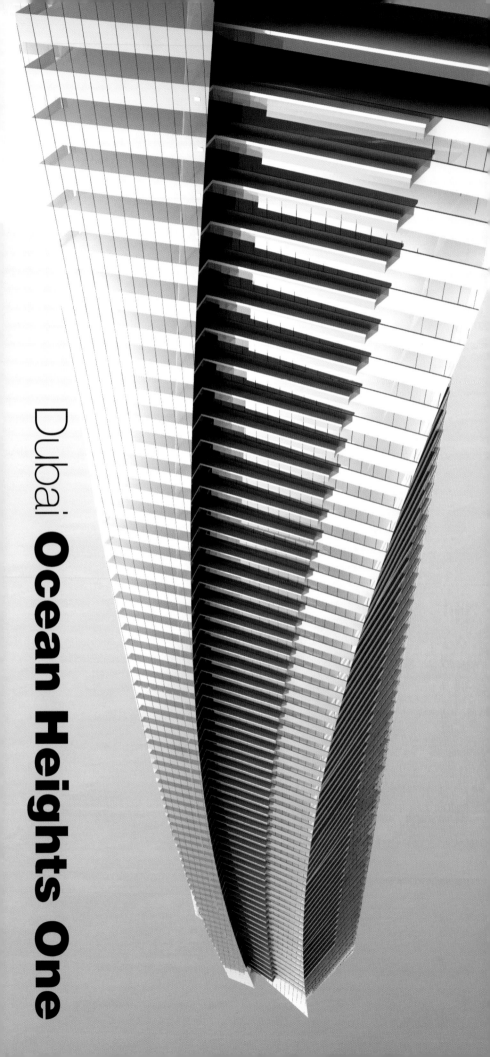

Dubai **Ocean Heights One**

## Dubai **Ocean Heights One**

Ocean Heights, located in Dubai Marina, United Arab Emirates, is a 310-meter residential tower. The project was the recipient of the Bentley 2006 "Best Architecture" award. The design evolved to maximize views toward the ocean with a deliberate twist on three of its faces. This allows the units, even in the back, a view toward the water beyond. The 82-storey tower is planned for completion in 2008.

The building immediately starts its twist of its three faces at the base. As it rises, the tower's floor plates reduce in size, allowing the rotation to become even more pronounced. At 50 stories, the building rises over its neighbors. This movement allows two faces of the building unobstructed views of the ocean. The tower breaks away from the orthogonal grid and reorients the project toward one of Dubai's Palm Islands to the north.

A challenging aspect of the design was accommodating the client's strict requirement of unit layouts within a changing envelope. What resulted was a rational four meter module, which tracks its way down through the entire building and only changes at the façade. This also considerably simplified the structural system of the project.

The shear walls were placed perpendicular to the mean of the two most extreme angles of the façade. This was done to soften the relationship between façade and partitions, minimizing how "off-perpendicular" the relationship becomes.

The shifts in geometry were taken as soft, gradual moves over the 310 meters of height resulting in a sculpted and dynamic object – but with a rationalized structural system and modulated façade – essential in the project's viability of common-sized residential units for Dubai's market ▪

■ Upper Floors

■ Middle Floors

▫ Lower Floors

■ Structure

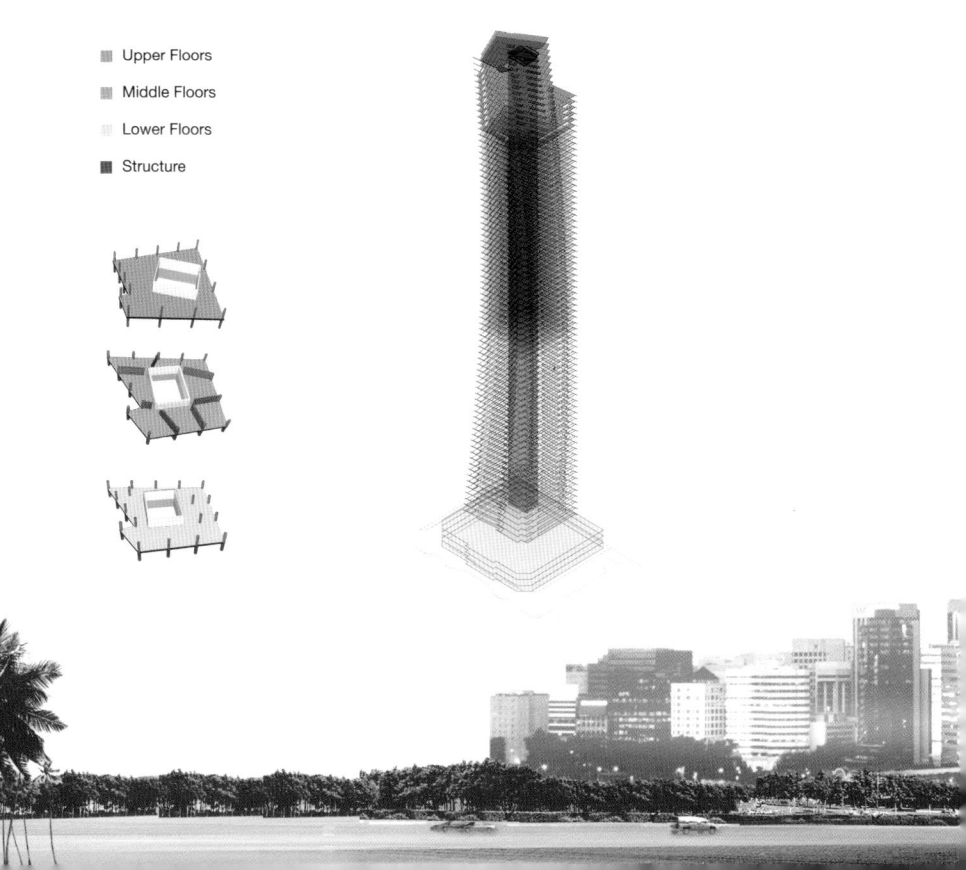

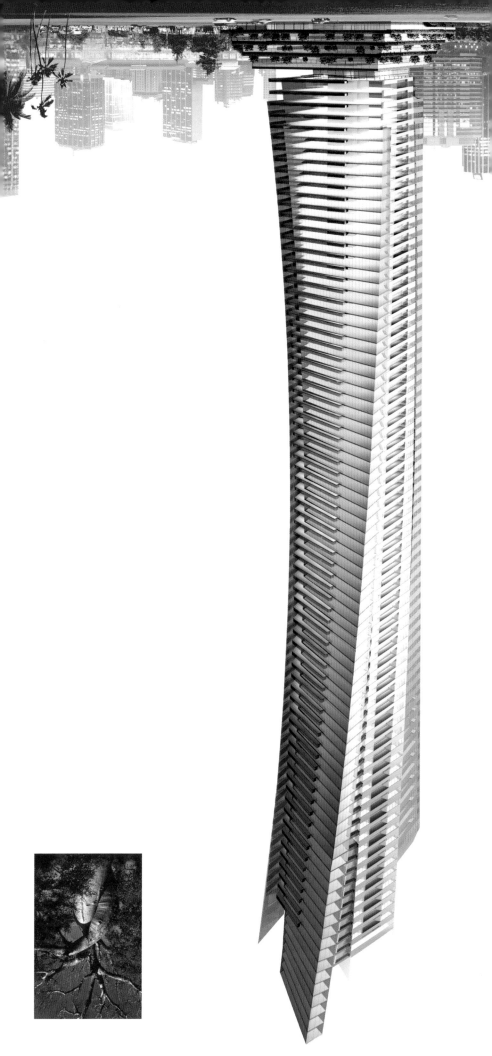

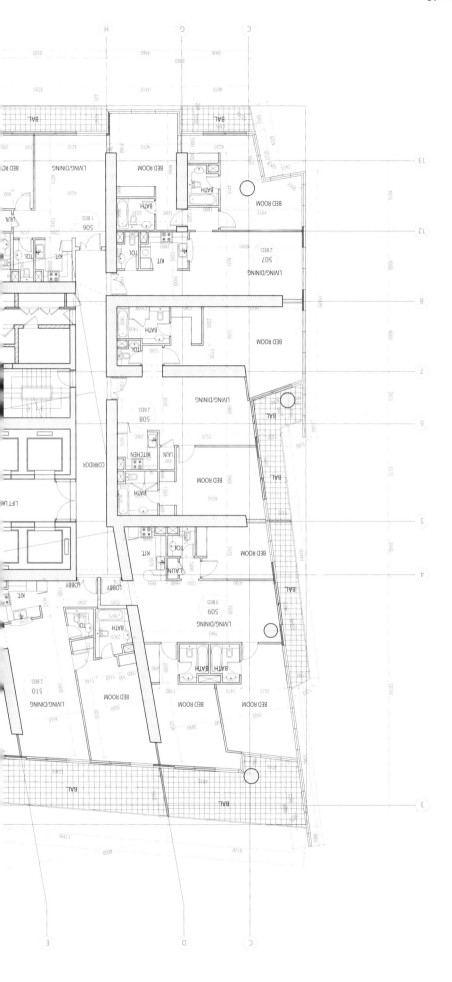

Under Construction

BAL.

BED ROOM
504
1 BED

LIVING/DINING

LIVING/DINING
505
1 BED
BED ROOM

KIT.
BATH
TOI.

KIT.
LAUN.
TOI.
LOBBY
LOBBY

BATH

BED ROOM
LAUN.
KIT.

503
1 BED
LIVING/DINING

STO.
STO.
CORRIDOR
LAUNDRY

BAL.

BATH
KIT.
TOI.

BED ROOM

502
1 BED
LIVING/DINING

STO.
TOI.
LOBBY
BATH

BAL.
BATH
KIT.
TOI.

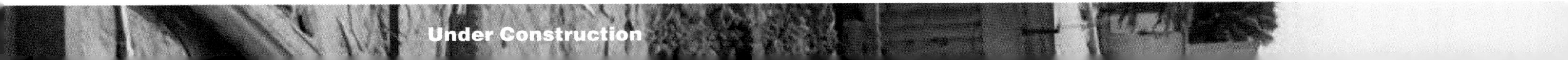

501
2 BED.
LIVING/DINING

BED ROOM

BED ROOM

BAL.

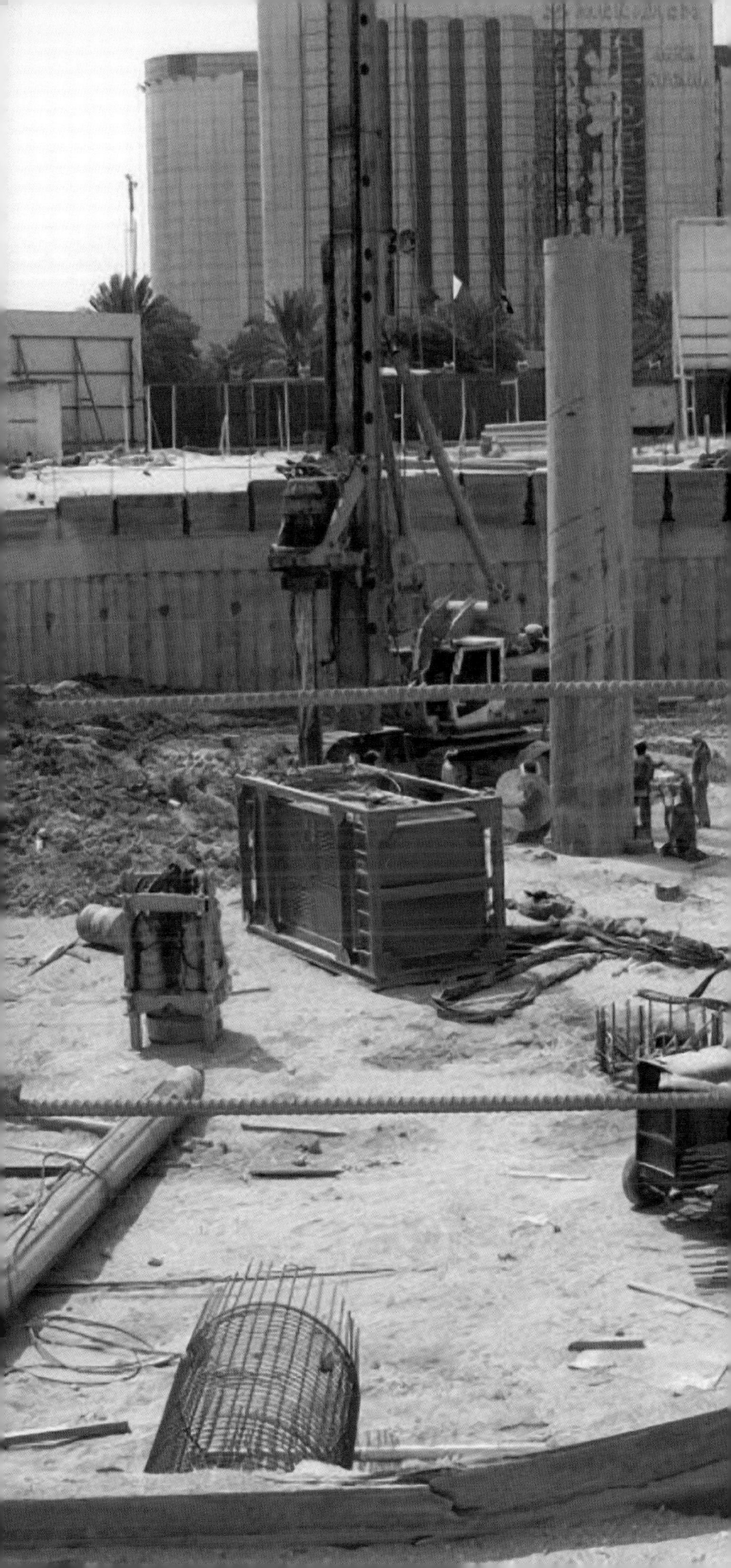

# Site Preparation
## for Ocean Heights One

see Page 234

CONSULTANTS

DRAWING TITLE

Ian Banham & Associates
CONSULTING ENGINEERS
Dubai P.O Box 23901 TEL: 04-2666939 FAX: 04-2661599

MEP CONSULTANTS

MEINHARDT
Consulting Engineers, Planners, Managers

STRUCTURAL / FACADE CONSULTANTS

Aedas

ARCHITECTS

ECG
ENGINEERING CONSULTANTS GROUP

MAIN CONSULTANT

DAMAC GULF PROPERTIES (L.L.C)
5th Floor, Al Moosa Tower 2
Formerly Palm Terrace (L.L.C.)
Sheikh Zayed Road, Dubai
P.O. Box 2195 Dubai, UAE
Tel: 971-4-332205 Fax: 971-4-3321874
www.damacproperties.com/oceanheights

CLIENT

OCEAN HEIGHTS
AT MARSA DUBAI - PLOT No. 392-188/A27A

CLIENT NAME

PROJECT

REVISIONS

| No. | Date | By | Revised Details |
| --- | --- | --- | --- |
| 0 | 12 Sep 06 | Aedas | Detailed Design Drawings |

ISSUES

| No. | Date | By | Issue Details |
| --- | --- | --- | --- |
| 0 | 12 Sep 06 | Aedas | Issued for Tender |

ELEVATION 3

ELEVATION 4

ELEVATION 1

ELEVATION

N

1. THIS DRAWING IS THE PROPERTY OF AEDAS LIMITED.
2. IT IS FORBIDDEN TO REPRODUCE IT, COMPLETELY, IN ANY FORM, EXCEPT FOR THE WRITTEN PURPOSE.
3. THIS DRAWING IS NOT TO BE SCALED.
DIMENSIONS ARE FOR SETTING OUT.
ATTENTION AND RESOLVED BY AEDAS LIMITED.
THE DISCREPANCIES ARE TO BE BROUGHT TO THE
BEFORE COMMENCEMENT OF ANY WORKS.

# Abu Dhabi Empire Tower

Empire Tower was challenged through a client request of not "pushing the limits" too far. The concern is that the residential project was located in the middle of a masterplan filled with potential icons. The design standardizes the units to accommodate the client request but manipulates the section to develop a very dynamic solution, which holds its own amidst the visual clutter of its neighbors. This was deemed important for the financial viability of this project that is dependent on pre-sales within a very competitive market.

The design maximizes the towers presence on the street with vertical layers spreading out to the property lines. The building then bends back away from the street across from a large commercial tower allowing for an enlarged view corridor between the central park of the community and the sea. The splayed vertical layers converge while rising up before bending forward together as the 249-meter tower rises toward the sky and maximizing its views between the park and sea ■

Initial Massing

Mass Divisions

Strip Shifting

Strip Bending

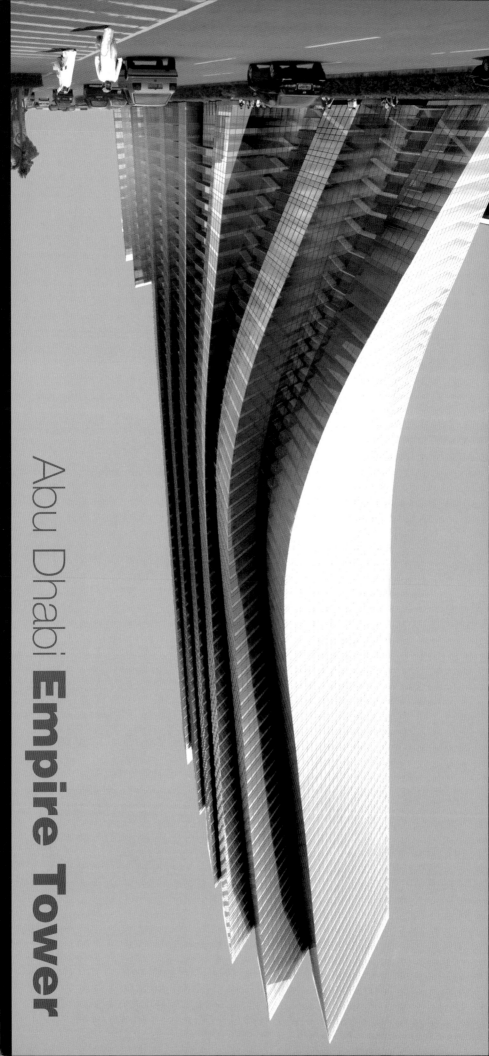

Abu Dhabi **Empire Tower**

## Dubai **Ocean Heights Two**

Ocean Heights Two is also located in Dubai Marina, UAE, along with its sister project, Ocean Heights One. Over 420 meters in height, it will be one of the tallest towers in its vicinity. However, unlike its predecessor, the requirements for more modulated units up to the 60th floor, forced a different approach while intending to maintain the spirit of its sister.

The first 60 floors of the tower needed to have the majority of units standardized. The curved shape of the tower improves views past its densely located neighbors. The playfulness of this tower was concentrated into the two most visible faces, allowing units to bend up the tower in two blades. These blades were still modulized up to the 60th floor before the tight restrictions of unit area fluctuations become more relaxed. At this point, the modules drop off and the blades continue, tapering and bending into the sky ▪

Program **Residential** Site Area **3,453sqm**
Floor Area **197,975 sqm** Building Height **420 m**

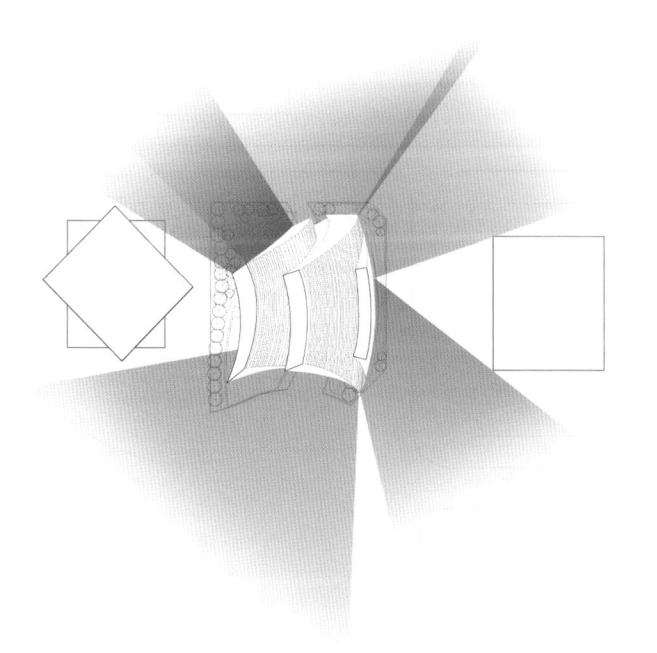

**View Diagram**

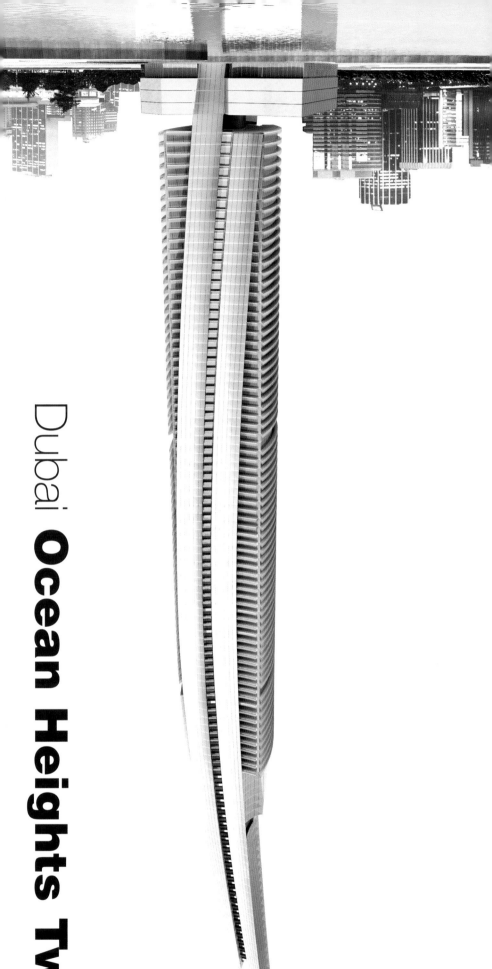

Dubai **Ocean Heights Two**

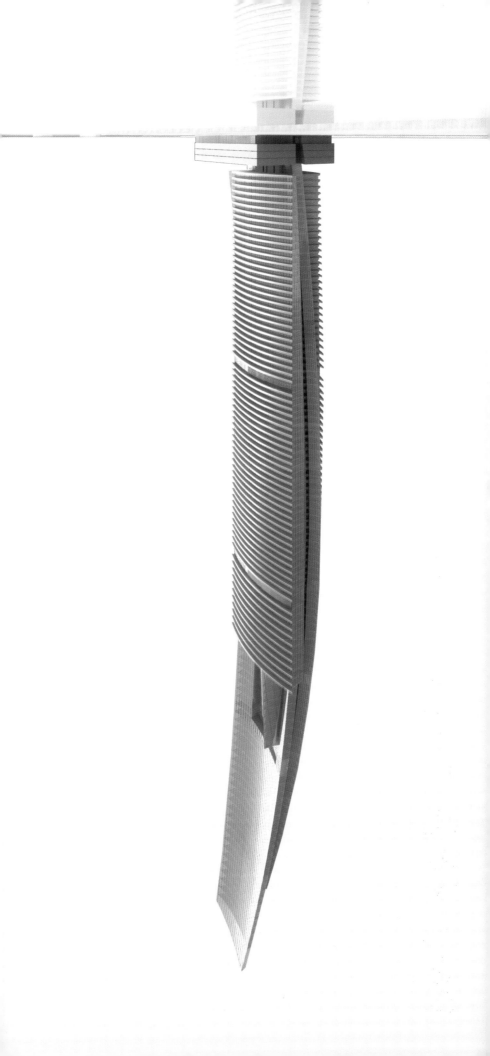

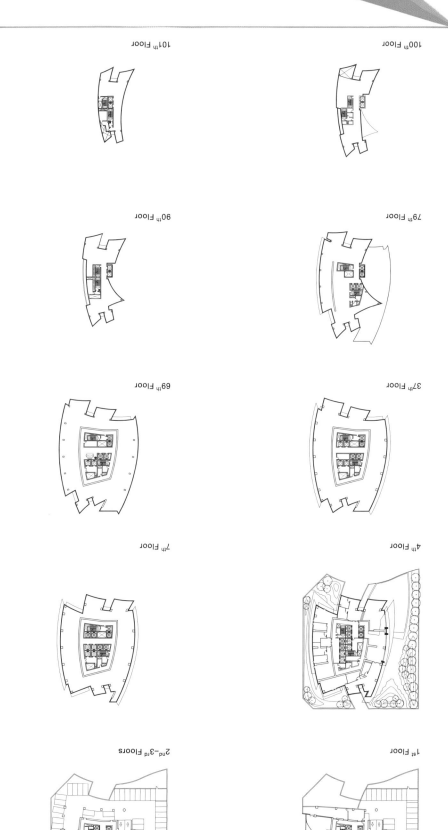

101st Floor

100th Floor

90th Floor

79th Floor

69th Floor

37th Floor

7th Floor

4th Floor

2nd–3rd Floors

1st Floor

# People's Republic of China **Zhongguan Plaza**

Zhongguan Plaza is sited at the confluence of the major vehicular and pedestrian paths into the Haidian District, enabling this project to become the new gateway and architectural icon of the community. Programatically, two separate office buildings were requested as a requirement for a service apartment/hotel. Both sites have a six-floor retail base, including two floors below grade. The design intends to unify all of these disparate forces under a unifying umbrella, strengthening its impact within the Haidian District as well as strengthening the internal vitality of the project ▪

Initial
Massing

Site
Restrictions

Outcome

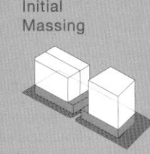
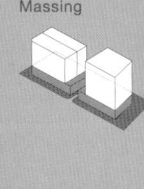

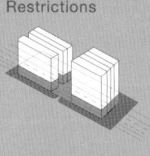
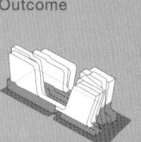
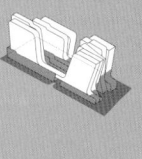

Program **Mixed Use** Site Area **12,950 sqm**
Floor Area **64,314 sqm** Building Height **79.3 m**

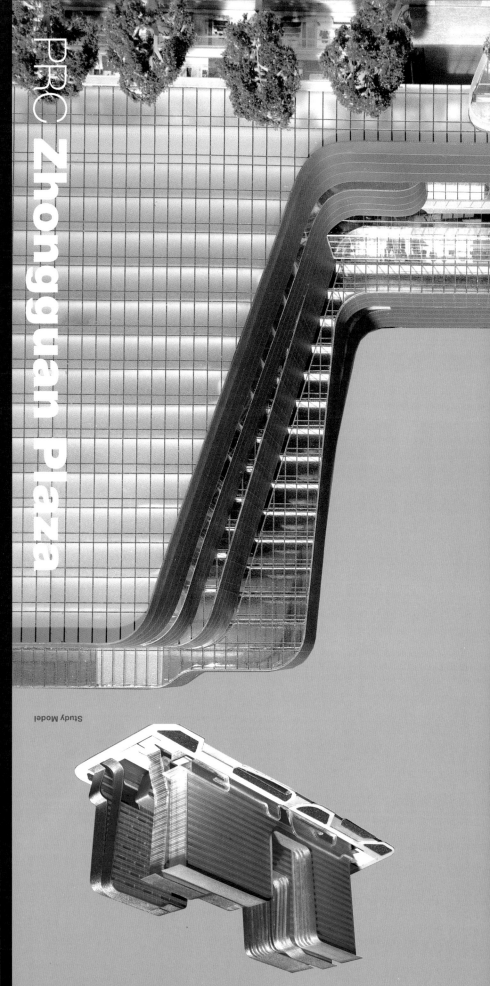

Study Model

Program **Mixed Use**  Site Area **4,180 sqm**
Floor Area **44,235 sqm**  Building Height **160 m**

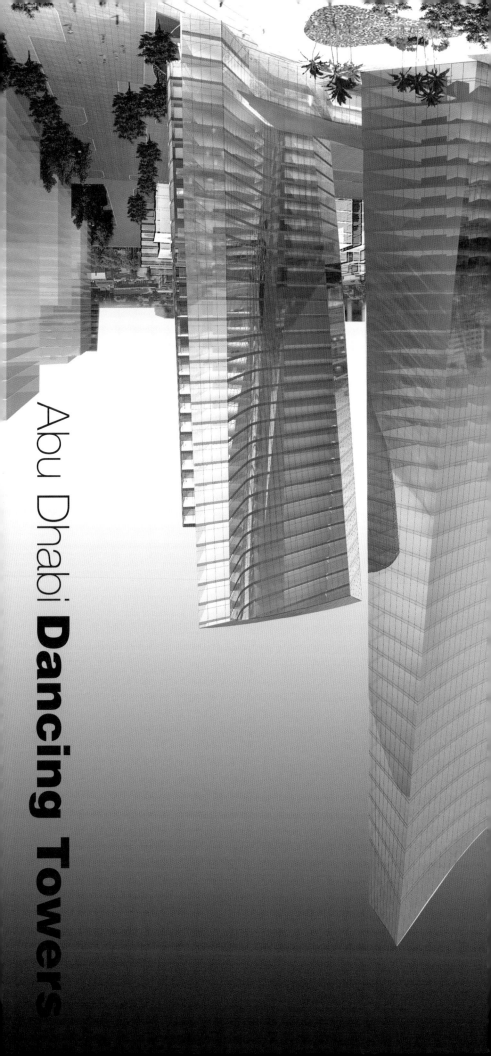

Abu Dhabi **Dancing Towers**

## Abu Dhabi **Dancing Towers**

Located in the heart of Abu Dhabi, Dancing Towers was designed to appropriately fit its surrounding neighbors in scale.

The challenge was how to achieve this when the project was only 70,000 square meters and adjacent properties were relatively small, averaging 900 square-meter floor plates. Two slender towers as opposed to one singular tower was the first step, but the site itself was constrained, forcing a close proximity between the two buildings.

This site constraint is intensified in achieving a viable connective retail podium between the commercial and residential towers, drop-offs to the lobbies and access to supporting functions. The buildings were placed deliberately to maximize the uses down below.

However, the two towers quickly lean, rotate, bend and warp to respond to each other, the adjacent sites and ultimately the view to the ocean at their horizon. These two figures fluidly respond to each other, dynamically engaged and flowing – and ultimately tied together in a passionate dance ▪

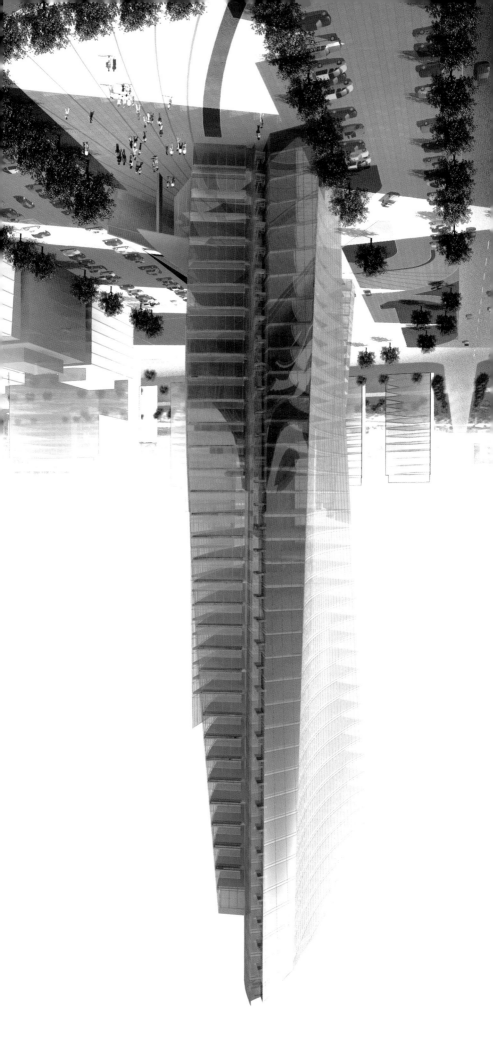

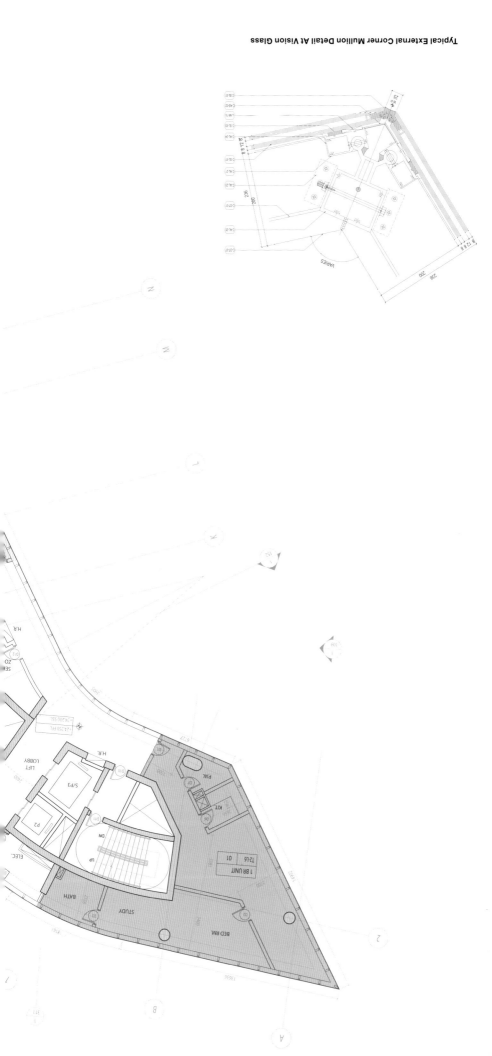

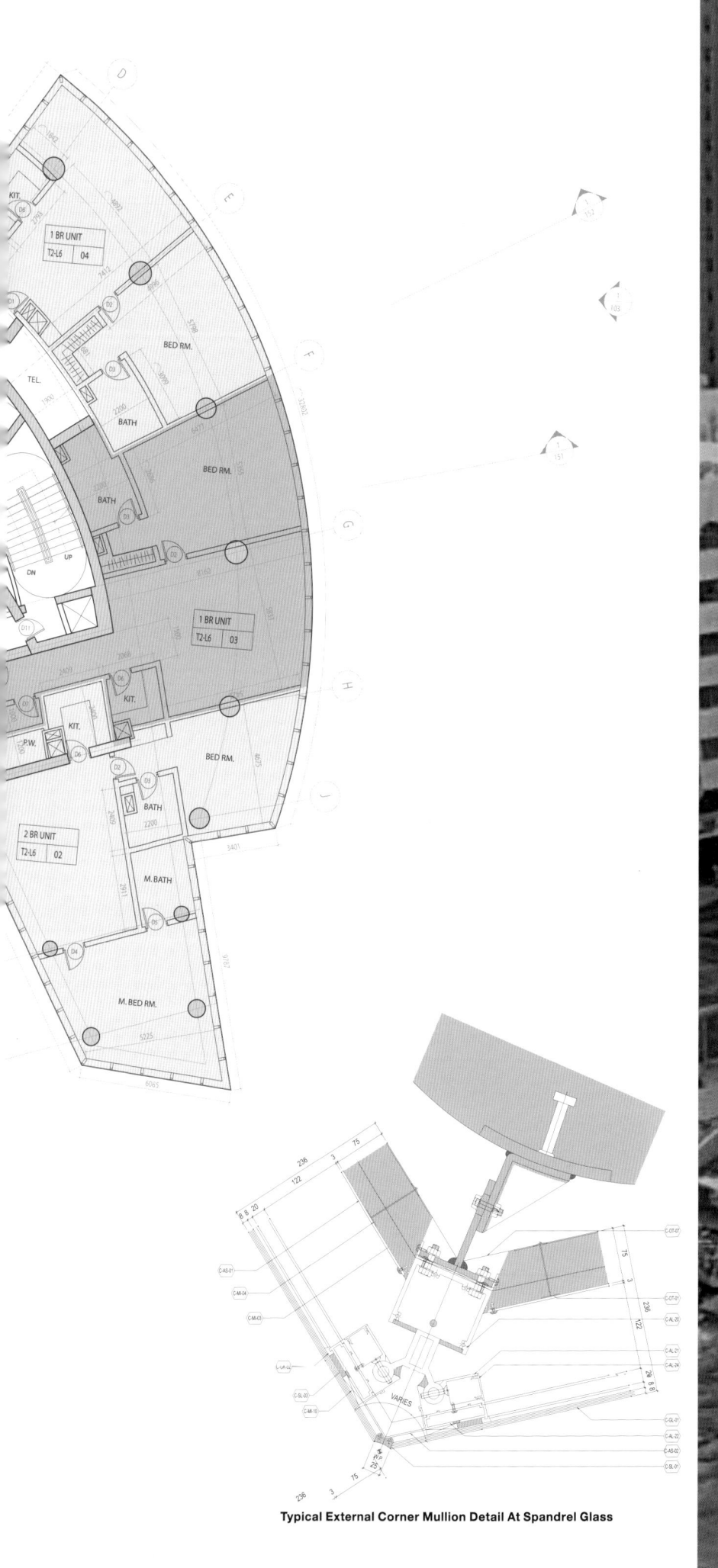

**Typical External Corner Mullion Detail At Spandrel Glass**

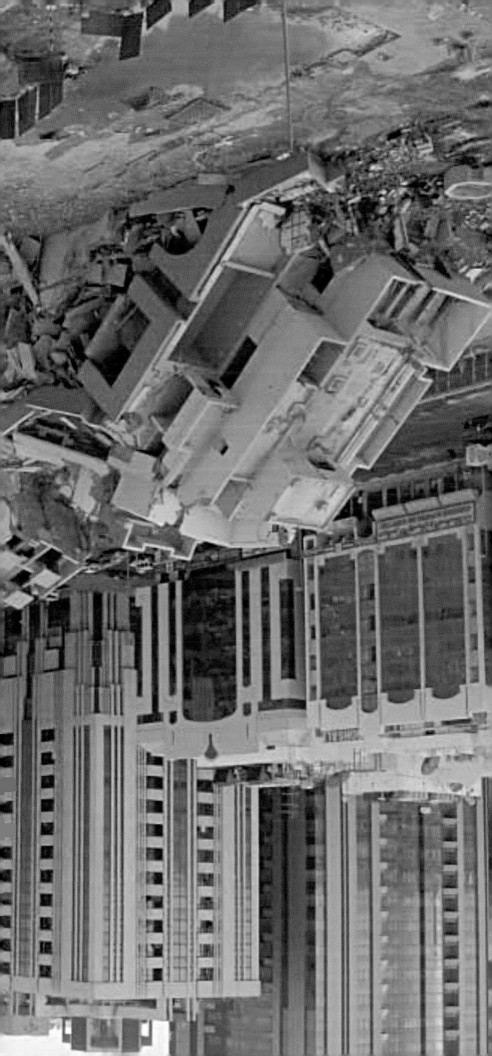

Site Demolition
for Dancing Towers

see Page 234

CONSULTANTS

CLIENT

NAME

QUANTITY
SURVEYORS
CONSULTANT
HANSCOMB CONSULTANTS INC.
PO BOX 4124 ABU DHABI
UNITED ARAB EMIRATES

FACADE
ENGINEERING
CONSULTANT
ALT LIMITED
RM 1803 WHEELOCK HOUSE
20 PEDDER ST
CENTRAL, HONG KONG

STRUCTURAL
MEP & FIRE
ENGINEERS
WHITBY & BIRD ENGINEERS
PO BOX 116921 DUBAI
UNITED ARAB EMIRATES

LEAD
CONSULTANT
ARCHITECT
AEDAS LTD.
19TH FLOOR 1063 KINGS ROAD
QUARRY BAY, HONG KONG

PROJECT
CONSULTANT
JAMES CUBITT & PARTNERS
PO BOX 46208 ABU DHABI
UNITED ARAB EMIRATES

PROJECT
MANAGER
PO BOX 28536
ABU DHABI
UNITED ARAB EMIRATES

CLIENT
FORESIGHT DEVELOPMENT AND
PROJECT MANAGEMENT

DANCING TOWERS OF ABU DHABI

AL KHALDIA COMPLEX

KEY PLAN

THE SITE

THE KHALDIA COMPLEX
DANCING TOWERS OF ABU DHABI

PROJECT NO.     05680

SCALE

DATE     13.11.06

DRAWING NO.

REVISION

DRAWING TITLE
AL KHALDIA COMPLEX

STATUS
TENDER

REVISION     DATE     DESCRIPTION

# Civic Approach

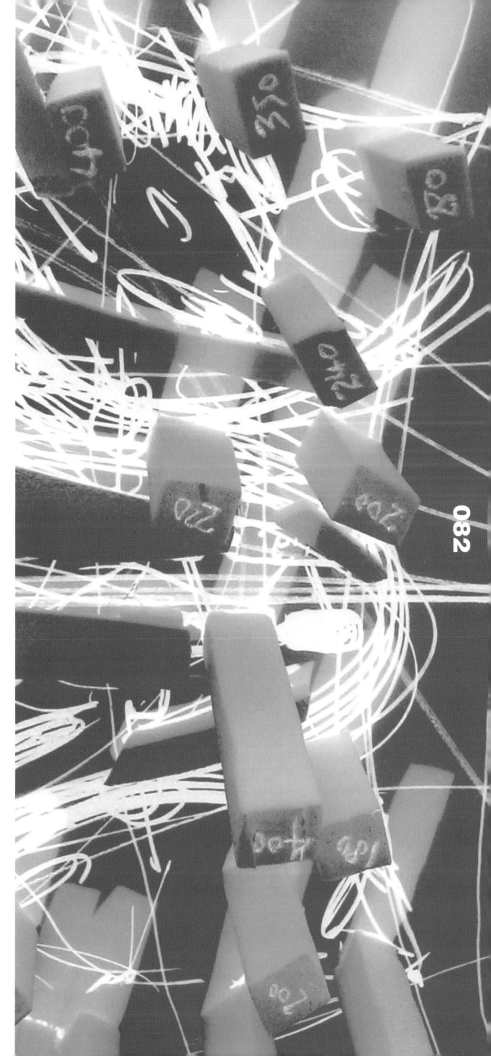

# Civic
# Approach

A "Civic Approach" places inherent values in the benefits a project has on the environment at large. It is neither defined by whether the project is publicly or privately executed, nor limited by its own criteria for success.

It is often true that projects that are considered "civic" are public, governmental, educational or cultural in use. In this regard, the West Kowloon Cultural District, shown in this chapter, would fit this archetype. The project contains five museums, five performance venues as well as a multitude of educational facilities. The use and type of the project, however, does not necessitate that the project is responding in a civic manner.

In this particular case, the civic response was in identifying a way to expand Hong Kong's urban open space, which was felt to be important to the community's well-being. The location of the project on Victoria Harbor and the sheer size of the 42-hectare site offered a perfect opportunity to give something back to the city. The entire project was

designed as a very large and central urban park, which also happens to house activities including the cultural center.

From a project viability point of view, the benefits of the project (which are both inward and outward in approach) are not immediately apparent. However, a building that is embraced by the public has enormous benefits for the project's viability. This is especially true with respect to commercial, hospitality, residential and retail, whose success is directly related to an ability to sell or be sold. In this respect, the "altruistic" goal of being "civic" can be sold to a client who may only care about profit.

Of course, projects such as libraries are truly public in nature and help define the public domain – in this respect, they can be deemed civic. It is this "public" component that needs to be nurtured. A project that can offer something to everyone will be used, enjoyed and experienced. The transition from public to private activities can be softened with varying degrees. This enables a multitude of opportunities for human interaction to be sustained within the project even with socioeconomic realities.

If a project is active, commercial components benefit. If a project is enjoyed, people will want to live, work and play within its walls. This is the formula and result of mixed-use projects. This is not a new formula, as Trajan's Market in Rome, dating back thousands of years ago, proves. A mixture of different types of activities are brought together in varying degrees, enticing public activity through commercial interaction, resulting in a rich and vibrant setting. Time cycles are increased and there is an impact of the project within the public domain.

Of course, the impact a project has on people's lives may be limited by accessibility, size and location. The degree of influence should not limit the importance and role of every project. "Civic Approach" goes beyond what is deemed civic, by instituting an obligation that every project try to improve and benefit the world we live in.∎

Program **Cultural** Site Area **40 Hectares** Open Space
Floor Area **1,734,871 sqm**  Building Height **155 m**

086

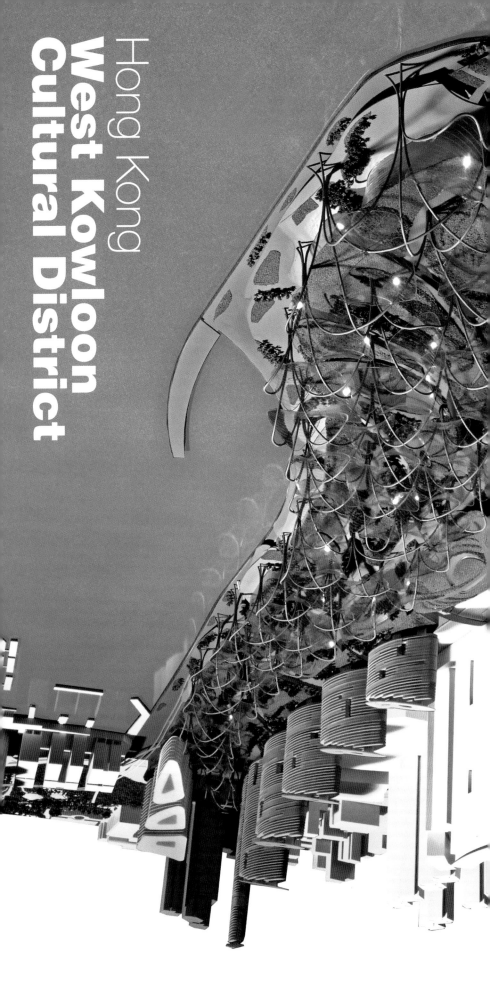

# Hong Kong **West Kowloon Cultural District**

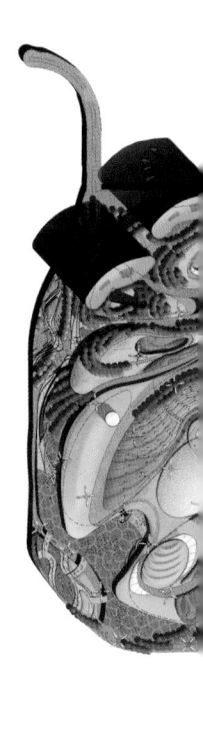

An approach to the public realm proposes a unique urban development in Hong Kong. On one level this will be a cultural district. On another level it will be a 40-hectare park, physically threaded into the life of the city and the harbour. This is a park in the sky, an undulating landscape affording all who visit – whether by day or by night – amazing views of the harbour and Central District's glittering citadels.

The normative urban model includes natural landscape features as occupants of the ground plane and building facades. In the normative model, buildings literally sit on the landscape, and the architecture divides and controls the urban spaces caught between. In this new conception, landscape becomes part of the experience of the city fabric, co-habiting with the built environment.

**1 Kilometer**

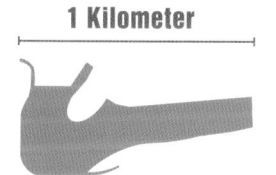

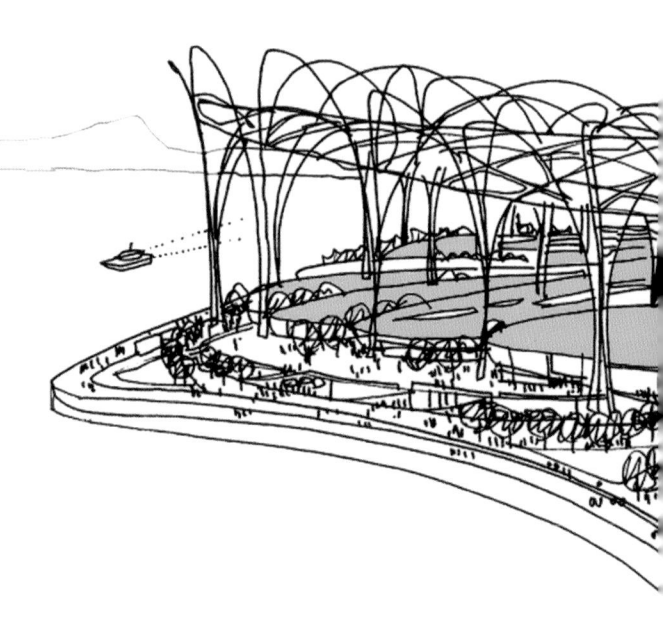

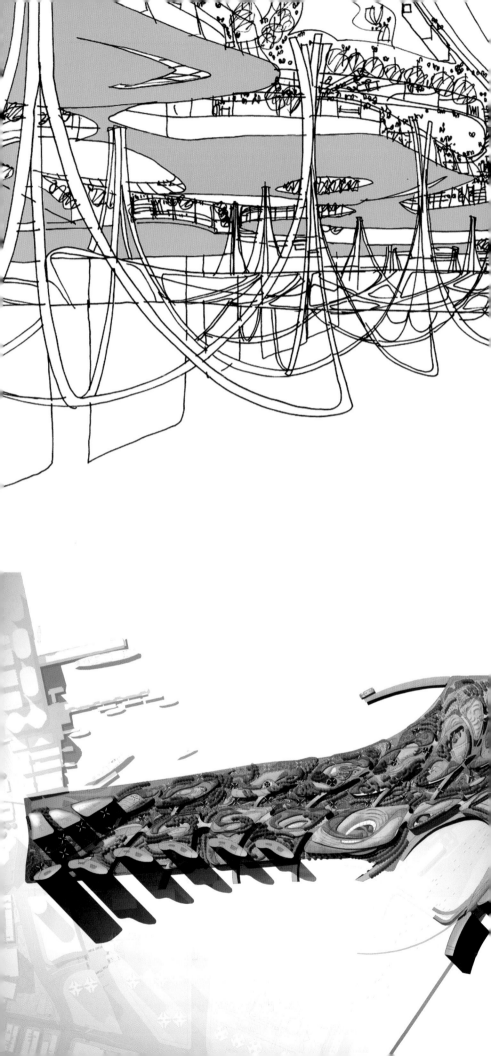

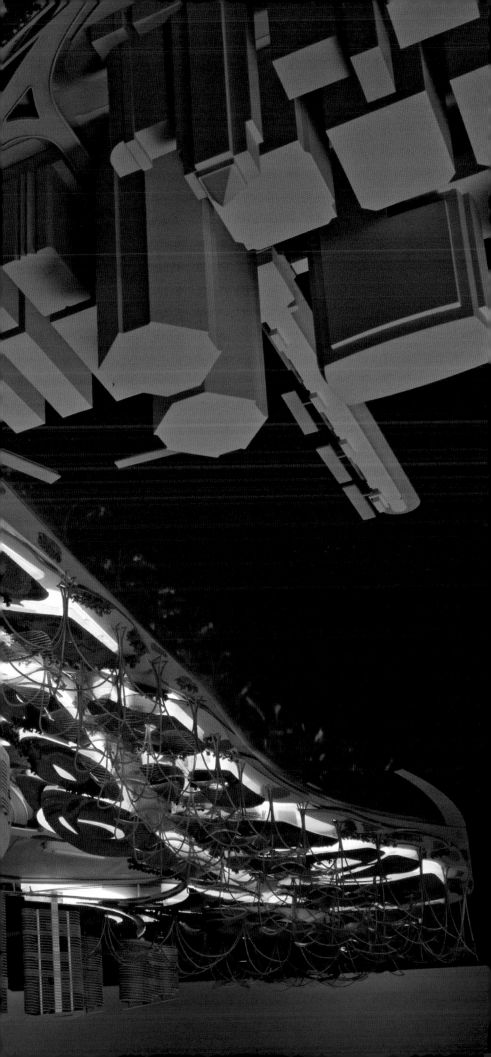

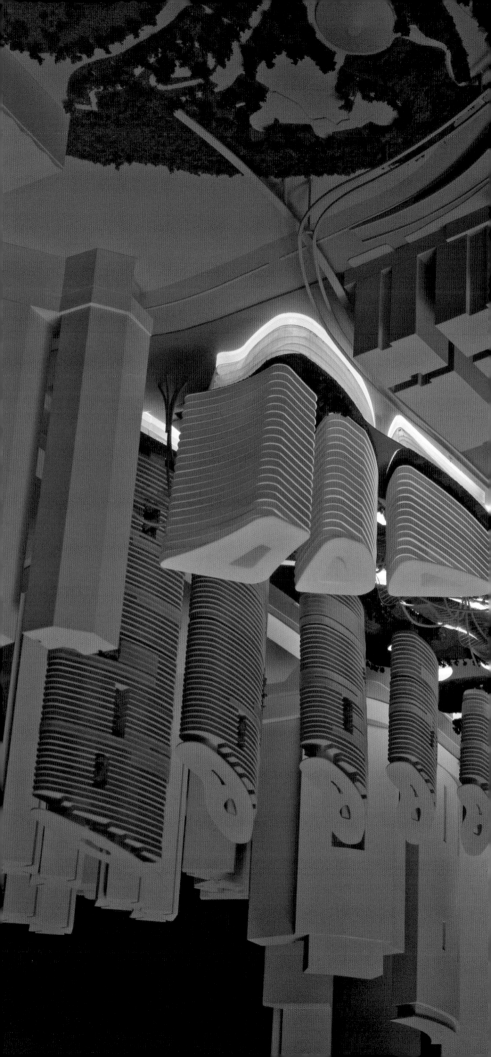

**10:00 AM**
Access through Central Promenade

**16:00 PM**
Performance Venue

**21:00 PM**
MITS: Museum of Information Technol

The groundscape references natural landscape formative processes. Water behaviour is the activator in this process, as it moves through the landscape and deposits materials on its journey to the sea. This process of attrition sculpts the different levels of ground, revealing layers of strata, subsurface water flows and durable landscape components. These components appear as architectural forms.

Carved through the landform are canyons, both narrow and wide, which give access to the buildings below the park. In the walls of these canyons are the performing arts venues, theatres and museums where Hong Kong's cultural heart is going to make its home.

The focal canyon, the central promenade, runs through the site in response to the desire lines of its visitors. Again, following nature's flow, this becomes the conduit through which nodes of activities and destinations are connected.

Powerful, iconic architectural forms rise up out of the central promenade, revealing the diverse cultural activities inside. Activities that would extend the hours of use within the district are introduced. This is no localised cultural ghetto, but a genuine district, where the diversity of use creates activity that starts in the morning and spreads long into the night.

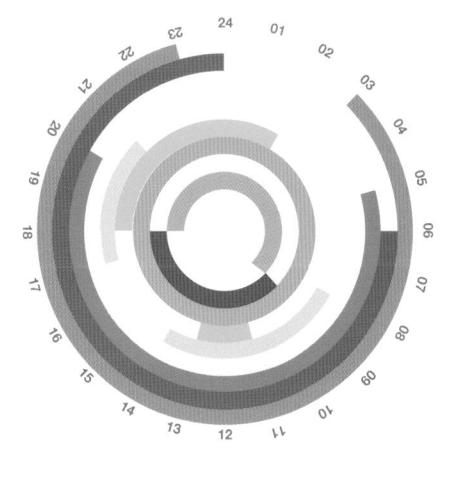

| | | |
|---|---|---|
| ■ Urban Park | ■ Museum | ■ Performance Venues |
| □ Food/ Beverage | ■ Piazzas | ■ Entertainment |
| ■ Hotel/ Conference | ■ Office | ■ Residential |

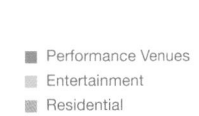

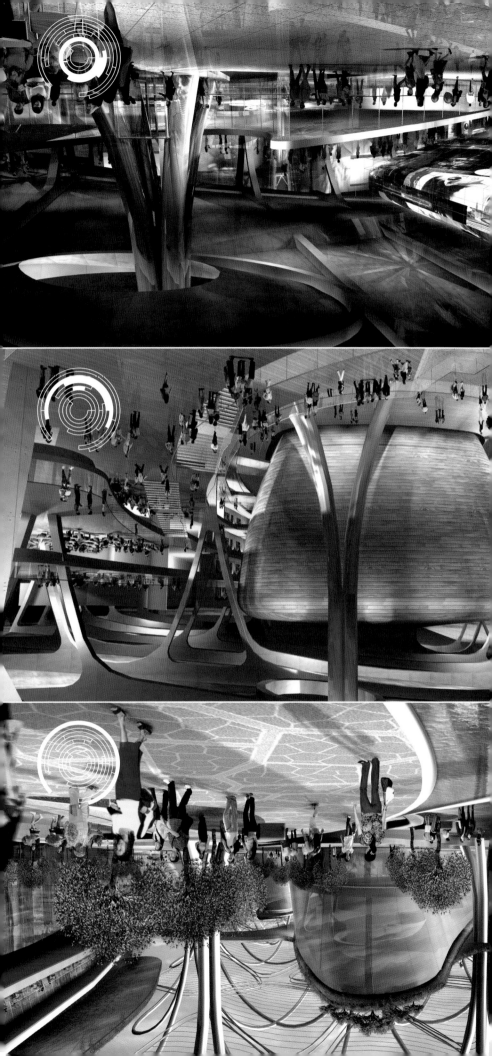

The canopy, as waves on water above the urban park, provides visual continuity along the waterfront as it floats uninterrupted over the buildings it covers. Organically tied to the master plan, the canopy hovering over the park is supported by an orchard of tree-like columns on an 80meter by 50meter grid. The roots of the columns disappear into the ground beneath. As the columns land, skylights and light-wells are created, allowing a gentle wash of light into the venues below.

The WKCD performing arts complex will be an exciting, inviting, vibrant and human space, full of life and activity. It will not only be a performing arts centre, but a true cultural district and a model for the performing arts in the 21$^{st}$ century. The attractiveness of these facilities will be greatly enhanced because they are intermingled with the museums of the cultural district. All the theatres and museums cluster between the waterfront and the central promenades and have frontage to at least one major piazza. Mixing the two types of venue into a single cultural cluster will create an energy that will extend far into the night ▪

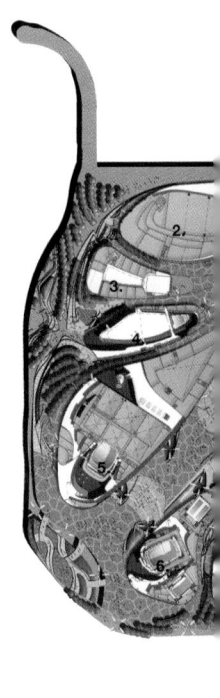

1.  Hotel
2.  Conference Centre
3.  School of Arts
4.  Art Exhibition Centre
5.  Large Theatre
6.  Concert Hall
7.  Education Centre
8.  Museum of Information/Technology
9.  Museum of Contemporary Art
13. Performance Venue
14. Centre Living Art/Design
15. Cultural Block A
16. Mall 1
17. Cultural Block B
18. Mall 2
19. People Mover Station
20. Mall 3
21. Office Tower

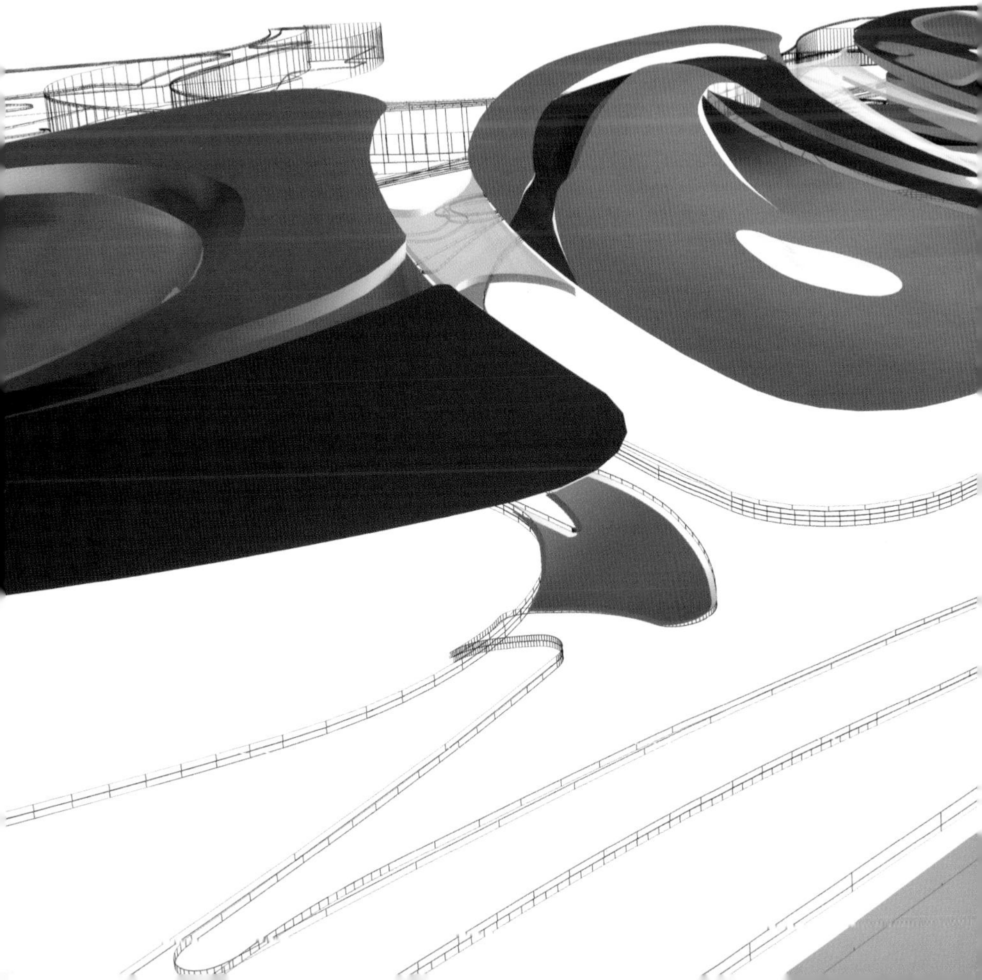

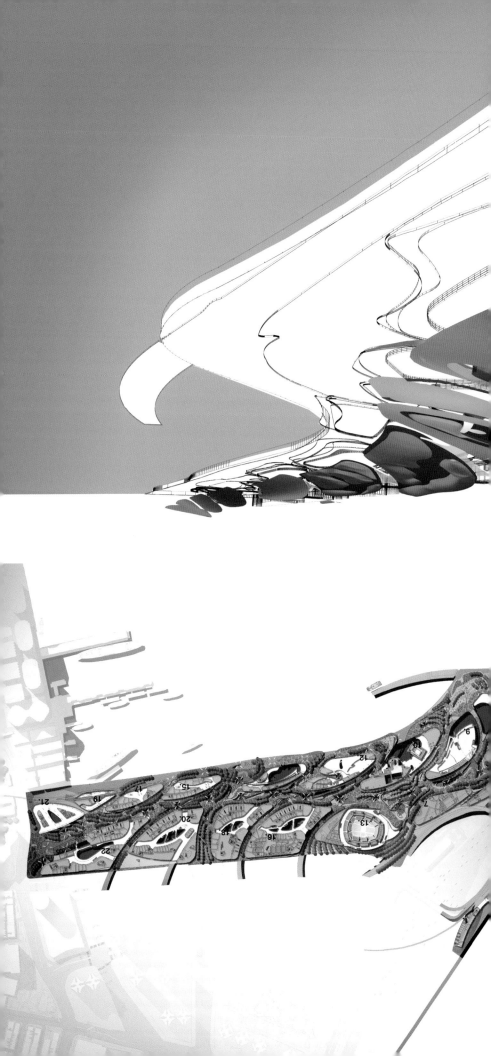

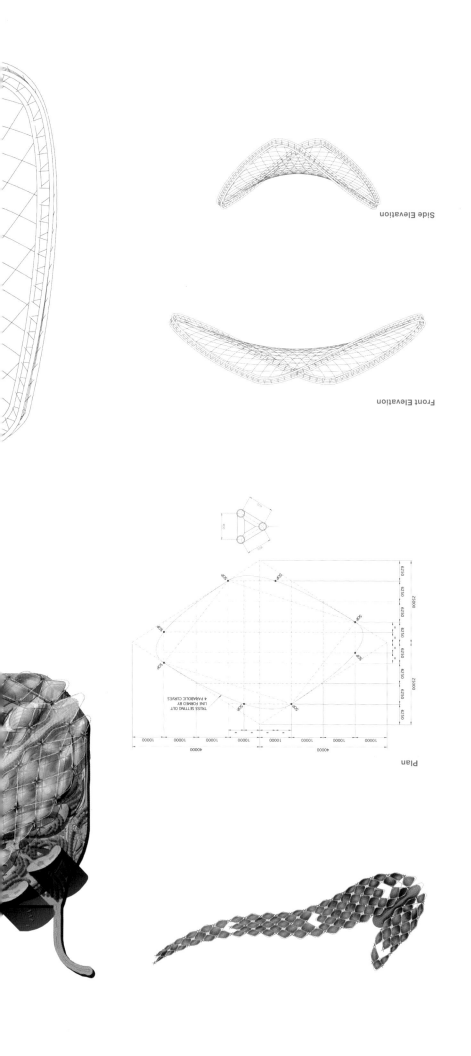

Side Elevation

Front Elevation

TRUSS SETTING OUT
LINE FORMED BY
4 PARABOLIC CURVES

Plan

44 mm. Dia Fully Locked
Cables (Pfeifer WS-2 Or
Similar) Heavy Galvanized
At 3 meter crs

450 x 240 x 16 Rhs Struts
At 1.6 meter crs

3 No. 508 x 40 Chs Chords
In Truss Approximately
3 M. Faceted Lengths
Connected Using Full
Penetration Butt Welds

ETFE Panels

Steel-Cast Clamp Detail

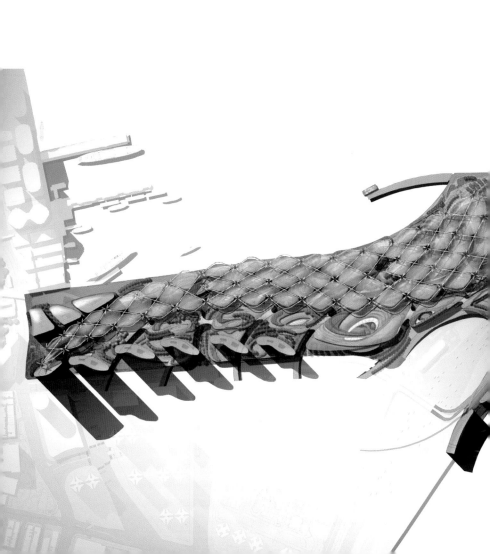

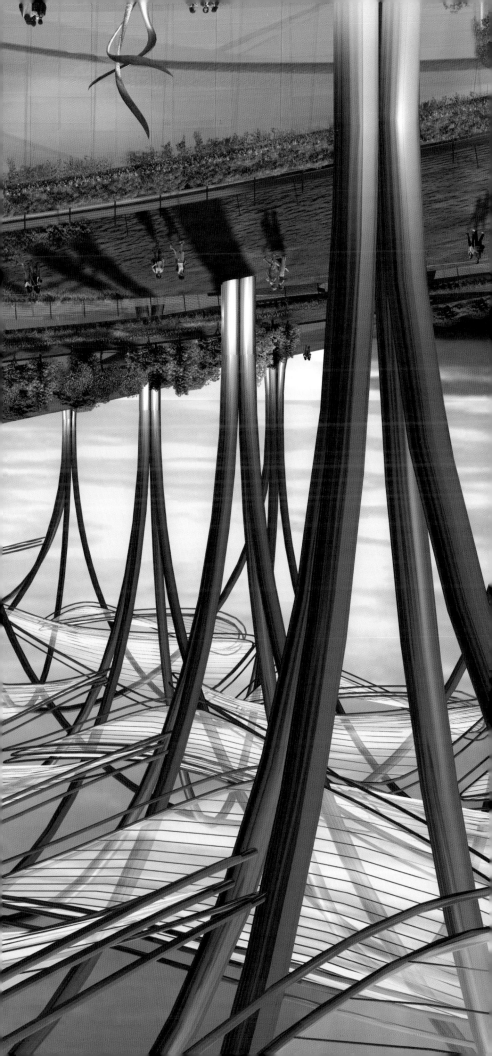

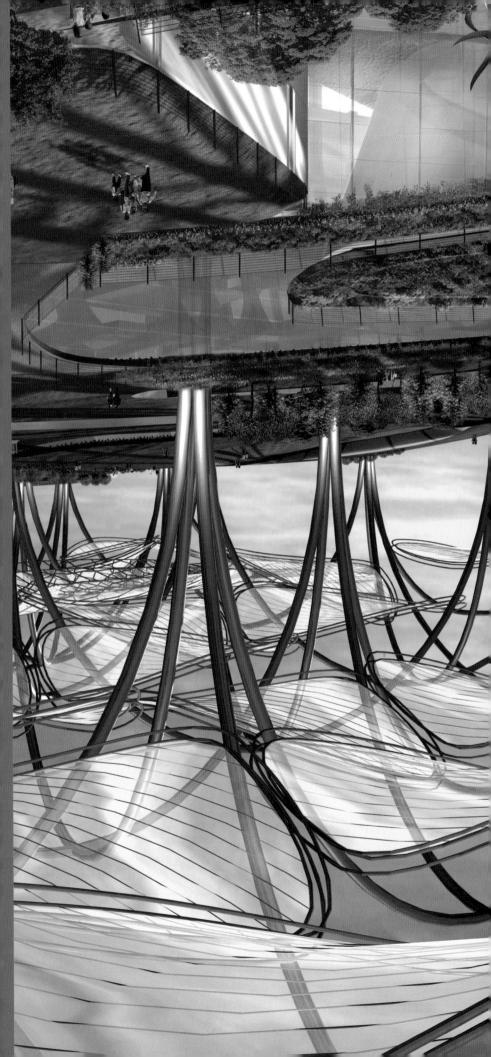

Program **Broadcast Studio/Office**  Site Area **39,756 sqm**
Floor Area **303,929 sqm**  Building Height **300 m**

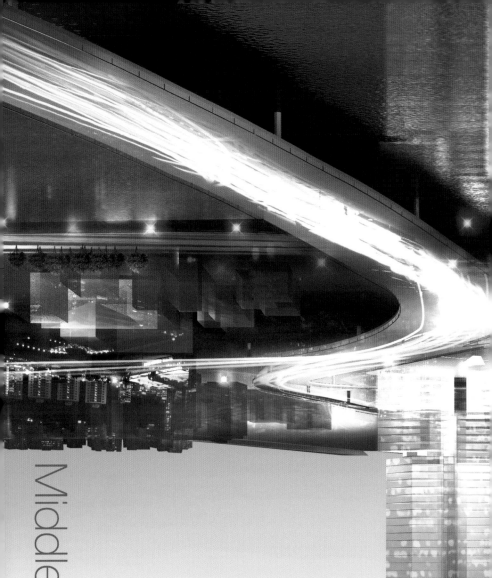

Middle East **Media Tower**

## Middle East **Media Tower**

As the importance of the Middle East is growing within the global realms of business and politics, what was once considered local media is now emerging into an international media network, with projected influence and audience levels in the next 10 years comparable to CNN or BBC.

The client's brief asked for a 12,000 square meter expansion, on a plot of land with limited availability, adjacent to the current station. By considering the design vertically, this land limitation was taken out of the equation, allowing for a building that meets the client's vision for the future, and providing over 120,000 square meters for the station alone.

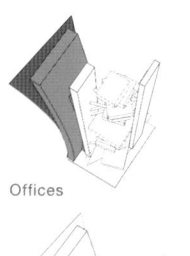

Offices

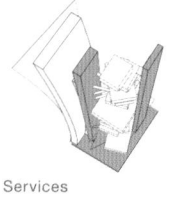

Services

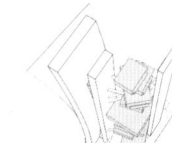

Studios

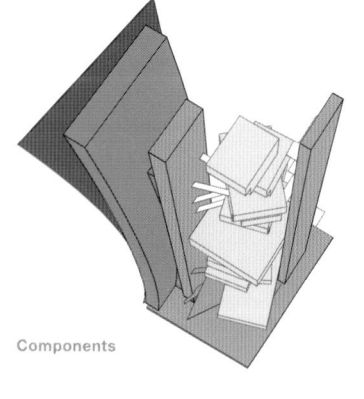

Components

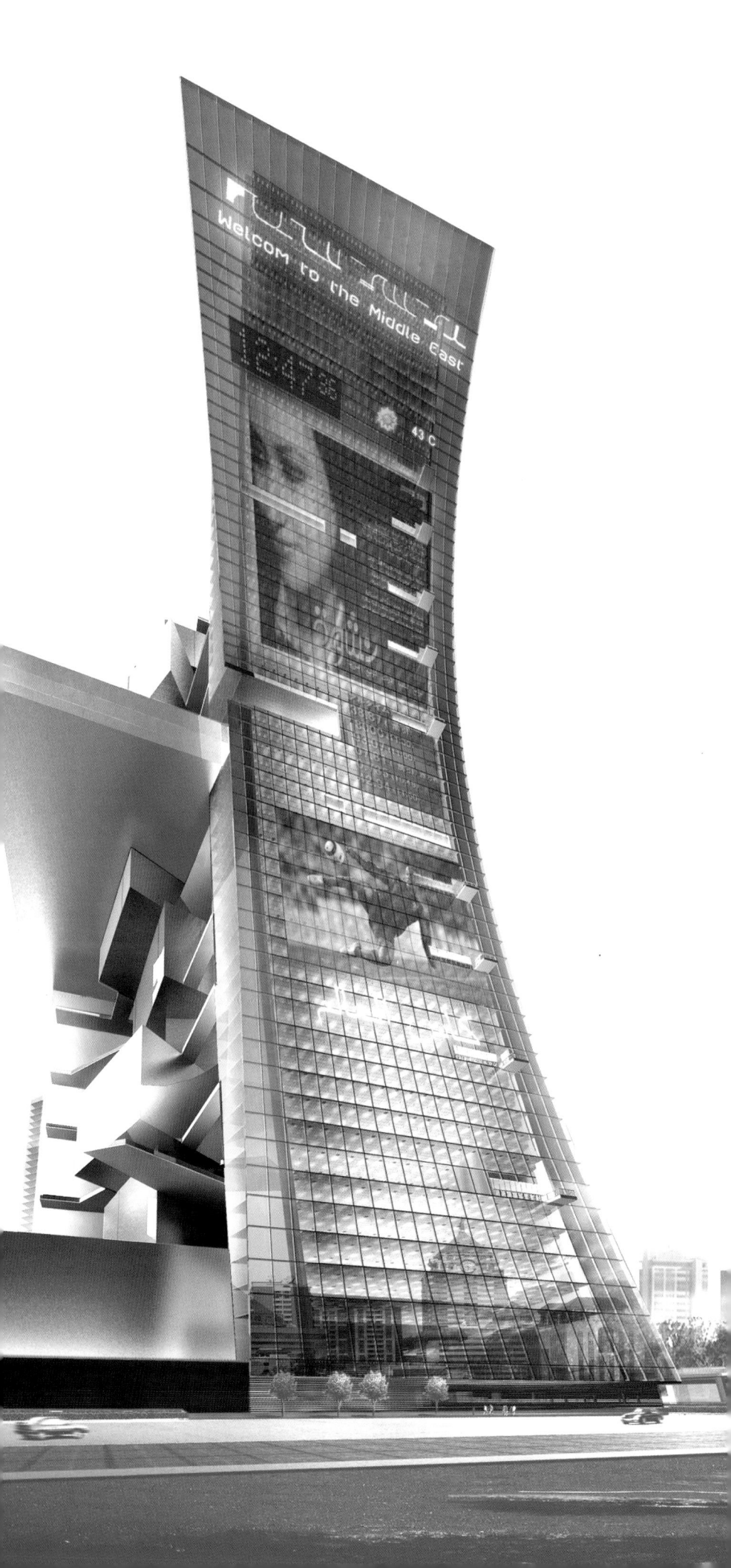

Ten studios were stacked on top of each other as giant television sets. The master control room, editing rooms and news studio are located in the middle of this stack. On one side of the studios are the technical support lifts, which connect conveniently to the workshops below. On the other side are all the office and commercial support spaces, overlooking a river. The office bar is shaped to become a 60m-by-300m-high LED screen visible from across the water, welcoming passengers on incoming planes.

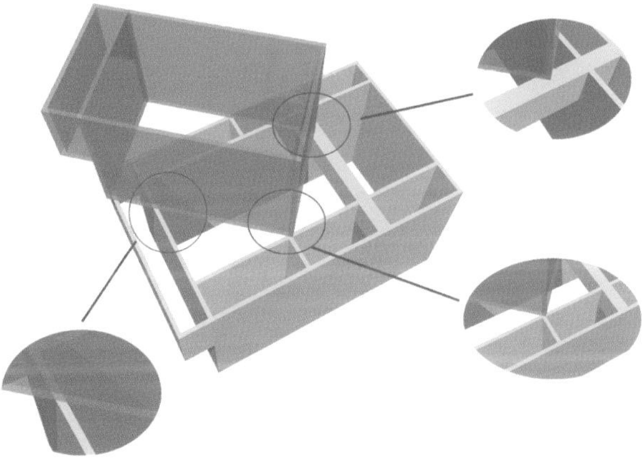

**Structure**

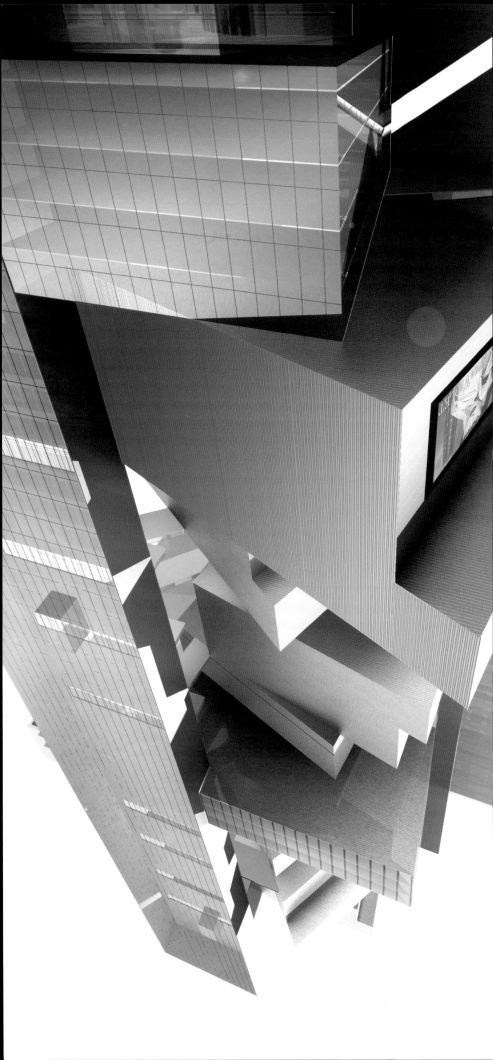

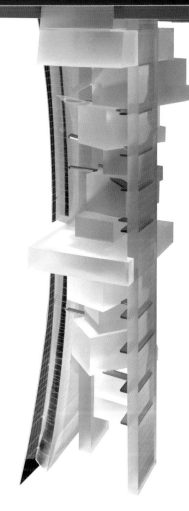

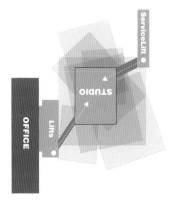

- Lifts
- Offices
- Studio
- Lower Studios

Snaking through the entire complex are the different circulation patterns between audience, actor, technical support, business, and the public spectator. All of these patterns pass and almost touch each other within the 100-meter-high central atrium. This allows the public the ability to freely see and comprehend the inner workings of the TV station without interruption to the business activities contained inside.

This educational desire is also presented outwardly to the surrounding city, revealing different aspects of the station, encouraging an exploration around the project, and ultimately luring the civic realm inside, to continue the awaiting discovery.

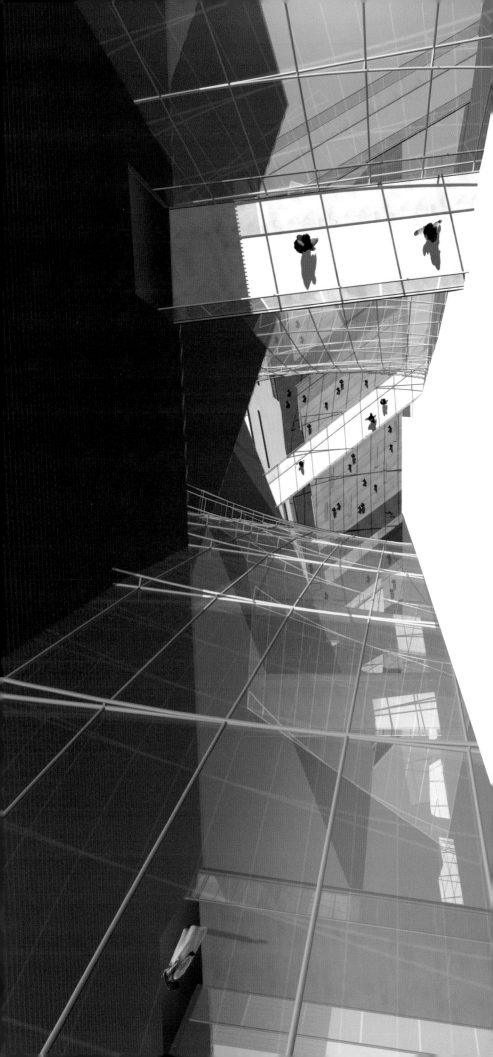

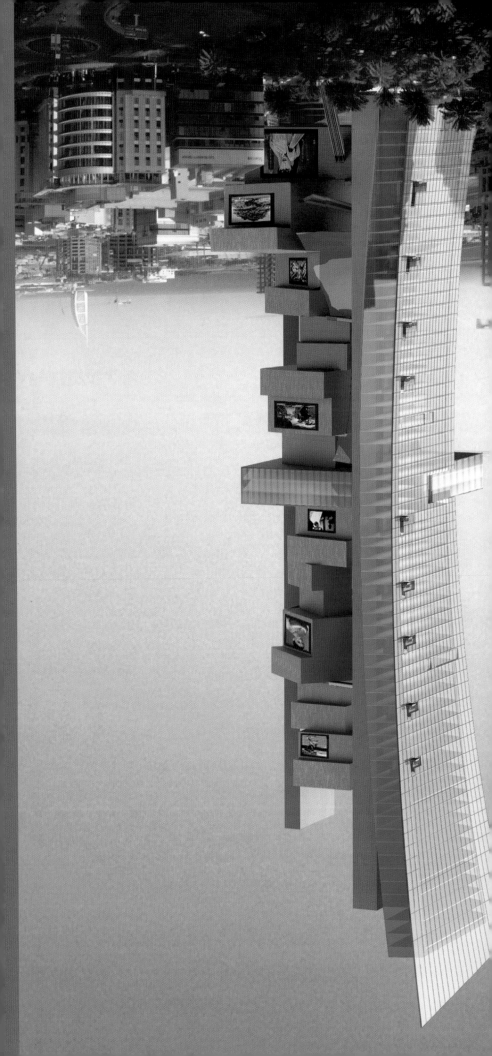

## United Arab Emirates **Multaka**

Multaka is an enormous master plan for 880 hectares located outside Abu Dhabi, the capital of the UAE, immediately adjacent to its expanding international airport. The scheme for a medium-density new town of 120,000 people responds directly to this relationship with the transport hub in both zoning and use.

The commercial hub meets the edge of the airport in a discrete corner on the south of the site and then stretches deep into the site. This is surrounded by its supporting population of high-density housing, which then reduces to medium and low densities as you move away from its "Manhattan" island. The different uses of the site are represented by a topography of dunes, separated by public recreational valleys or public waterways ▪

Program **Urban Planning** Site Area **9,795,000 sqm** Area **6,611,625 sqm** Population **50,248**

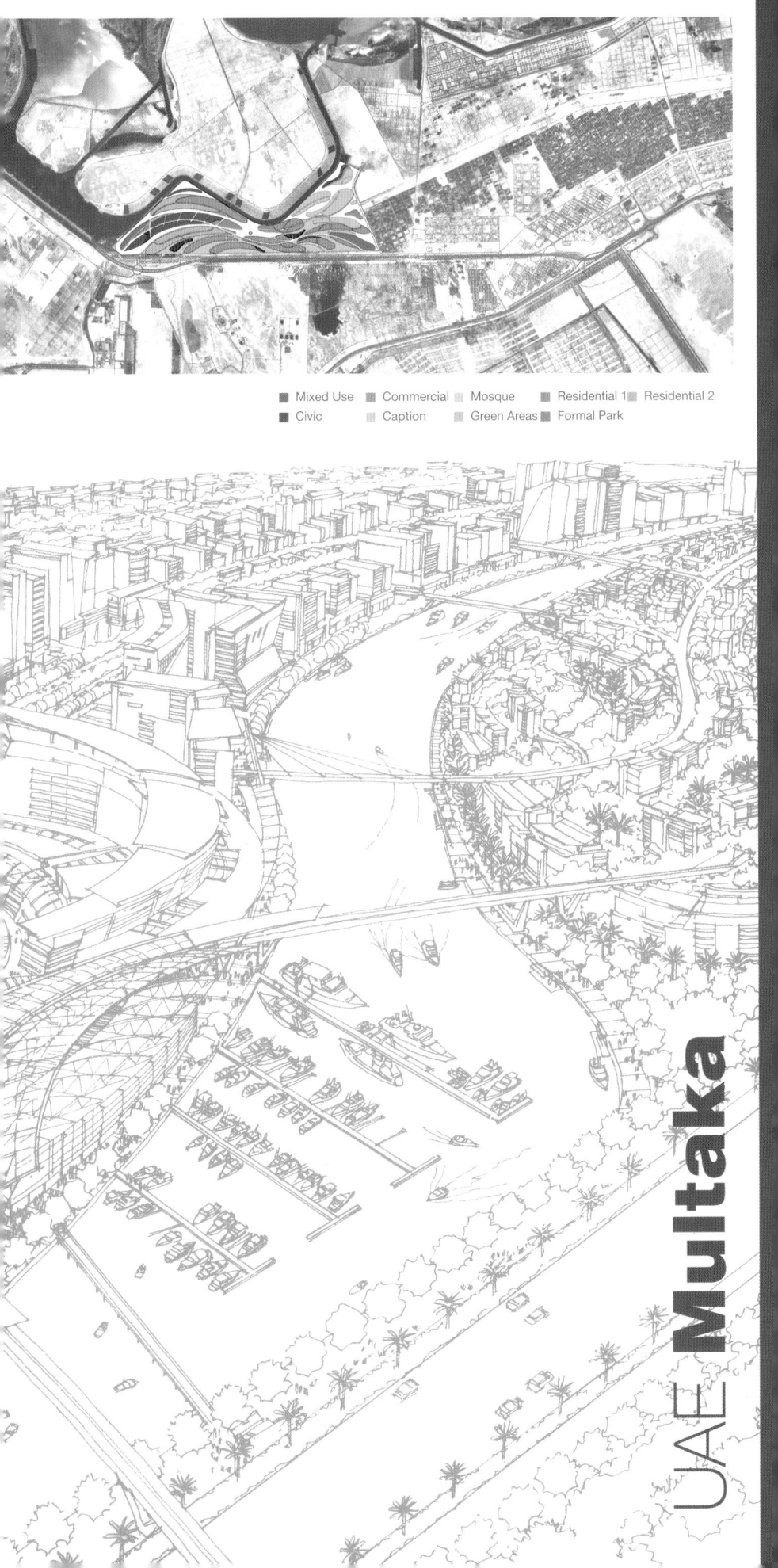

■ Mixed Use  ■ Commercial  ▦ Mosque  ■ Residential 1 ▦ Residential 2
■ Civic  ▦ Caption  ▦ Green Areas ■ Formal Park

UAE Multaka

# Dubai **U-BORA Towers**

The U-BORA Tower Complex is a mixed-use development located in the heart of Business Bay, Dubai, UAE. The design has given equal attention to its three different uses – office, residential and podium – in order to maximize their opportunities and viabilities within the site's context.

The office-tower position is rotated from the orthogonal at the street level to help focus the office space down the future view corridors toward the water and past the surrounding developments. As the tower increases in height, its four faces respond directly to their three-dimensional context. They all twist at varying degrees and angles to reorient their faces to maximize available views.

The residential block deliberately does not compete with the surrounding towers in height, and instead, keeps low and focused to the adjacent water body to the south.

Office Tower Circulation ■
Residential Circulation ▦
Openings ▨
Public Spaces ▪

Program **Mixed Use**  Site Area **19,883 sqm**
Floor Area **119,298 sqm**  Building Height **263 m**

Dubai **U-BORA Towers**

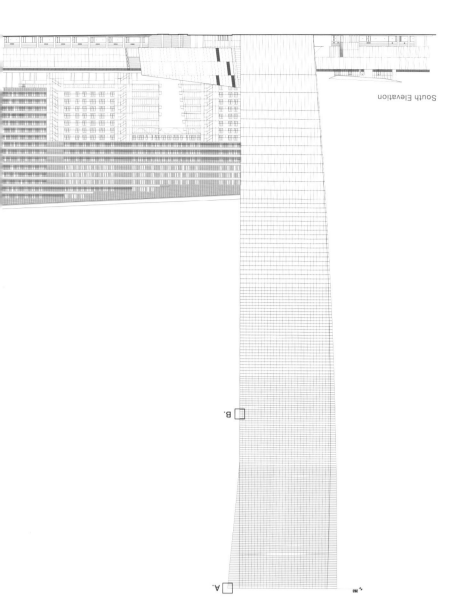

By designing the block as a linear bar rising from 12 stories at the tower end to 15 stories at the western end, a significantly greater percentage of units get an uninterrupted view of the water.

All three components are glued together with a 10,000 square-meter public, densely landscaped deck that has accessibility from all three exposed sides of the project. Two monumental stairs lead up from either side of the office tower with a third passing through a large "gateway" within the residential block down to the water edge to the south.

The U-BORA Tower's Mixed-Use offers something to everyone, and in a complementary way, balances its three major components of office, residential and retail in order to maximize the site's vibrancy. The architecture is powerful, pure and dynamic and will become a focal development in a setting of competing attention. The project will be unique to its setting in Business Bay and will also become a model development for the entire region ▪

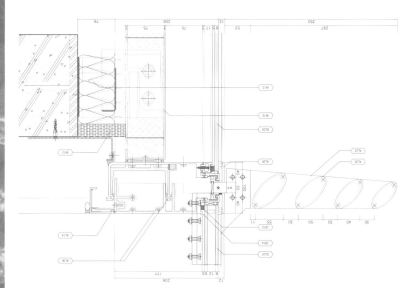

B. Façade Detail at Mid-Level

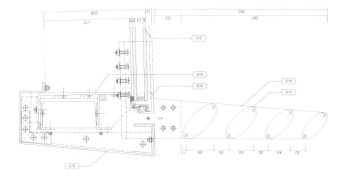

A. Façade Detail at Roof

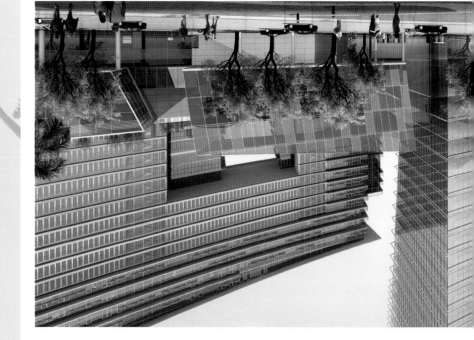

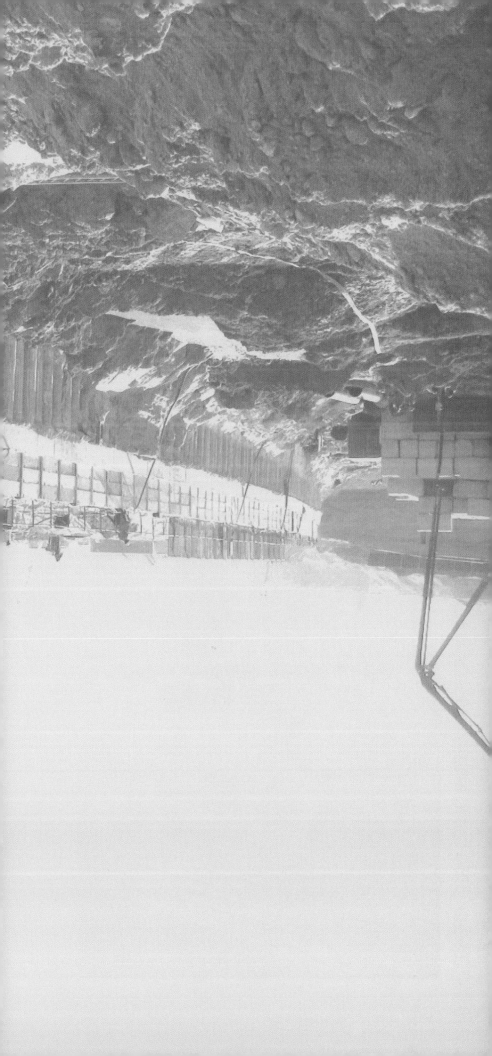

DATE
03 DECEMBER 2006

DRAWING NO.
727D029

REVISION
–

TITLE
PODIUM G.A. PLAN P3
EAST

FILENAME
AED-7727-P-P3-N

PROJECT NO.
06727

APPROVAL

ORIGINAL SIZE
A1

CHECKER

AUTHOR

SCALE
1 : 200

CURRENT ISSUE SIGNATURES

STATUS
ISSUE FOR TENDER

| ISSUE | DESCRIPTION | DATE |
|---|---|---|
| – | FIRST ISSUE | 31.10.06 |

TRAFFIC CONSULTANT
MAUNSELL CONSULTANCY
SERVICES
P.O. BOX 9103
DUBAI, UAE
TEL +971-4 335 3545

FACADE CONSULTANT
ALT CLADDING INC.
7TH FLOOR, WASL CENTER
SHEIKH ZAYED ROAD
P.O. BOX 112500
DUBAI, UAE
TEL +971-4 338 6151
FAX +971-4 338 6152

INTERIOR DESIGN CONSULTANT
POINT OF DESIGN

STRUCTURAL ENGINEER
WHITBY & BIRD ENGINEERS
P.O. BOX 115550
DUBAI, UAE
TEL +971-4 332 4545
FAX +971-4 332 4546

QUANTITY SURVEYOR
GROUP CONSULT INTERNATIONAL

LANDSCAPE & DRAINAGE
AEXAD LIMITED

DESIGN
RANCO E&C LIMITED

CONSULTANT

CLIENT

U-BORA TOWER
MIXED USE DEVELOPMENT AT
BUSINESS BAY, DUBAI, UAE
PLOT No. A06,A25

NAME

## Thailand **Office Park**

Thailand Office Park recalls the temples of the ancient capital, Ayattaya. The purity of these temples becomes fragmented in the ground plane through the surrounding urban and commercial forces. The project's faceted shape maximizes spatial diversity for the retail-podium portion of the project, complete with indoor and outdoor spatial fragments. A family of crystalline towers extrudes and tapers from the angled podium. Although both the tower and the podium originate from this fractured geometry, the towers rising with a slight taper evolve into simple extrusions, allowing for high efficiency on all levels, as required by the client. The two tallest towers link together with a sky-bridge and hold public functions 300 meters above the streets. The overall result is a distinctive complex that is contemporary and references Thai architecture, while maintaining the challenging economic restrictions of the client. ▪

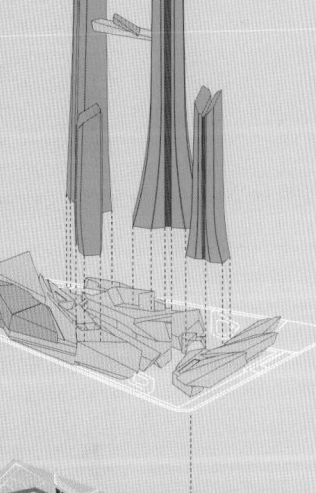

Outdoor Public Circulation ▫

Indoor Public Circulation ▪

Retail ▫

Specialized Retail ▪

Towers ▪

Verticle Circulation ▪

Program **Mixed Use** Site Area **54,519 sqm** Building Height **420 m**
Floor Area **679,697 sqm**

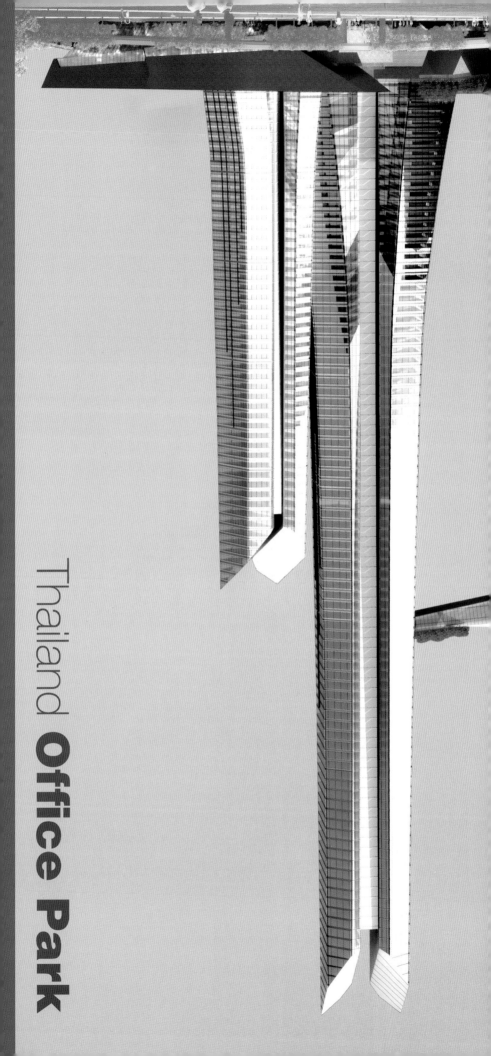

Thailand **Office Park**

## People's Republic of China **Crowne Plaza Hotel**

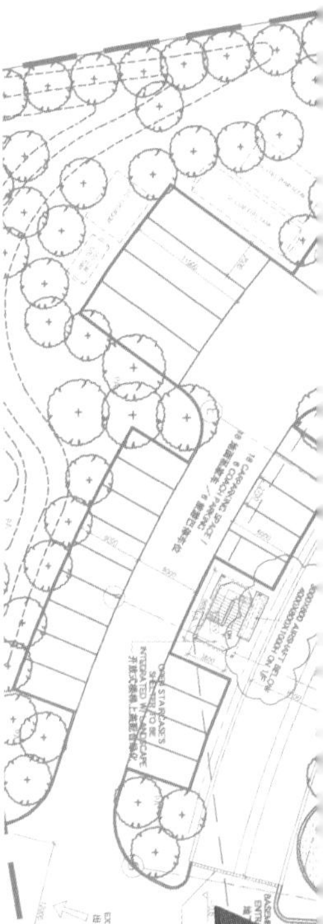

The client, located in the center of Huizhou within the Guangdong region of China, was asked by the city to create a focal development five-star hotel across from the civic square. As a civic hotel, the project was weighted heavily in the supporting facilities beyond the 365 rooms. This includes five major restaurants, ballroom, function rooms, business center, spa and sauna activities.

The project, being highly visible on all faces, toward one main street, and thus maximizes the open space on the other side, enabling the project to knit with the open space of the civic square. The project gestures and curves softly in response to the changing views and approaches both from and toward the hotel ▪

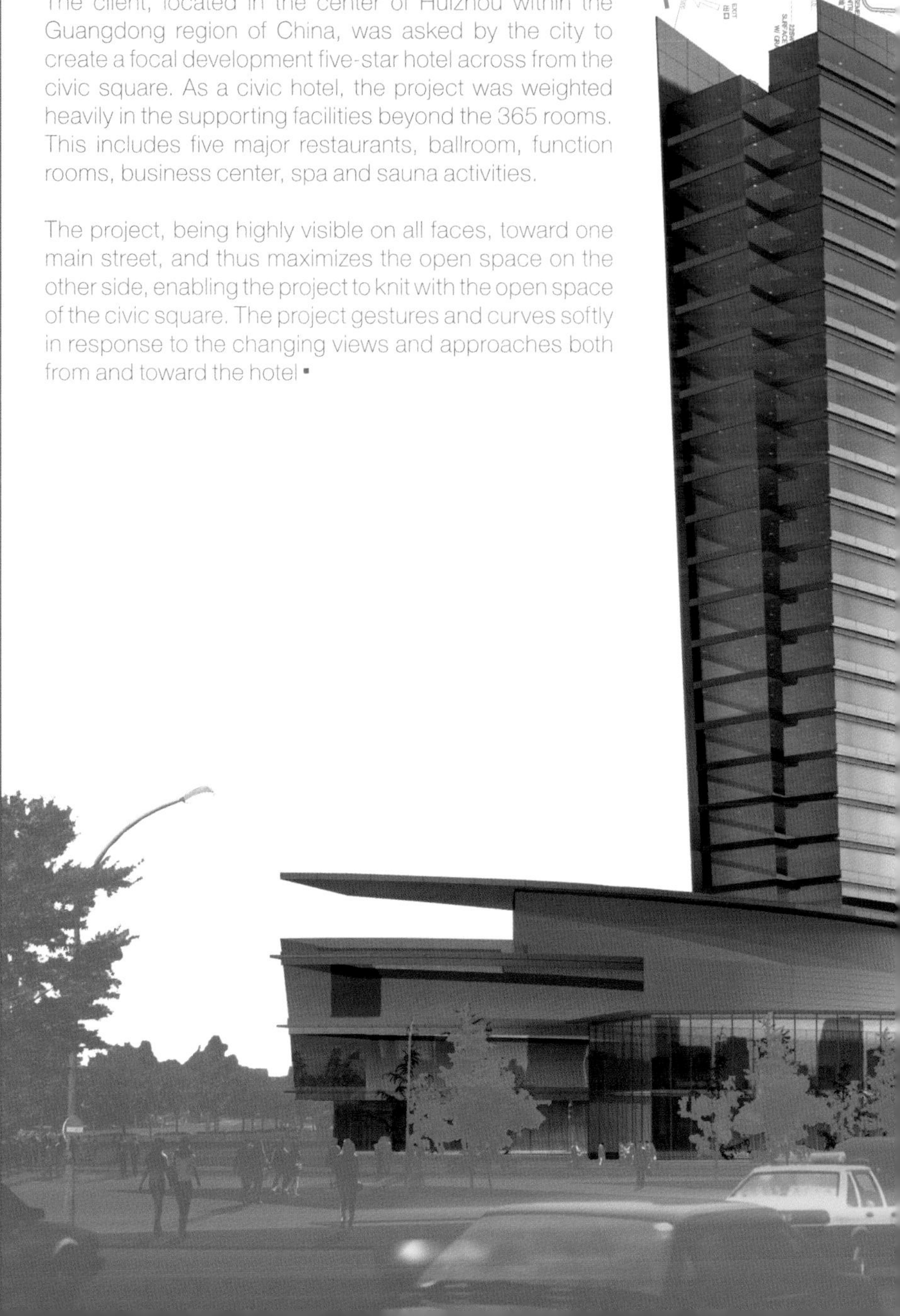

**120**

Program **Hotel** Site Area **9,904 sqm** Building Height **97 m**
Floor Area **84,237 sqm**

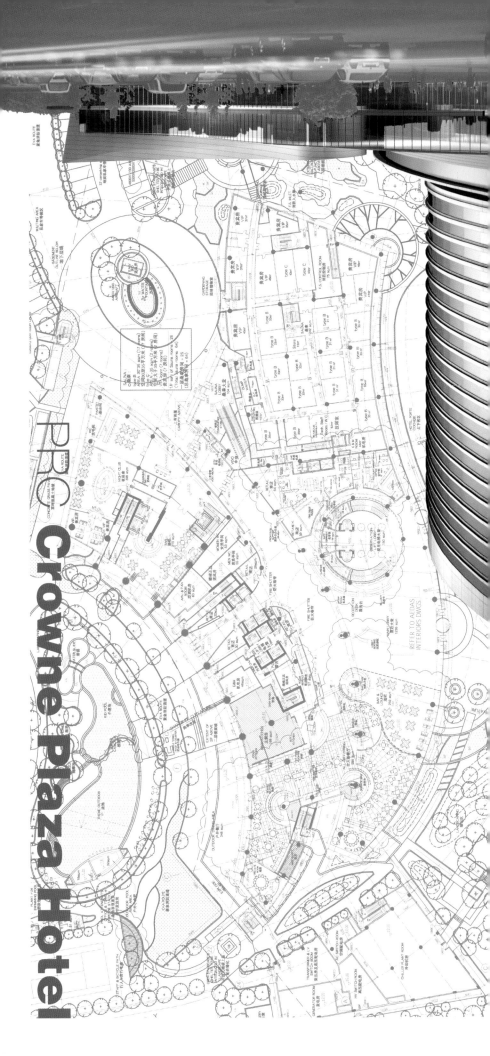

PRC **Crowne Plaza Hotel**

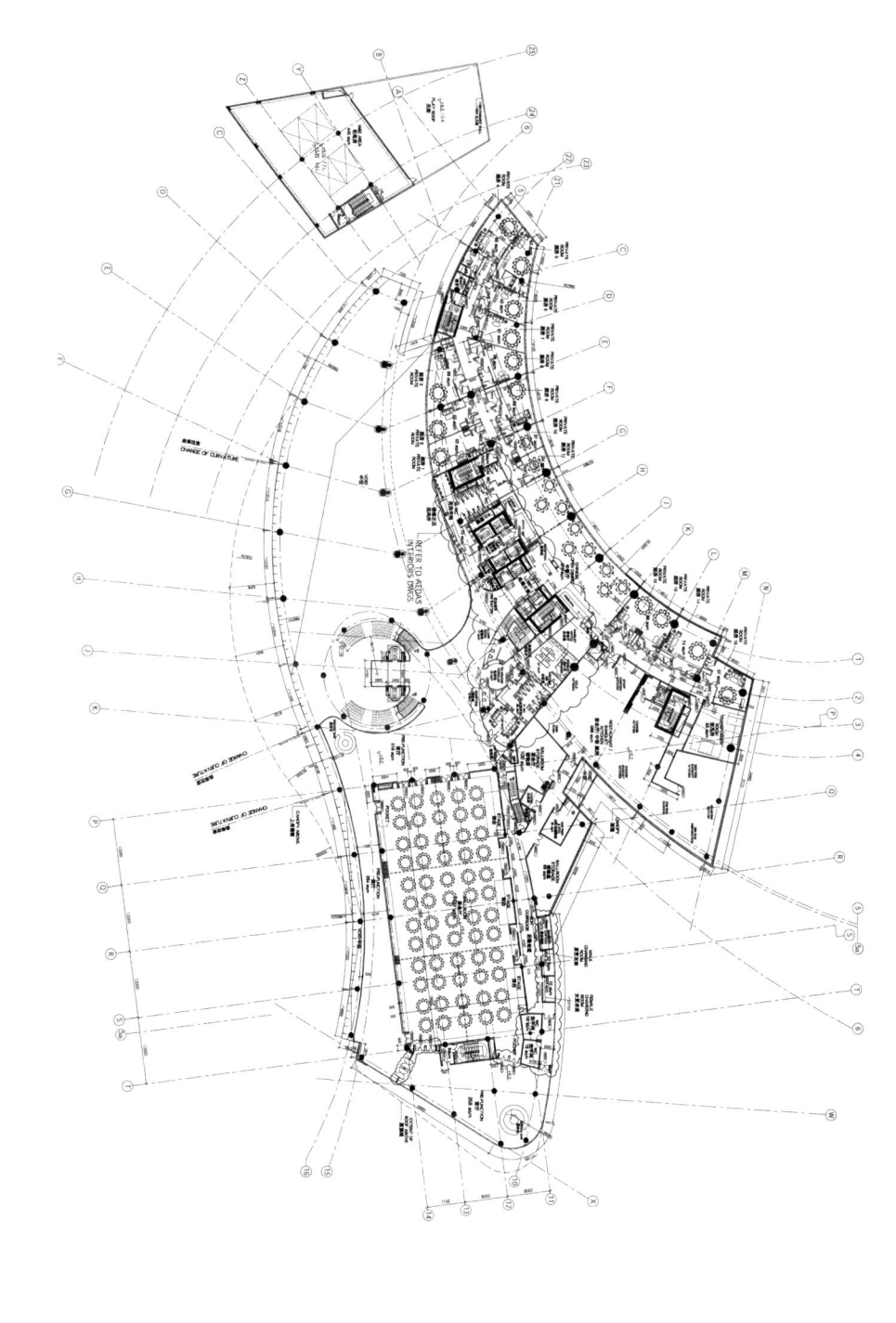

Plan Level - 2

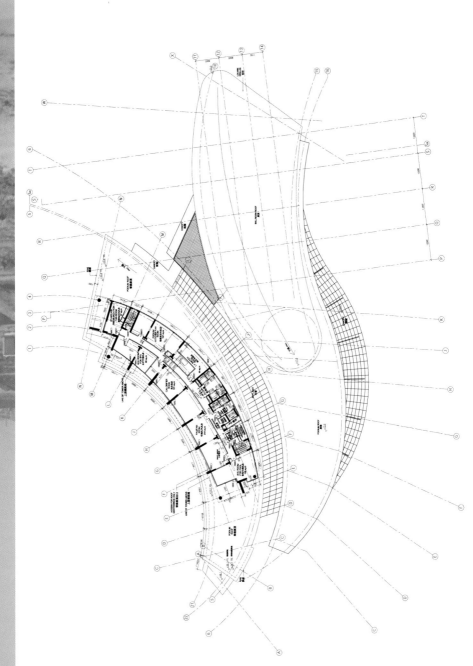

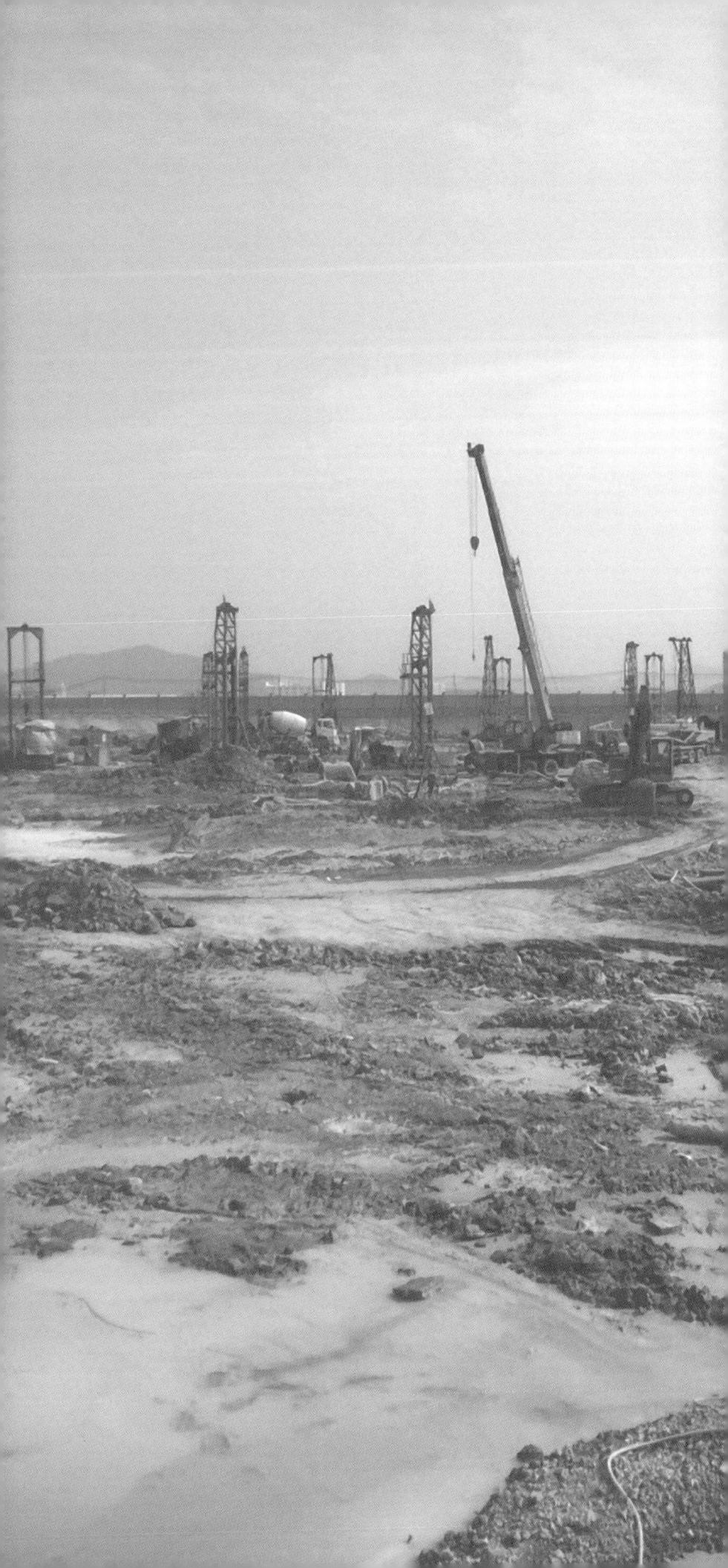

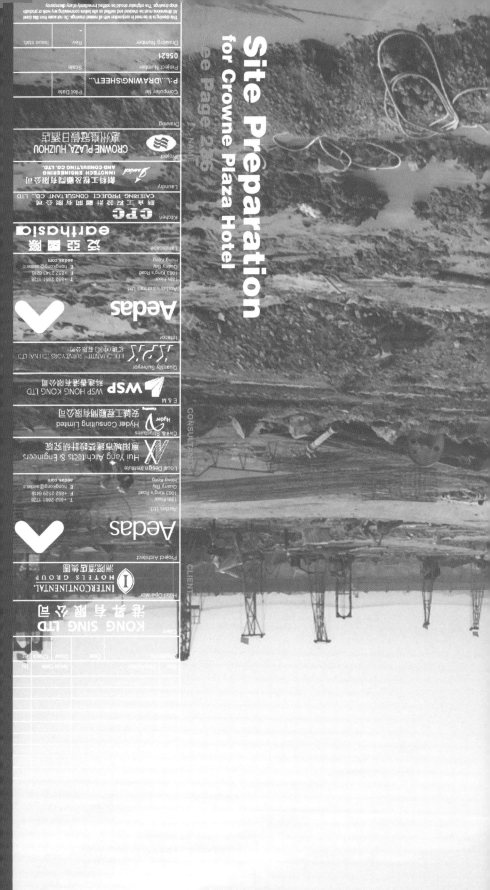

# Site Preparation
## for Crowne Plaza Hotel

See Page 296

NAME

CONSULTANTS

CLIENT

This drawing is to be read in conjunction with all related drawings. Do not scale from this sheet. All dimensions must be checked and verified on site before commencing any work or production of shop drawings. The originator should be notified immediately of any discrepancy.

Drawing Number    Rev    Issue Date

Project Number
05621

Computer file    Scale
P:\...\DRAWING\SHEET...

Plot Date

Drawing

**Project**
CROWNE PLAZA, HUIZHOU    惠州皇冠假日酒店

**Laundry**
INNOTECH ENGINEERING
AND CONSULTING CO., LTD.
創科工程顧問有限公司

**Kitchen**
CPG
CATERING PROJECT CONSULTANT CO., LTD
柏基工程設計顧問有限公司

**Landscape**
earthasia
泛亞國際

**Interior**
Aedas
Aedas Interiors Ltd
18th Floor
1063 King's Road
Quarry Bay
Hong Kong
T +852 2861 1728
F +852 2143 6216
E hongkong@aedas.c
aedas.com

**Quantity Surveyor**
KPK
KPK QUANTITY SURVEYORS (CHINA) LTD
科進利比(中國)有限公司

**E & M**
WSP
WSP HONG KONG LTD
科進香港有限公司

**Civil & Structures**
Hyder
Hyder Consulting Limited
海德工程顧問有限公司

**Local Design Institute**
Hui Yang Architects & Engineers
惠陽城市建築設計研究院

**Project Architect**
Aedas
Aedas Ltd
19th Floor
1063 King's Road
Quarry Bay
Hong Kong
T +852 2861 1728
F +852 2529 6418
E hongkong@aedas.c
aedas.com

**Hotel Operator**
INTERCONTINENTAL
HOTELS GROUP
洲際酒店集團

**Client**
KONG SING LTD
港成有限公司

For    Check    Draw    Date    Description    Rev
[nt]    Issue Date

Drawing Number

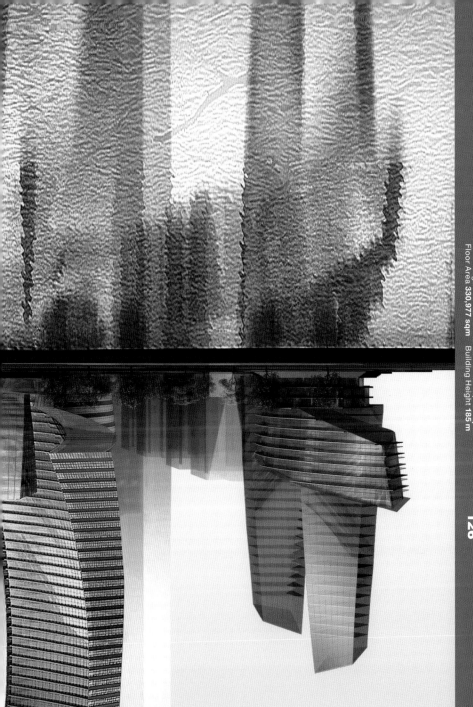

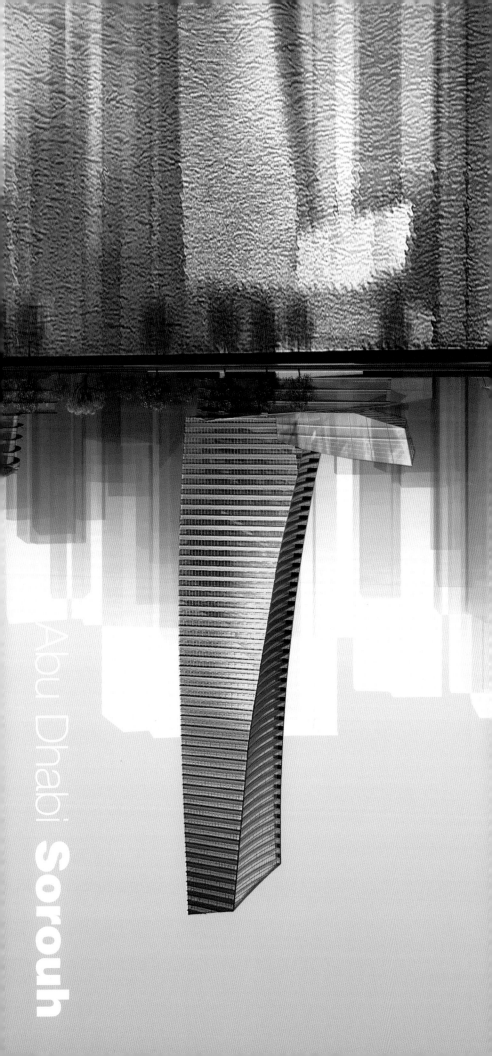

Abu Dhabi **Sorouh**

# Abu Dhabi **Sorouh**

The design for this residential project strives to symbolize the boldness of the overall master plan and represent its contemporary vision and innovation enthusiastically. As the northern tip of Reem Island, this design is challenged by its status as an icon, which will give identity to the entire Sorouh development. The importance of the site is accentuated by its location as the terminus of both the vehicular loop road and the internal canal walk system.

The two focal towers frame the developments to the south, with two arms opening up to the sky. These towers, which twist to provide spectacular views across the water, transition below to become two other arms of the podium. The podiums embrace the heart and focus of the project, which is where the canal and loop road come together. This space becomes a very important and prominent civic node in the Upper Village of Sorouh ▪

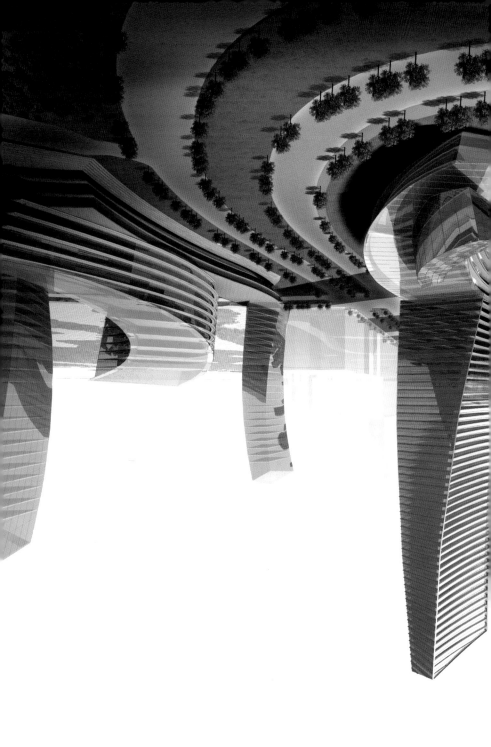

Master Plan

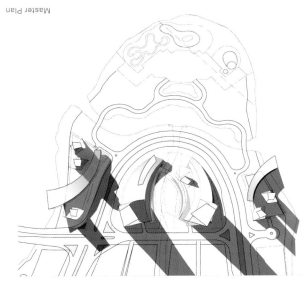

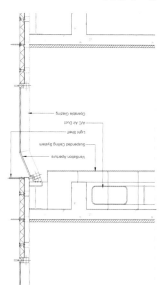

**Façade Detail**

Operable Glazing
A/C Air Duct
Light Shelf
Suspended Ceiling System
Ventilation Aperture

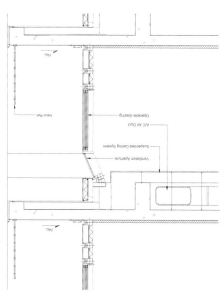

**Façade Detail with Aperture**

Hand Rail
Operable Glazing
A/C Air Duct
Suspended Ceiling System
Ventilation Aperture
FALL
FALL

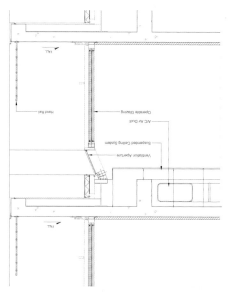

**Balcony Façade Detail with Large Aperture**

FALL
Hand Rail
Operable Glazing
A/C Air Duct
Suspended Ceiling System
Ventilation Aperture
FALL
FALL

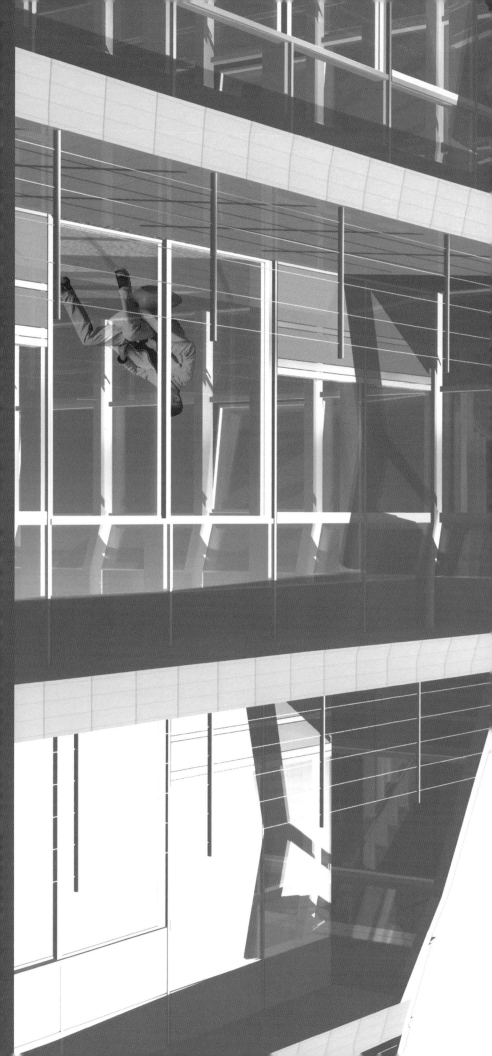

Program **Mixed Use** Site Area **43,000 sqm**
Floor Area **139,641 sqm** Building Height **35 m**

■ Incoming Wind Stream

■ Outgoing Wind Currents

▨ Operable Canopy

In a region of extreme temperatures, this project redefines an urban open space within an ecologically tempered environment. Located in the Deira side of Dubai, the project is strategically placed between the old Souks and the airport. The site for Union Square is both the symbolic heart of the city as well as a major node on the city's future subway system.

An existing underutilized park was replaced with a mixed-use development and a reinterpretation of the open space. This becomes the focus and activator of the development. Surrounding this open space is a complex of hotels, retail, restaurants, residential and performance venues.

# Dubai **Union Square**

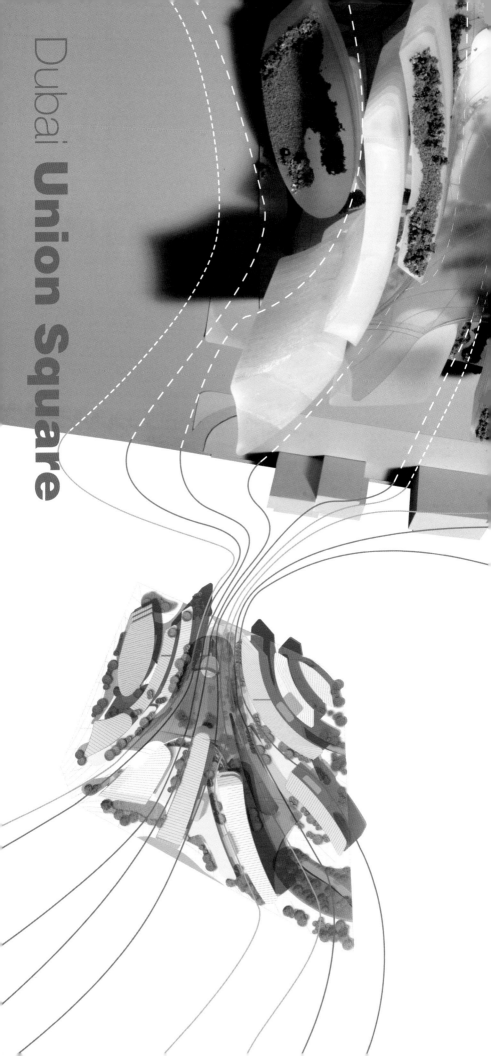

Dubai **Union Square**

The design is based on wind currents in the region, with the buildings placed and shaped to enhance and control these breezes to help temper the ambient temperatures of the desert heat. An environmental canopy covers the complex, containing the breezes and protecting the 14,000 green terraces below ▪

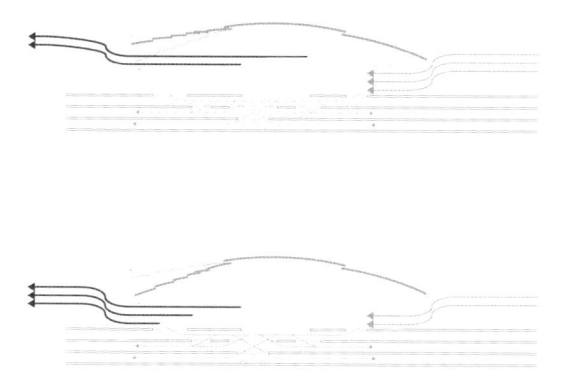

▨ Operable Canopy

■ Outgoing Wind Currents

▨ Incoming Wind Stream

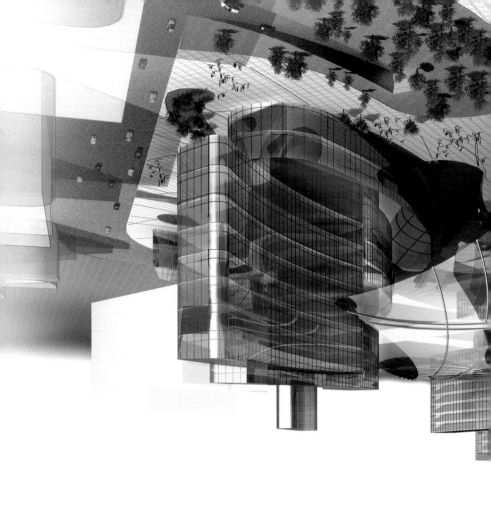

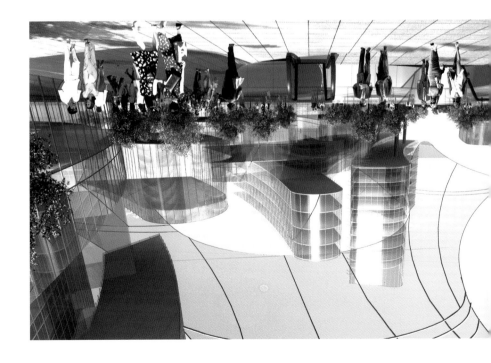

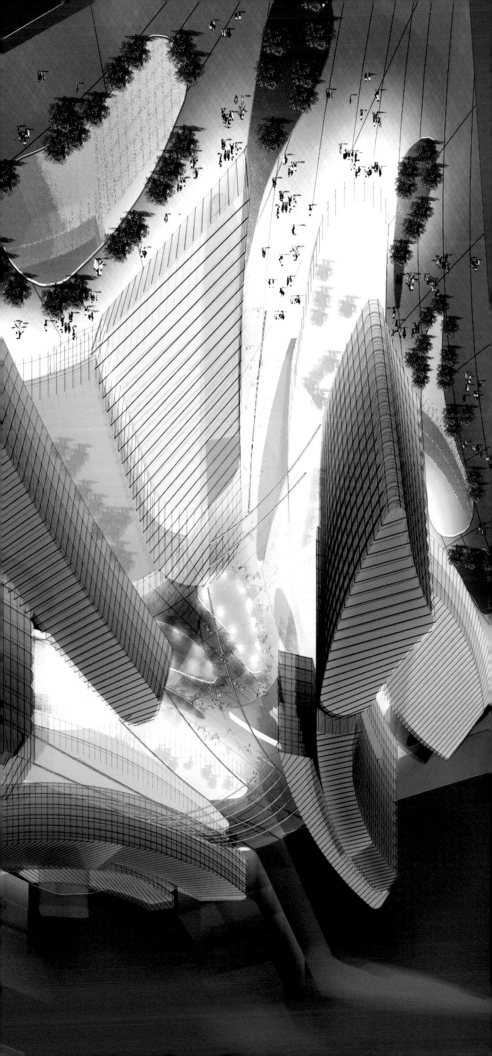

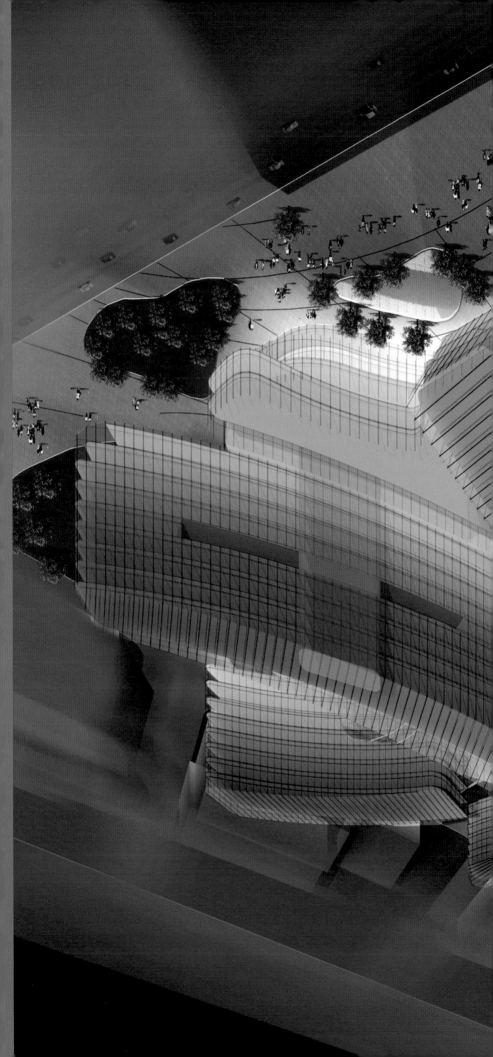

## People's Republic of China **Foshan Media Centre**

The Foshan Media Centre, being both civic and commercial, is ideally located between the Foshan Sports Centre and the new urban center's commercial axis. The design for the Media Centre will knit and merge these two edges together, as a physical manifestation of both. The center becomes a theatre complex, a museum of media and a multimedia library. All of this is contained within an efficient and viable complex of functioning media businesses which themselves are presented to the public as an exhibit. Ultimately, the Foshan Media Centre is a center of learning about media and the business of the media, as well as the world in which we live – today, yesterday and tomorrow ▪

Program **Media Centre** Site Area **63,600 sqm** Building Height **81.7 m**
Floor Area **87,696 sqm**

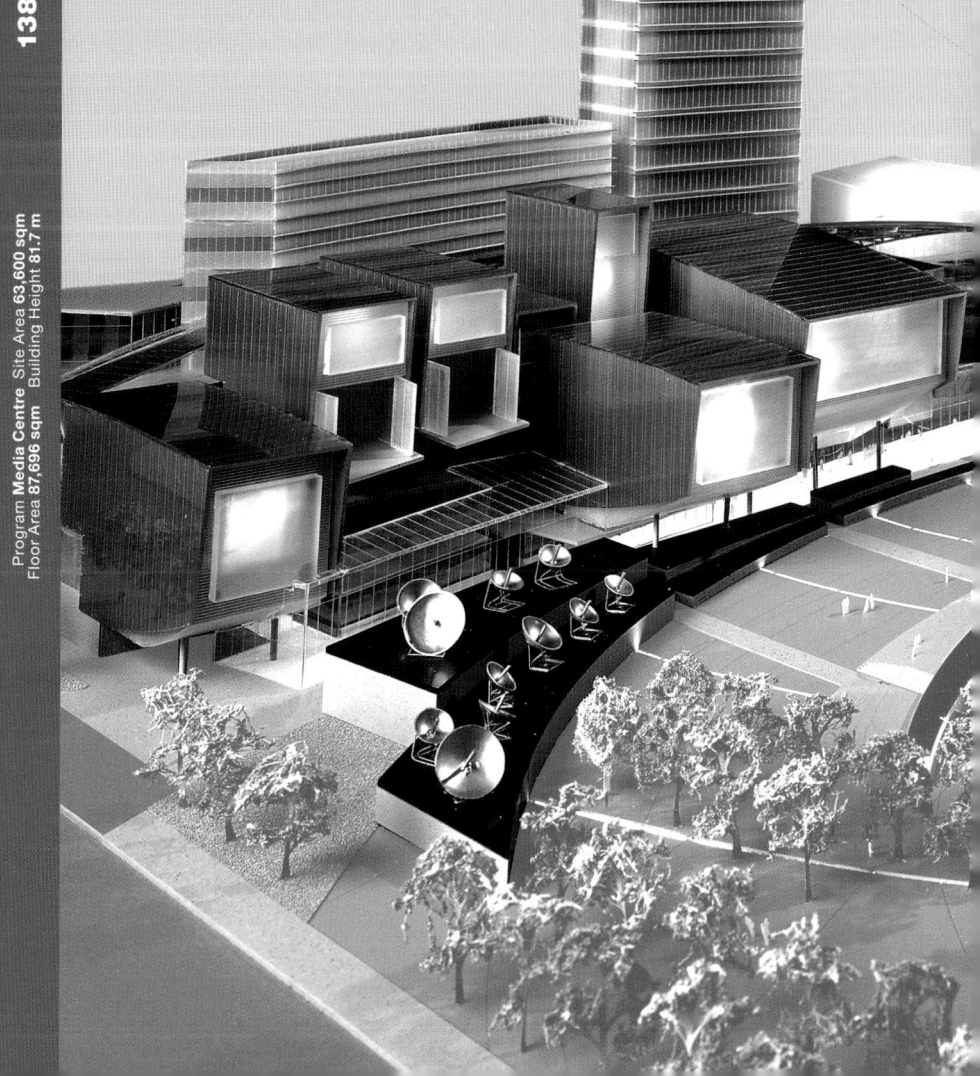

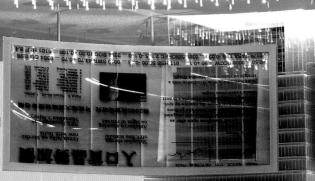

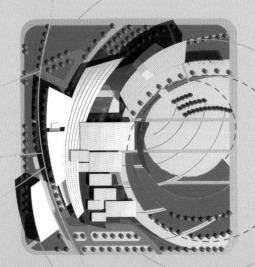

Program **Mixed Use**  Site Area **2,525 sqm**
Floor Area **161,780 sqm**  Building Height **107 m**

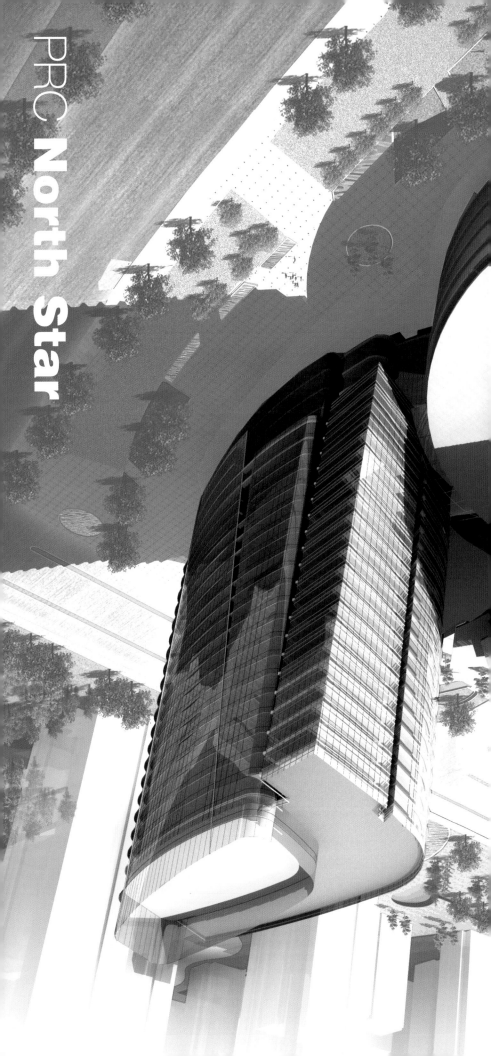

## People's Republic of China **North Star**

Anchoring the overall development, this project engages the natural forces of the site and celebrates their potential. The project addresses the park as a "quiet zone." Its eastern face looks out at the main street's "loud zone" and its northern civic edge relates to the master plan corridor, where most retail and commercial functions are planned. The southeast corner of this site is linked to a future train station.

The commercial and residential towers anchor each side of the site, and natural movement is caught between them. Northstar's 100-meter office tower stands on the intersection corner as a landmark while the apartment tower is on the southwest corner, oriented towards the park and southern light. Daylight pours through skylights between the towers towards the ground, highlighting entrances in the north, south and west sides of the site ∎

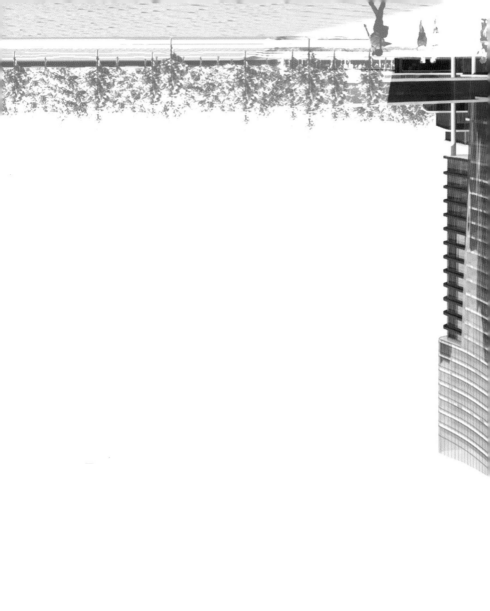
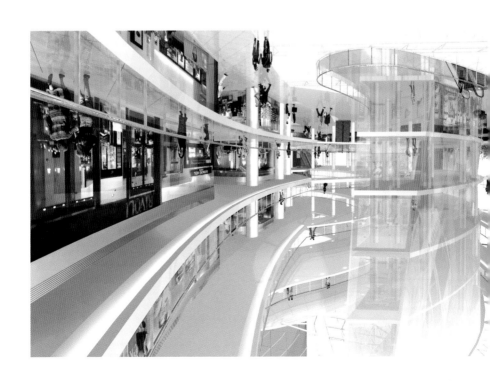

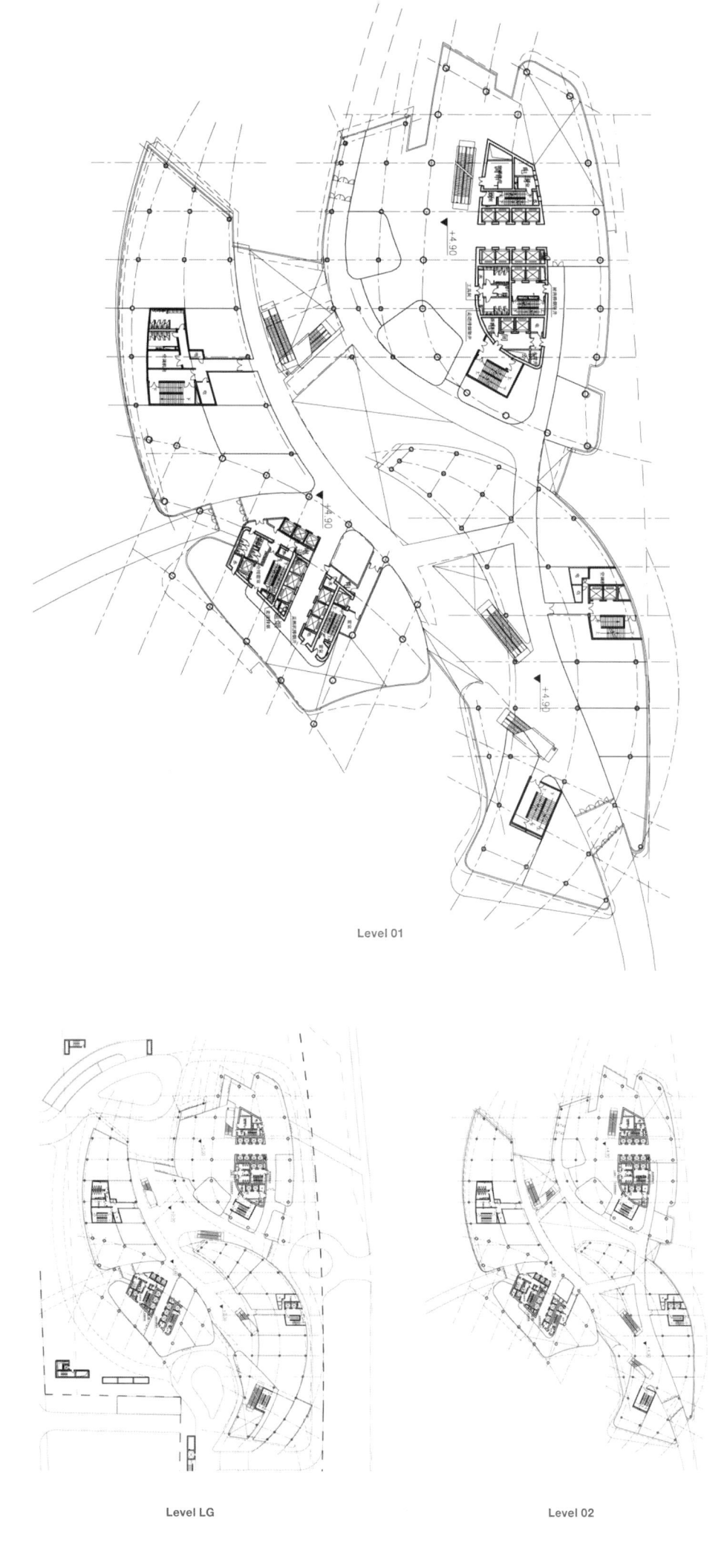

Level 01

Level LG                                        Level 02

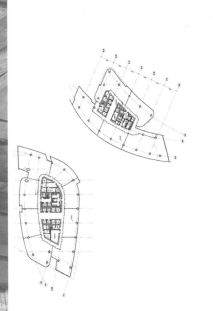

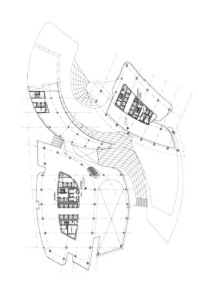

**Under Construction**

Schematic Design Model

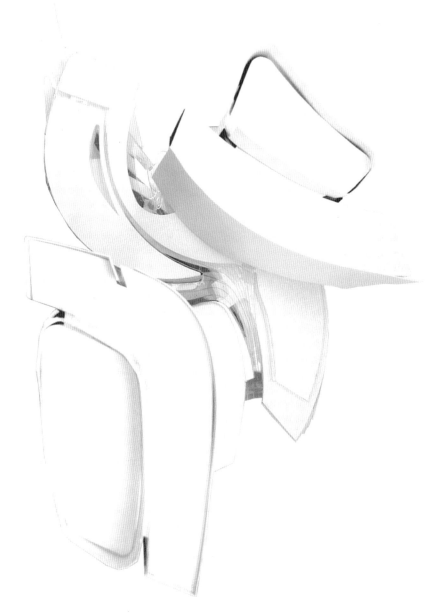

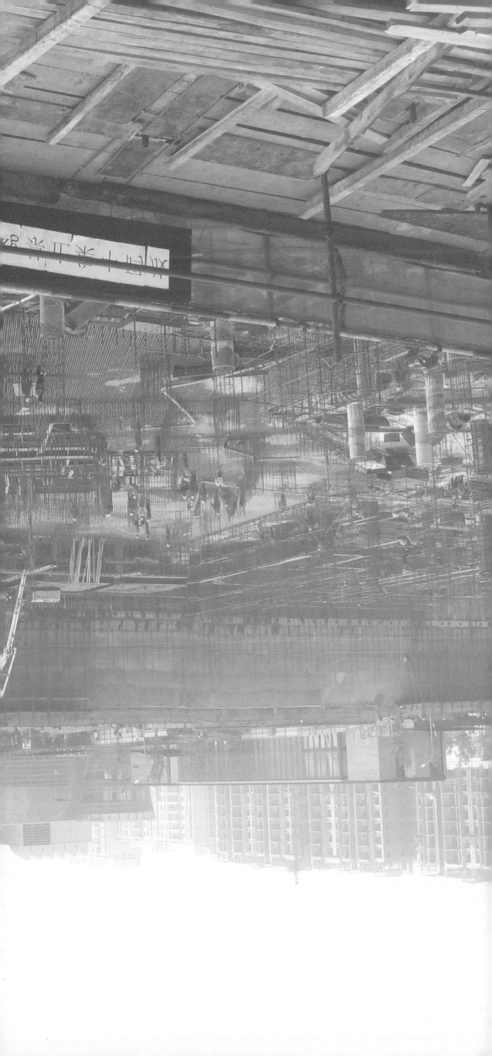

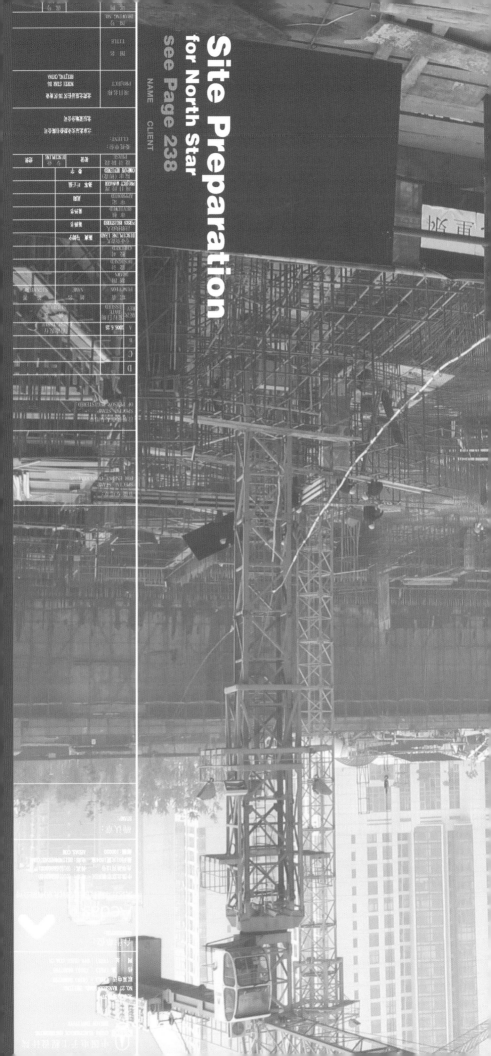

# Site Preparation
## for North Star

See Page 238

Program **Theater/Mixed Use**  Site Area **19,270 sqm**
Floor Area **54,000 sqm**  Building Height **60 m**

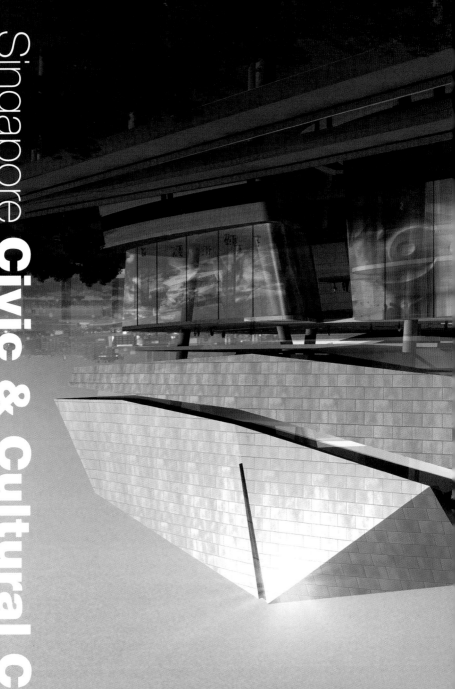

Singapore **Civic & Cultural Complex**

## Singapore **Civic & Cultural Complex**

Civic & Cultural Complex does not present one singular expression but celebrates the rich and varying activities inside with a dynamic design that blurs the boundaries between the public/private realms and between the retail/cultural components. These transitions are soft and flowing, encouraging discovery and resulting in a highly public, energetic civic node within One-North and beyond.

The civic and public components of the project are paramount and outwardly expressed. The south elevation is completely opened up presenting the inner workings of the facility as a section visible from the exterior. The mass of the theatre floating above is faceted with glass fissures, and utilizes titanium cladding. All of this helps dissolve and break down the mass above, playing with a composition of positive and negative readings, in balance with the lower portions use of solid and void.

**Cultural Program**

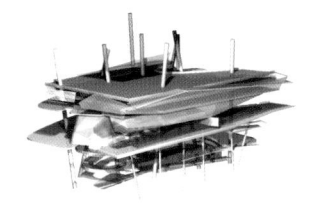

**Civic Program**

**Retail Program**

SUBSTATION

9m  8m

8m

BV MRT STATION

PMS

VISTA XCHANGE GREEN

VISTA XCHANGE GREEN

BV CENTER

MRT STATION

BUONA VISTA PARK

BUSINESS HOTEL

ROCHESTER DRIVE

BUONA VISTA PARK

8m

10m

NORTH BUONA VISTA DRIVE

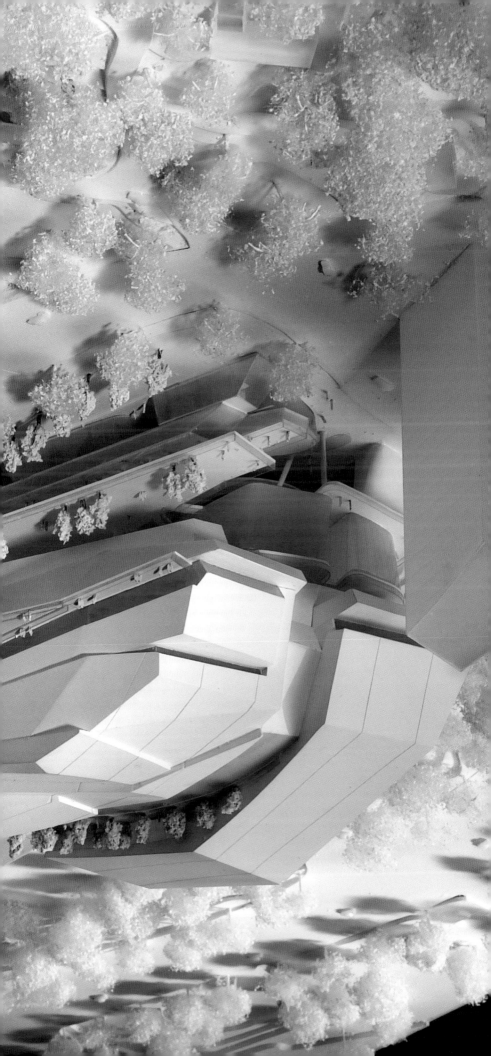

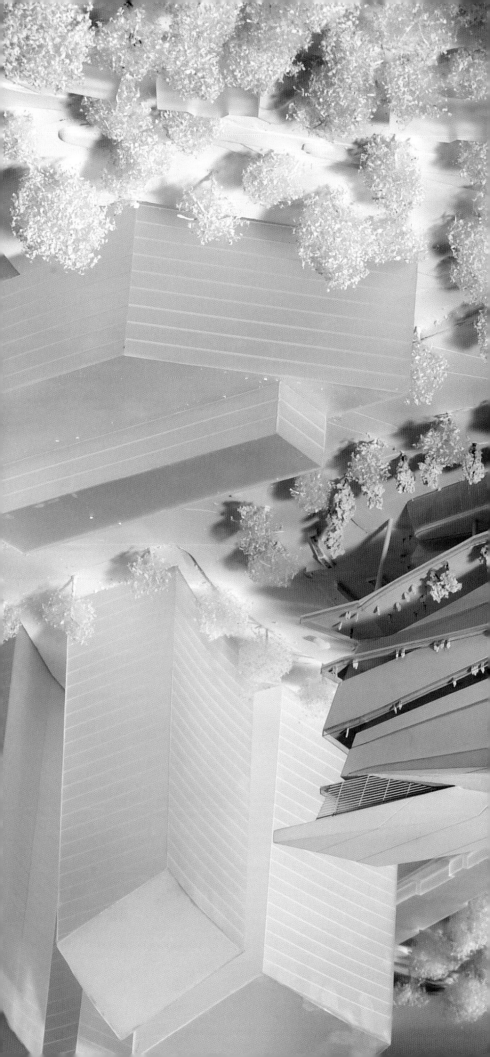

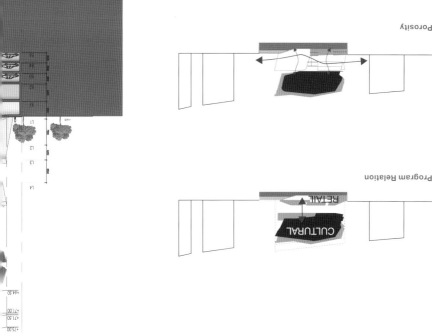

RETAIL

CULTURAL

The civic building is an organic object open to public discovery. One can crawl under, move through, transverse around and climb onto the complex through a series of ramps, escalators, terraces and public gardens. All circulation, movement and internal forms are soft and sinuous as if the civic activities have polished the inside.

The cultural/retail components are bound together with the volume of the 40m high, "Grand Foyer". The importance these two components have on each other is celebrated by blurring the divisions between them while maintaining functionality. This soft transition occurs vertically from the most public of the open retail into the perceptual privacy of the theatre. This entire sequence and transition is linked visually and spatially to the "Grand Foyer" connecting the sunken retail below up through the glass floor of the theatre's main lobby exposing its volume floating above.

The design is highly sustainable through its approach to minimize air conditioned spaces. The retail, civic square, outdoor theatre as well as the pre-function of the banqueting and meeting room facilities are all open air along with the "Grand Foyer". This thereby encourages air movement through the volume and results in a shaded environment that can be enjoyed year round. As well as stimulating air circulation that cools the suspended mass above.

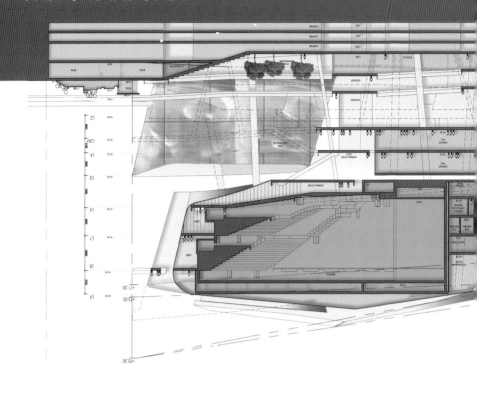

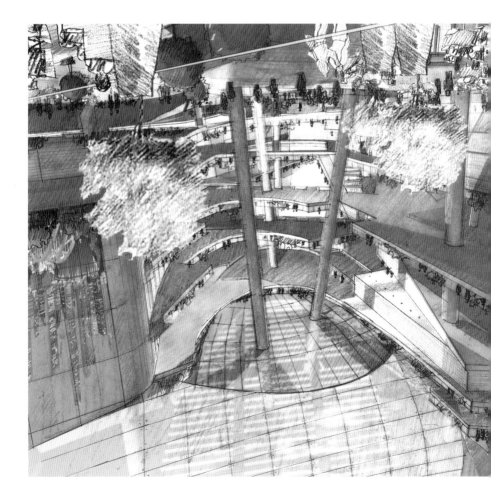

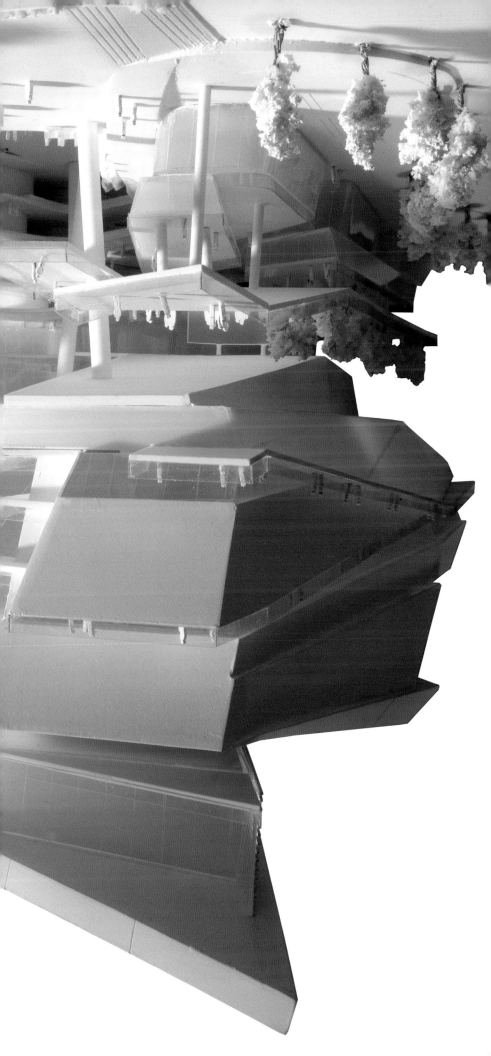

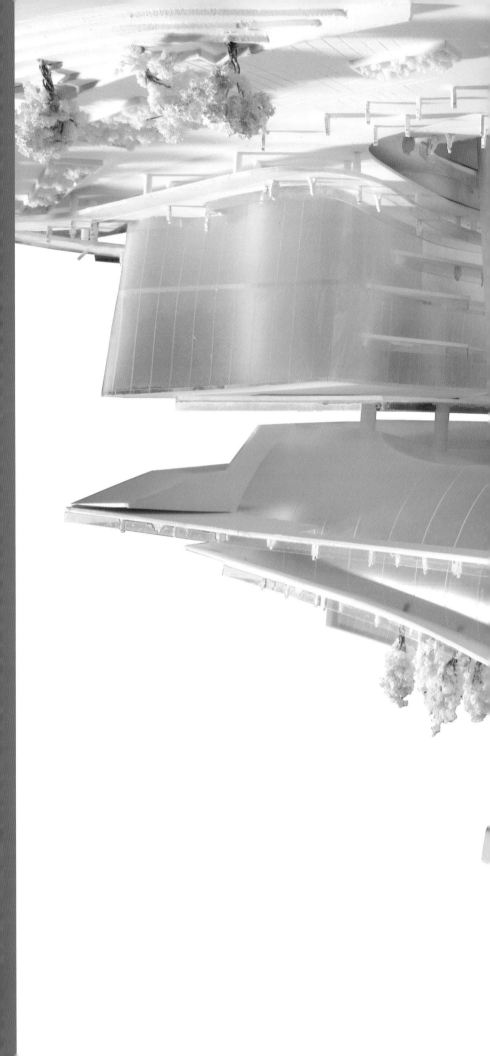

# Contextualism

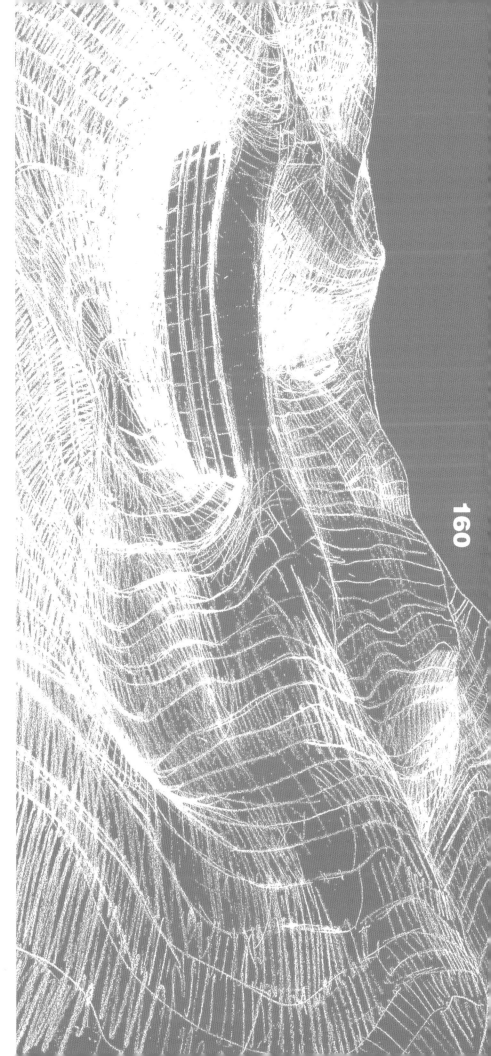

# Contextualism

A building's influence on its environment is equally influenced by the context in which it co-exists. How one balances and prioritizes these influences becomes significant in developing meaningful designs.

Every building should be a statement and a story that, when read, can reveal what has defined and shaped the design. Some of these moves will be more obvious than others – for instance, how a building responds to a view in the distance or relates to the warming rays of the sun. Some moves may not be apparent but are equally important – such as preferred circulation patterns through and around the project.

Of course, a building will not be able to do everything. What has been placed as secondary concerns are just as important to the story and the statement that this building is making, as are the governing forces. The moves should not be arbitrary but deemed to possess some sense of importance and restraint.

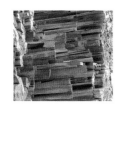

172

The interpretation of these moves may be obvious and rational or they may be intuitive and subjective. Both are justified, as comprehension of value in this world is not always apparent and can definitely be elusive.

A project may be conceived to find harmony with its environment or may be a response to sustain itself within its own setting. Two extreme examples, which are shown in this chapter, are Jebel Hafeet and Pentominium.

Jebel Hafeet is located in a landscape of indefinable beauty. It was important to find a solution in which the natural beauty was preserved and the hotel co-existed with it. The design actually allows opportunities to discover this beauty more accessibly and with more variety than if the project never existed.

On the other end, Pentominium Tower is a 618-meter building that sits just 20 meters away from its 380-meter neighbor. The immediate proximity to this other tower, which is a pure extrusion, forced a design which allows the two to exist together more comfortably. The design softens the relationship between the two giants, improving the lives of the residents in both projects, but still preserving (and quite possibly increasing) the power and marketability of the project.

Contextualism is one aspect of the design process that places immediate value on a design. The building is site-specific and has a return effect on its environment. Often these conditions are mandates for the design, with shadow casting and preserved-view corridors being examples. The immediate context may have a significant effect on the cost and execution of the building, such as traffic flow and wind-tunnel tests.

Contextual influences are varied and diverse – being physical, cultural, environmental and even subjective. A project should respond to these conditions deliberately, with the motivation of improving the value of the project and the quality of its surroundings, as well as enriching the lives of the people it affects and raising awareness of the world we live in today. ∎

Beirut **Solidere**

180

Dubai **Boulevard Plaza**

188

Program **Residential**  Site Area 2,200 sqm
Floor Area **2,000,593 sqm**  Building Height varies

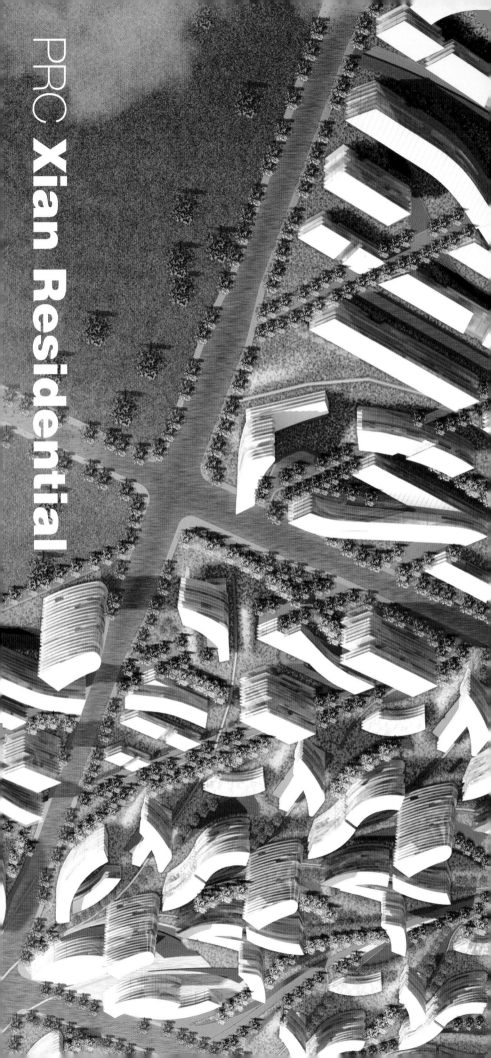

PRC **Xian Residential**

Located in historic Xian, the heart of the development is a former ammunitions storage site. A wall contains the ammunition bunkers that are located throughout the site and serviced by a railway system. Xian's modern city grid cuts through the site. Our proposal for this site seeks to reuse the existing elements: namely, the city wall, the ammunition bunkers and the railway tracks – while seeking to harmonise these elements with the modern city grid.

The grid has been softened as it moves into the site, evolving and taking on a more fluid character. The city wall echoes outwards into the site, becoming a modern adaptation of the ancient Chinese "ring road" system.

The ammunitions bunkers become the community centres and nodal transport points throughout the site. The existing tracks are reused and extend outwards. This system becomes the spine of the site, incorporating an energy-efficient tram system into the existing tram track, also allowing for an extensive pedestrian network •

■ Wall

▦ Rail Tracks

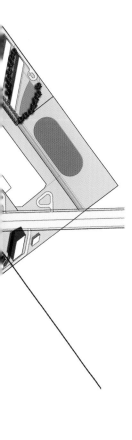

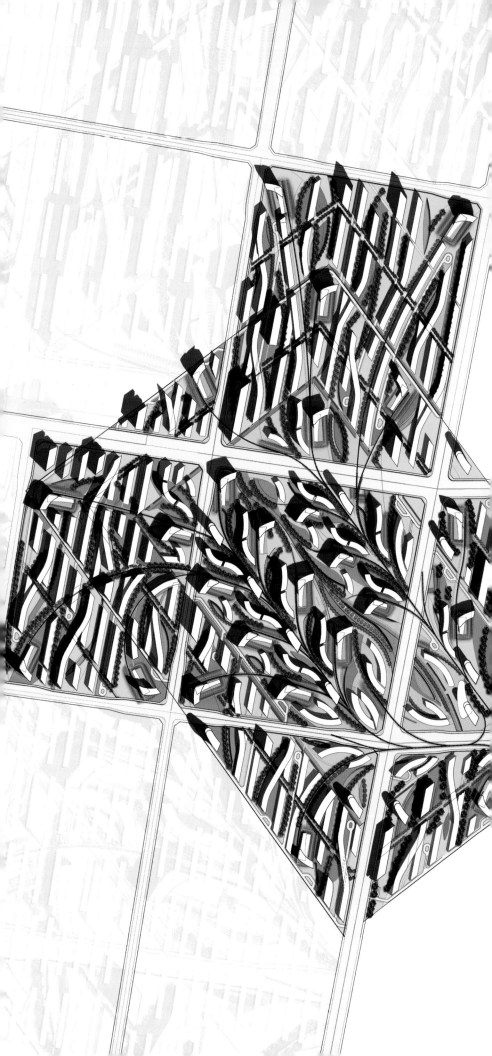

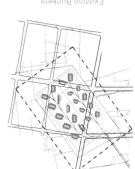

Existing Bunkers

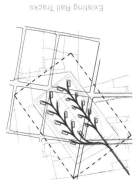

Existing Rail Tracks

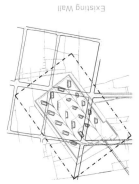

Existing Wall

Existing

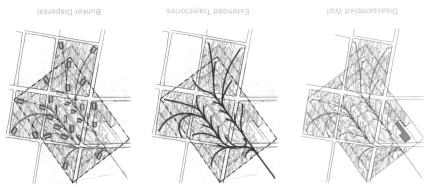

Bunker Dispersal

Extended Trajectories

Disassembled Wall

Strategy

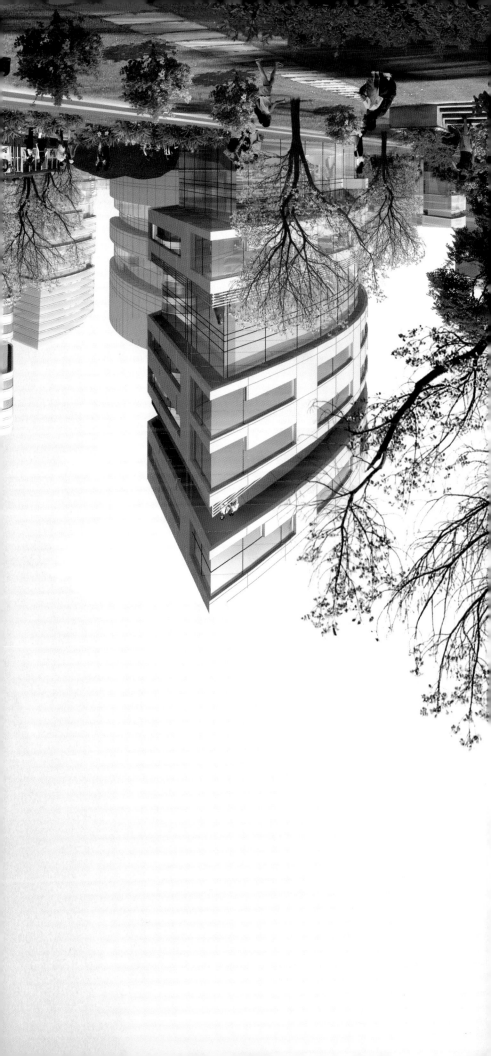

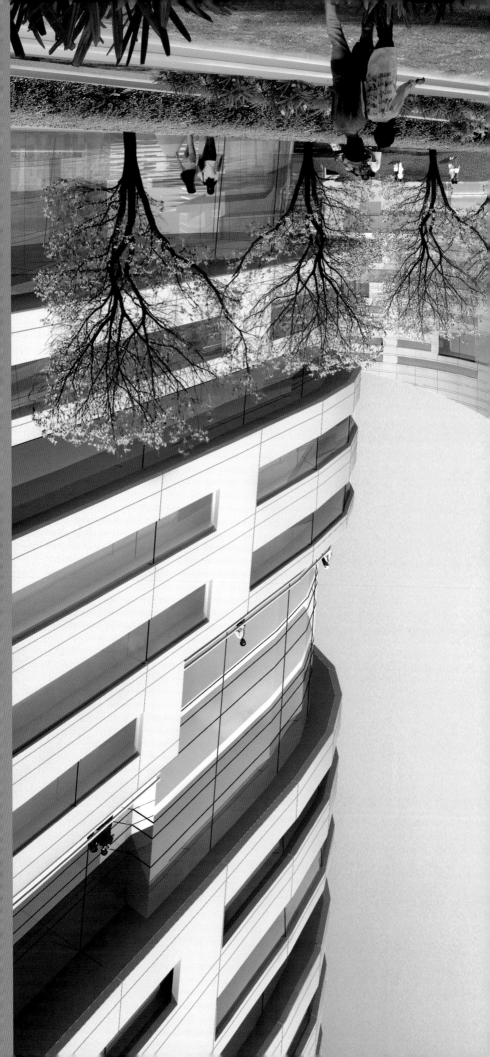

Program **Mixed Use**  Site Area **54,519 sqm**
Floor Area **351,684 sqm**  Building Height **428 m**

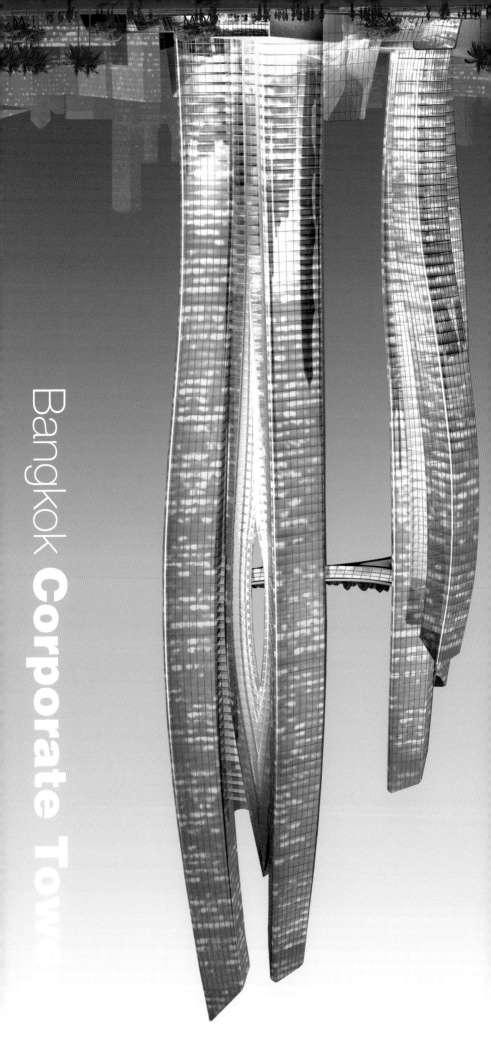

Bangkok **Corporate Tow**

# Bangkok **Corporate Towers**

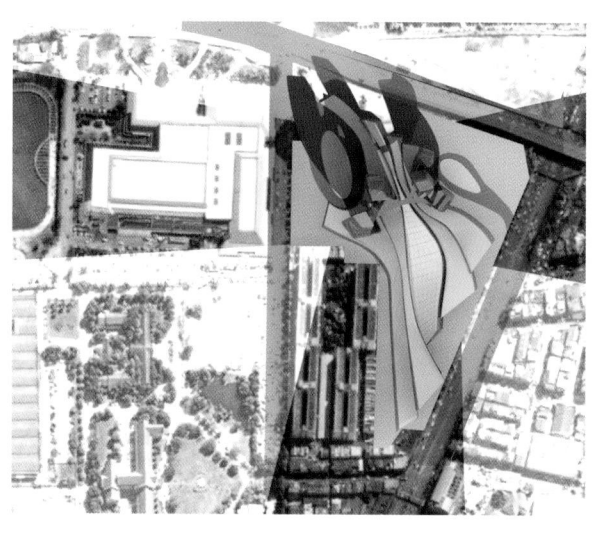

The two towers were influenced by a culturally contextual response to the softness and fluidity of Thai culture. The mixed-use project was to become an extension of the natural landscape that still exists in the hectic environment of Bangkok. The towers flow out of the ground as thin reeds rising and bending toward each other, gesturing to the city and its inhabitants in the traditional "Sawadeeka" Thai greeting.

With the year-round hot temperatures, the project had an opportunity to give back to the city with an introduction of a ventilated bridge park 216 meters above the ground. This element functions as a public space and as bridge connecting the two towers with restaurants and cafes. At this height both towers splay open, funneling the delicate Bangkok breezes across the public, open space to further cool down the outdoor environment and increase visitors' comfort.

The bridge connecting the two buildings links the upper lobbies of the smaller office tower to the hotel, as well as to the service apartments and residential facilities of the taller tower. These towers are 433 meters and 316 meters, respectively, so will inevitably become an identifiable symbol in the Bangkok skyline. They were designed to interact playfully with each other in order to offer an ever-changing image that can be perceived from different locations in the city around them ▪

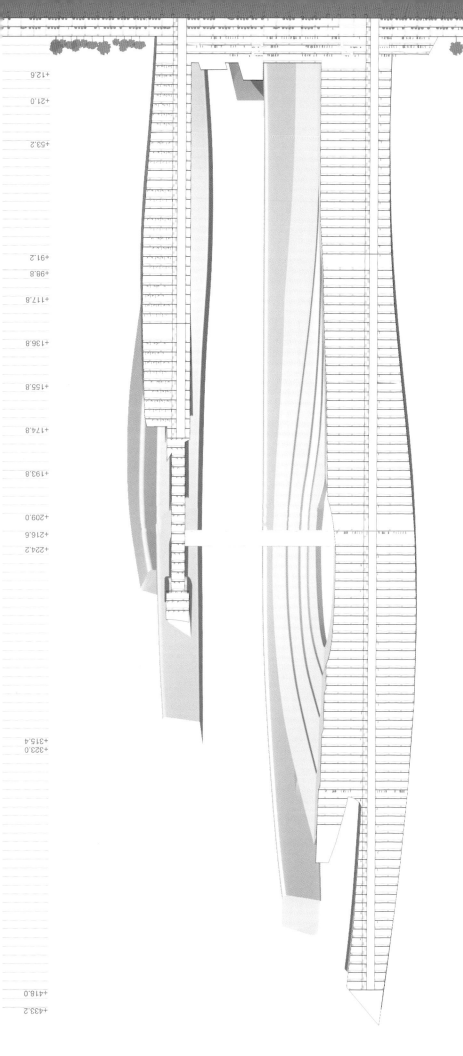

+12.6
+21.0

+53.2

+91.2
+98.8

+117.8

+136.8

+155.8

+174.8

+193.8

+209.0
+216.6
+224.2

+315.4
+323.0

+418.0

+433.2

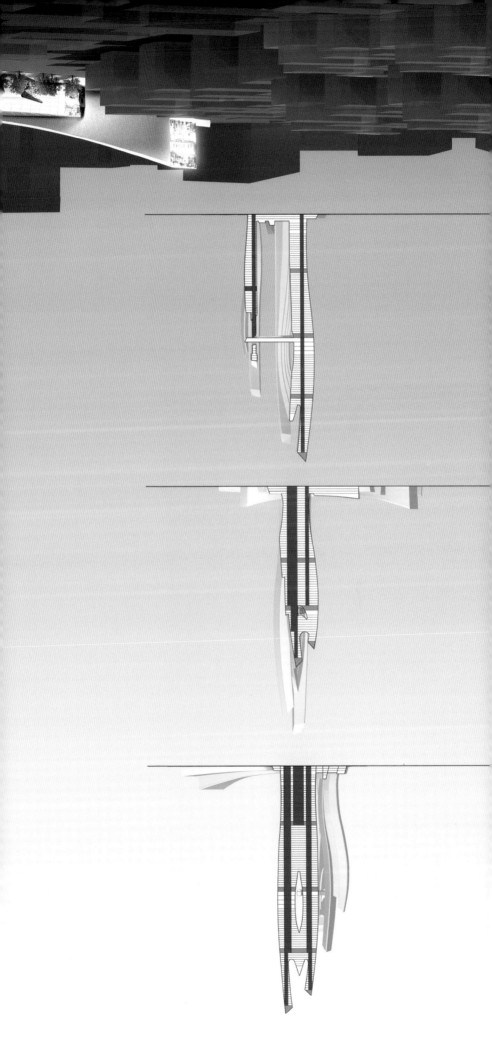

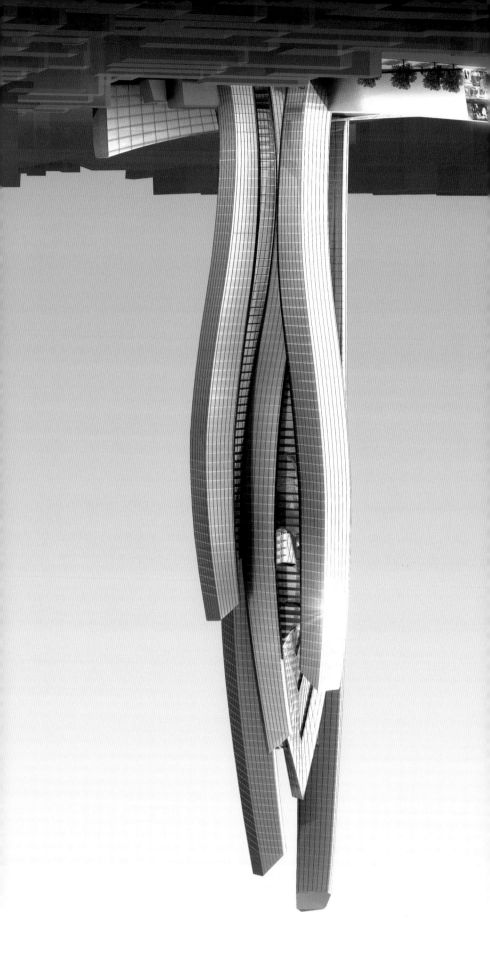

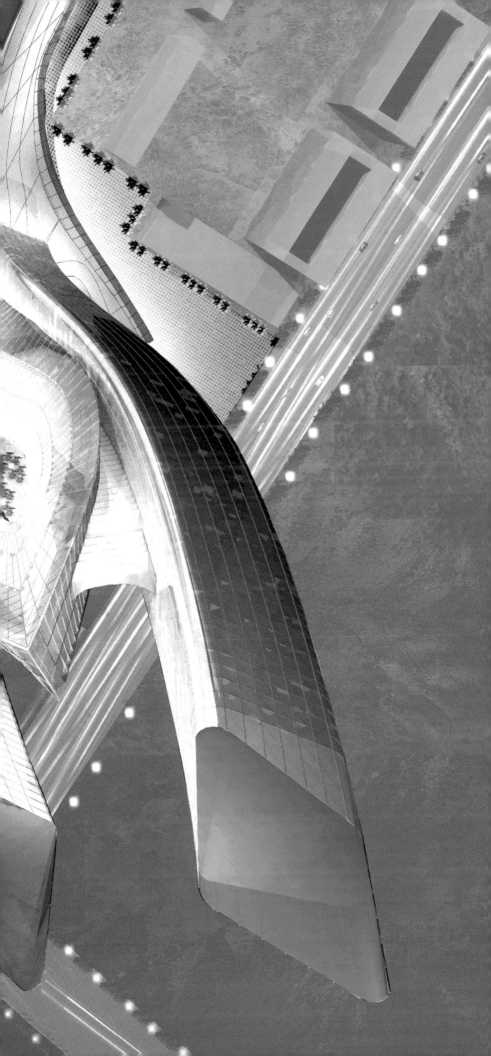

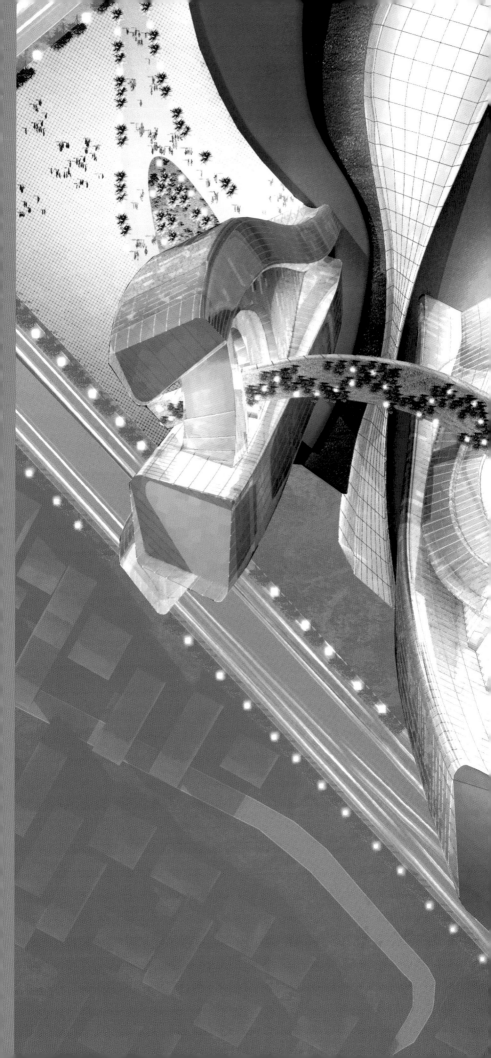

# Beirut **Solidere**

Located in the historic district of Beirut, the Solidere residential development takes its form from the nearby stone quarries, which have supplied the city with its traditional yellow limestone.

Oriented toward the Mediterranean Sea, the four units per floor, conceived as four vertical shards of stone, jockey for position down this limited view corridor while rising out of the limestone plinth below. The project's scale and materiality fit appropriately within the district, but the complex is still unquestionably contemporary in both form and movement ▪

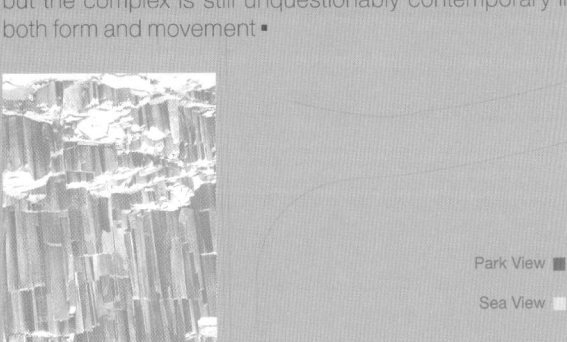

Park View ▪
Sea View ▫

Program **Residential**  Site Area **2,711 sqm**
Floor Area **43,987 sqm**  Building Height **120 m**

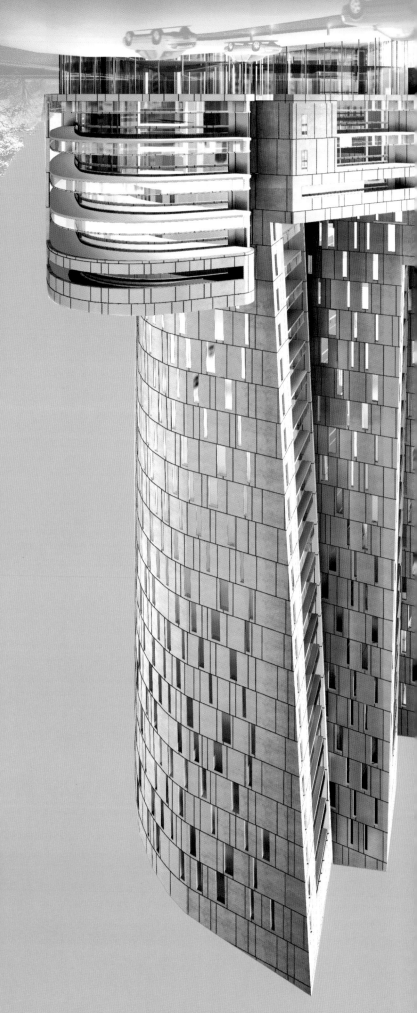

Beirut **Solidere**

Program **Hotel**  Site Area **345,000 sqm**
Floor Area **60,927 sqm**  Building Height **varies**

# Abu Dhabi Jebel Hafeet Resort

Rising out of the United Arab Emirates' desert, Jebel Hafeet Resort blends harmoniously into the barren, rocky hills near Oman.

Clusters of rooms and individual villas are either placed strategically into the steep terrain or bridged over its valleys. The resort maximizes privacy for its guests while enhancing the experience of the natural environment. An intricate weave of hiking trails intermixed with a pocket oasis, along with the resort itself, results in an almost "non-architectural" landscape solution. The lines indicating where the mountains meet the hotel are completely blurred, encouraging a journey of quiet discovery within this unique landscape ■

1.1 Main Buildings

Abu Dhabi **Jebel Hafeet Resort**

3.1 Villa

2.2 Hotel Cluster 2

2.1 Hotel Cluster 1

Vehicular Circulation
Golf-Cart Circulation
Pedestrian Paths

Circulation Plan

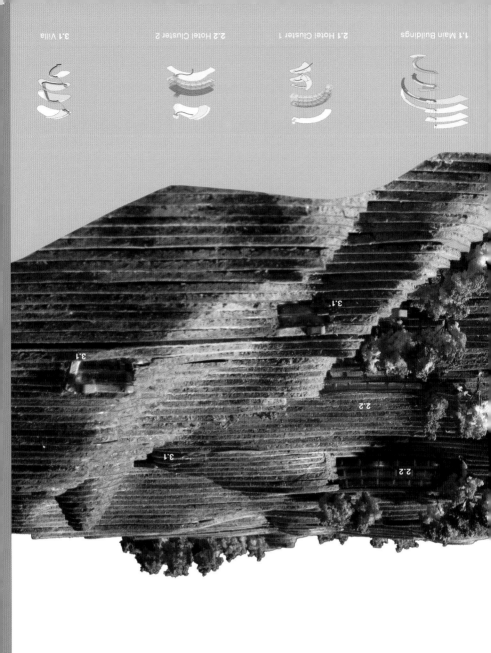

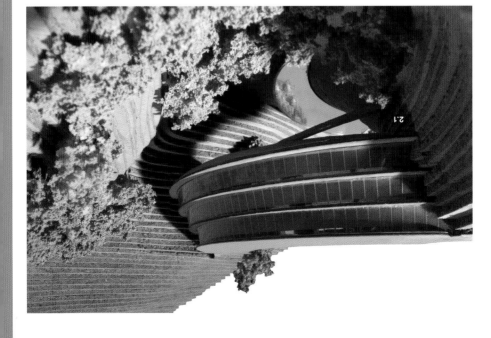

# People's Republic of China **Luo Xi**

The Luo Xi Residential Development is a direct response to client wishes and site constraints. The project is located on the southern bank of the river running through Guangzhou, China. Achieving southern light in the residential units of this region is fundamental to their marketability. However, the views of the river, which are also important, are to the north of the site. The client was hoping two-thirds of the units could retain river views. In developing the scheme through units that step back from the river, 85 percent of the units have achieved both southern light and river views. The gardens and holes, strategically cut into the elevation, enrich the environment for the users as well as help reduce the overall mass of the project ▪

Wind Movement ▪
Sun Rays ▦

Program **Residential**  Site Area **32,090 sqm**
Floor Area **90,050 sqm**  Building Height **45 m**

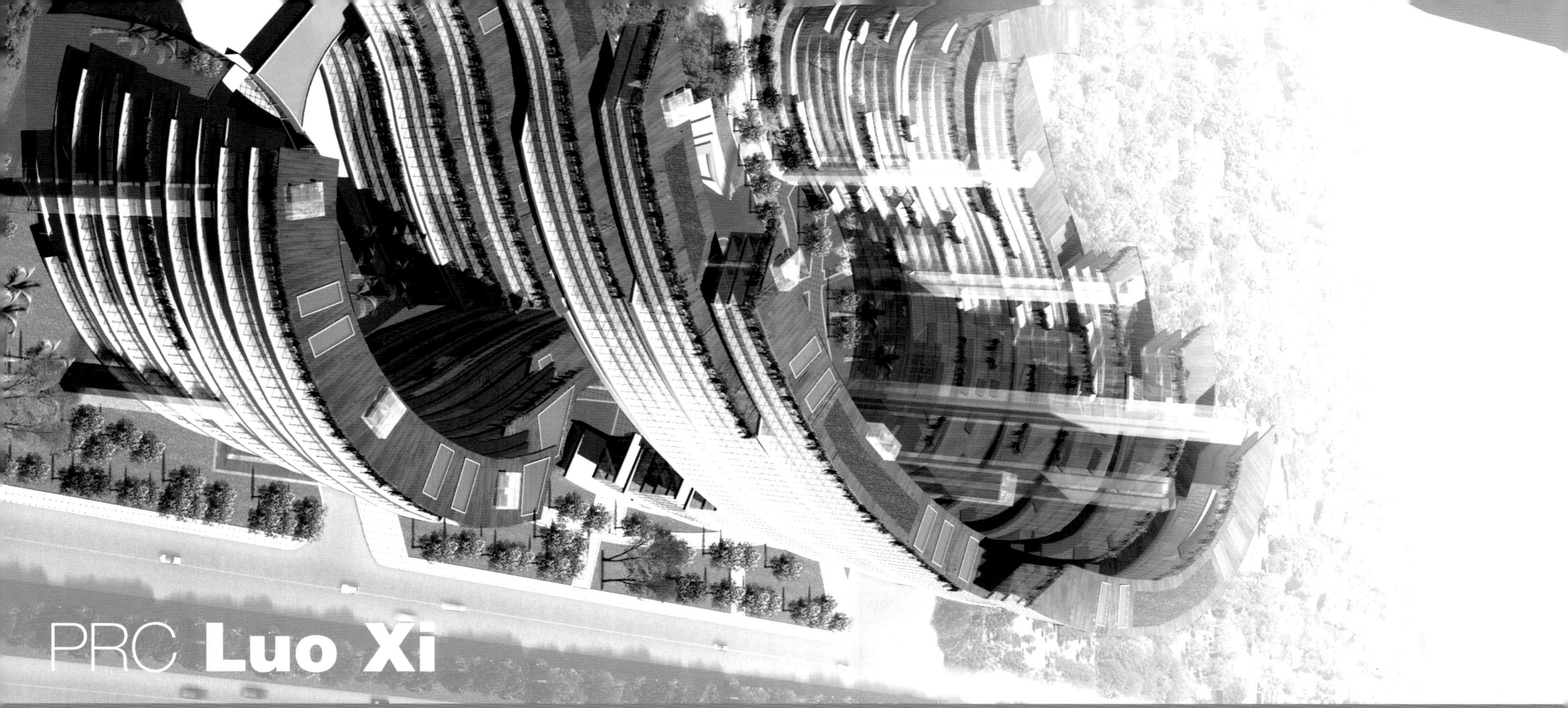

# PRC **Luo Xi**

Program **Mixed Use** Site Area **17,200 sqm**
Floor Area **60,927 sqm** Building Height **173.7 m**

188

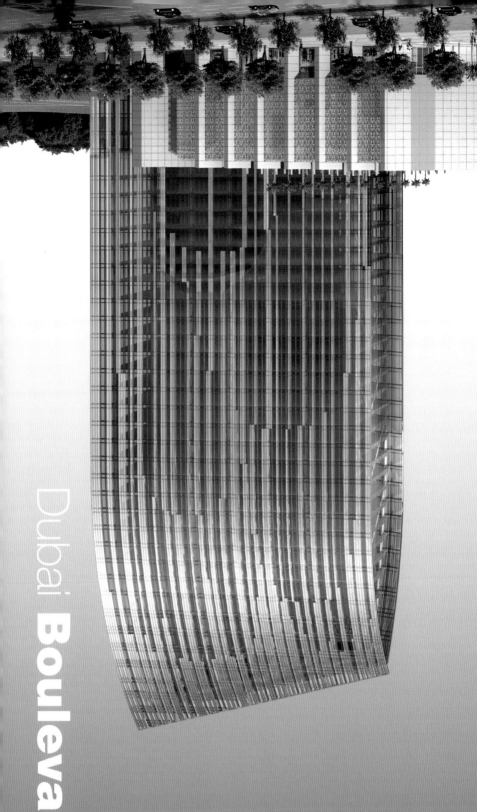

Dubai **Boulevard Plaza**

## Dubai **Boulevard Plaza**

The Boulevard Plaza Towers stand at the gateway
into the Burj Dubai development. The importance of
the site is accentuated even more by being located
immediately across the street from the future tallest
tower in the world – Burj Dubai Tower. The design strives
to fit appropriately into this development as a respectful
icon for the community. The relationship of the forms and
their articulation derive from both a contextual response
and the building's symbol representing modern Islamic
architecture set appropriately within the most modern
Islamic city in the world – Dubai.

Both towers point toward the main entry to greet the
visitors. As one continues into the site, the towers rotate
their orientation as a gesture of respect to the lofty
neighbor across the street. The two towers of 42 and 34
floors contain grade A+ office space, looking out to take
advantage of the views toward and around the Burj Dubai.
The towers are clothed with an articulated skin recalling
the veils and layers of traditional Islamic architecture.
As the figures rise, they bend inwards, forming two deep,
shadowed arches up to the sky and beyond – toward the
top of the Burj Dubai ▪

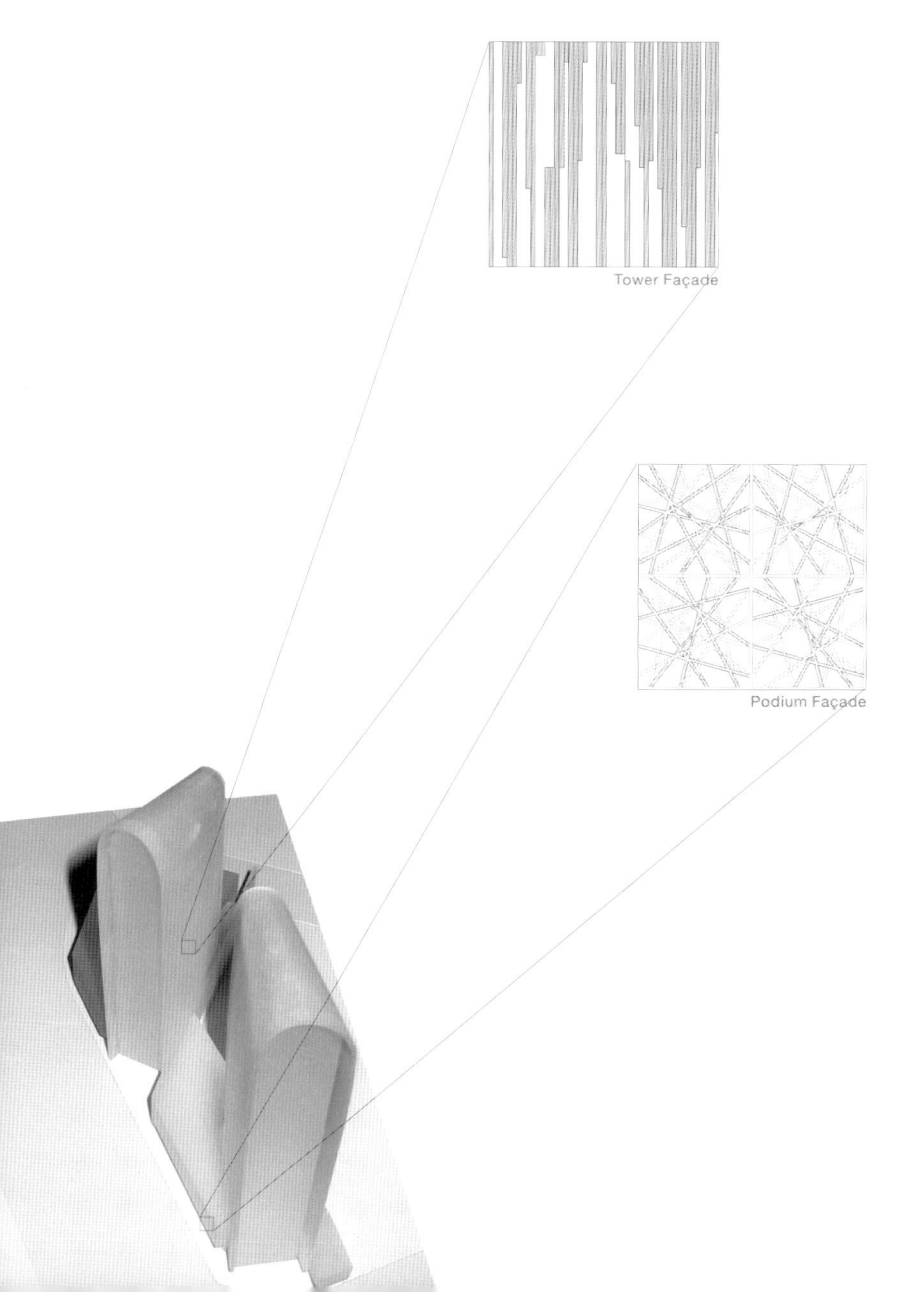

Tower Façade

Podium Façade

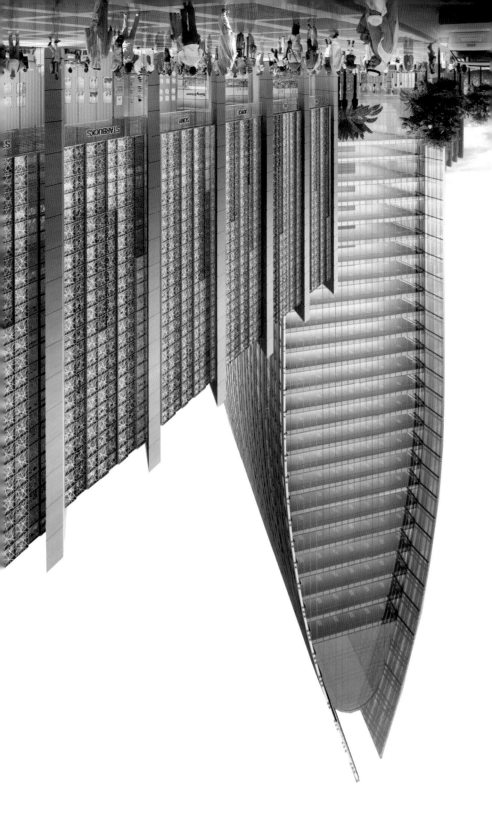

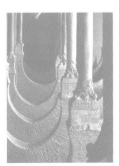
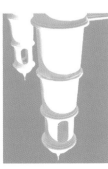

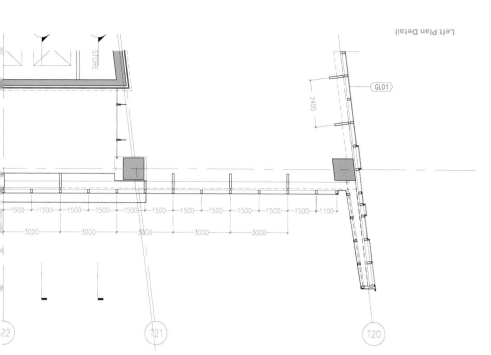

STORE

GL01

2400

1500 1500 1500 1500 1500 1500 1500 1500 1500 1500 1100

3000 3000 3000 3000 3000

T22 T21 T20

Level 22

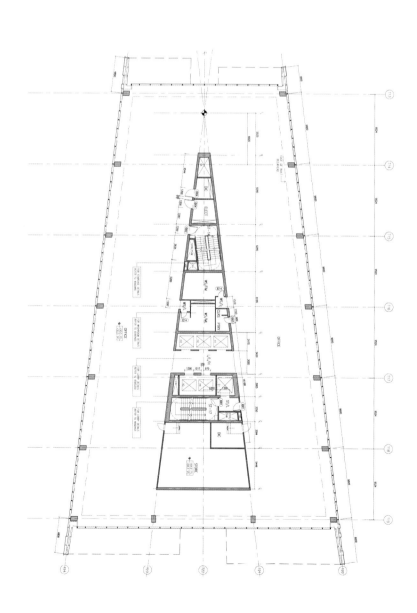

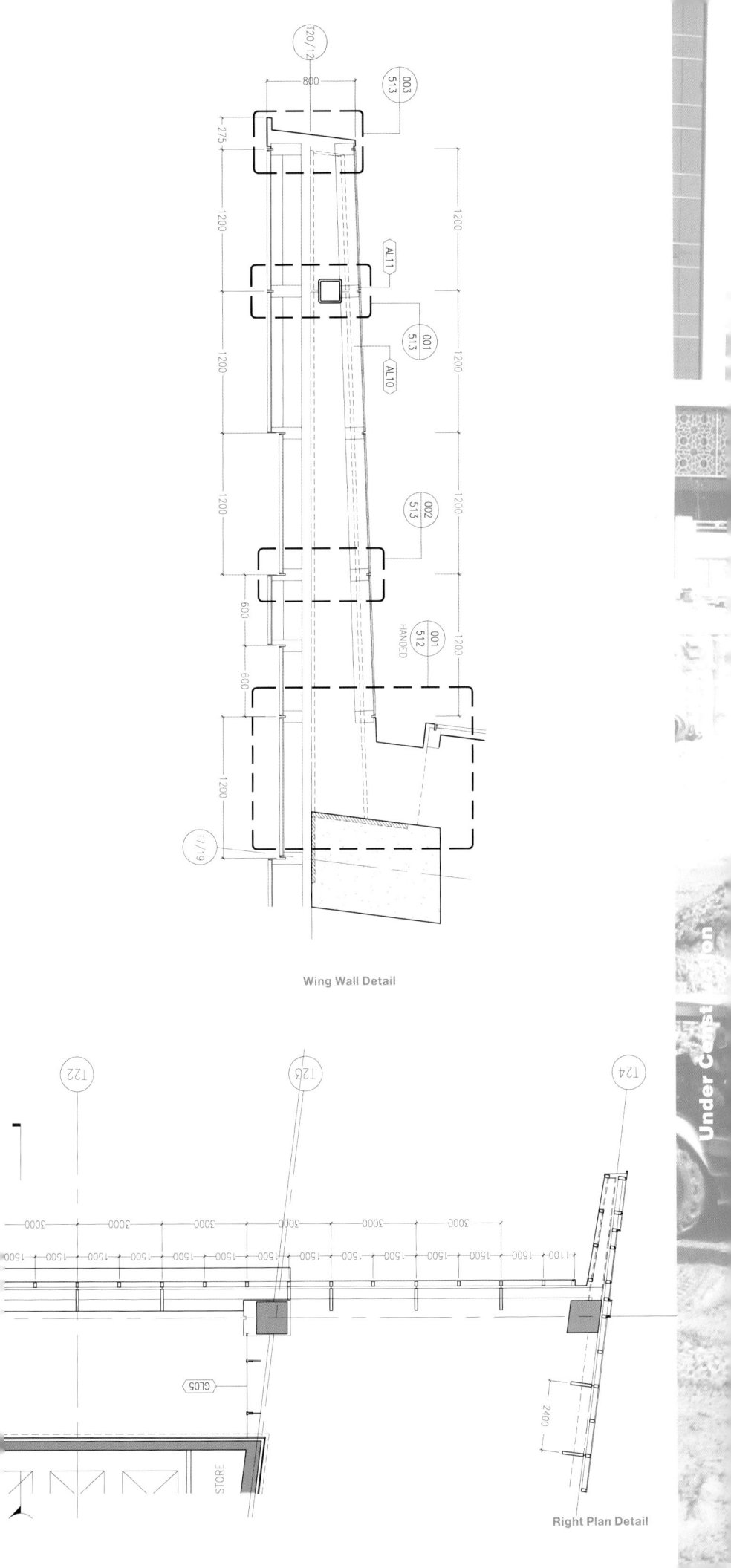

Wing Wall Detail

Right Plan Detail

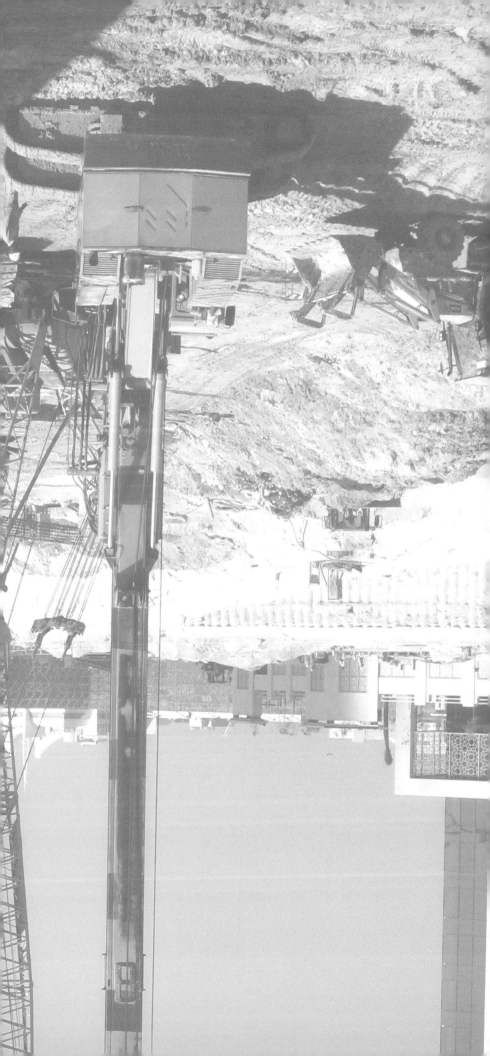

# Site Preparation
## for Boulevard Plaza

See Page 238

PROJECT NO   05656

DATE   31 JULY 2006

DRAWING NO   656D036

TITLE   G.A. PLAN L1 FLOOR (SHEET 1)

FILENAME

GRID

DATUM   APPROVAL

ORIGINAL SIZE   A1   CHECKER

SCALE   1:250   AUTHOR

CURRENT ISSUE SIGNATURES

STATUS   TENDER ADDENDUM

| ISSUE | DESCRIPTION | DATE |
|---|---|---|
| - | FIRST ISSUE | 31.07.06 |

PACKAGE   ATT LIMITED
CONSULTANT   ENGINEERING
1600 WHEELOCK HOUSE, 20 PEDDER ST.,
CENTRAL, HONG KONG
TEL.   +852 097 9762
FAX   +852 097 9762
EMAIL   attlt@attbuilding.com

ENGINEER   HYDER CONSULTING (ME) LTD
P.O. BOX 62790
DUBAI
U.A.E.
TEL.   +971 (04) 324 2532
FAX   +971 (04) 324 2531
EMAIL   hong@mwhhyderme.ae

ARCHITECT FOR RECORD   BREWER SMITH & BREWER GULF
P.O. BOX 30897

LANDSCAPE ARCHITECT   AEDAS LIMITED

CLIENT   EMAAR PROPERTIES PJSC
P.O. BOX 9440
DUBAI, U.A.E.

CLIENT

NAME

# BURJ DUBAI
## PLOTS 12 AND 13

Pentominium Tower, located in Dubai Marina, will potentially be the tallest residential tower in the world. This tower had a unique challenge, in that it had to respond to two different conditions on the site: the density/proximity of the neighbors and the extreme environment pressures of Dubai. Therefore, the building has two different sides that center around a shared core.

One side is a simple extrusion that reaches the full height of the building. This side is primarily southern-oriented and utilizes a system of balconies and a vertical layer of glass to mitigate solar gain. As the building rises this layer of glass becomes wider and functions as a wind break.

Dubai **Pentominium**

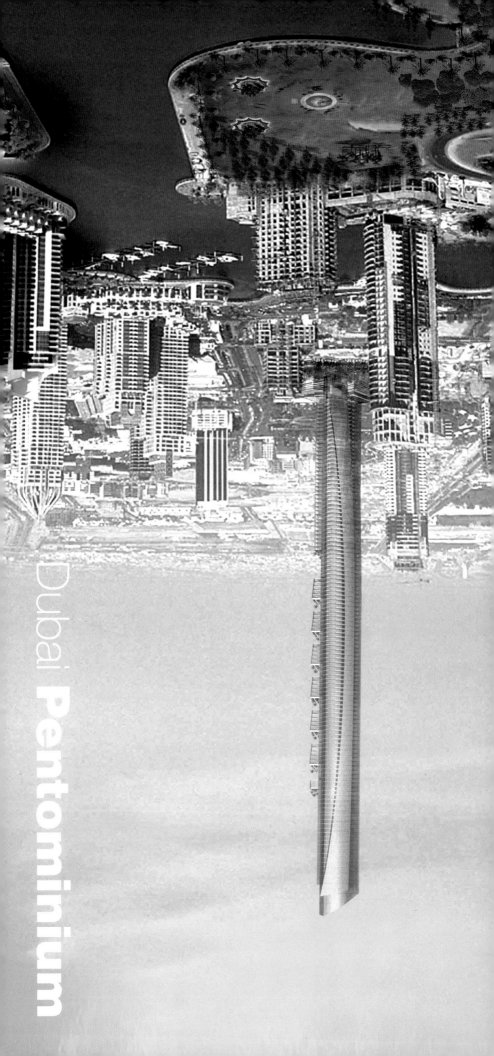

Dubai **Pentominium**

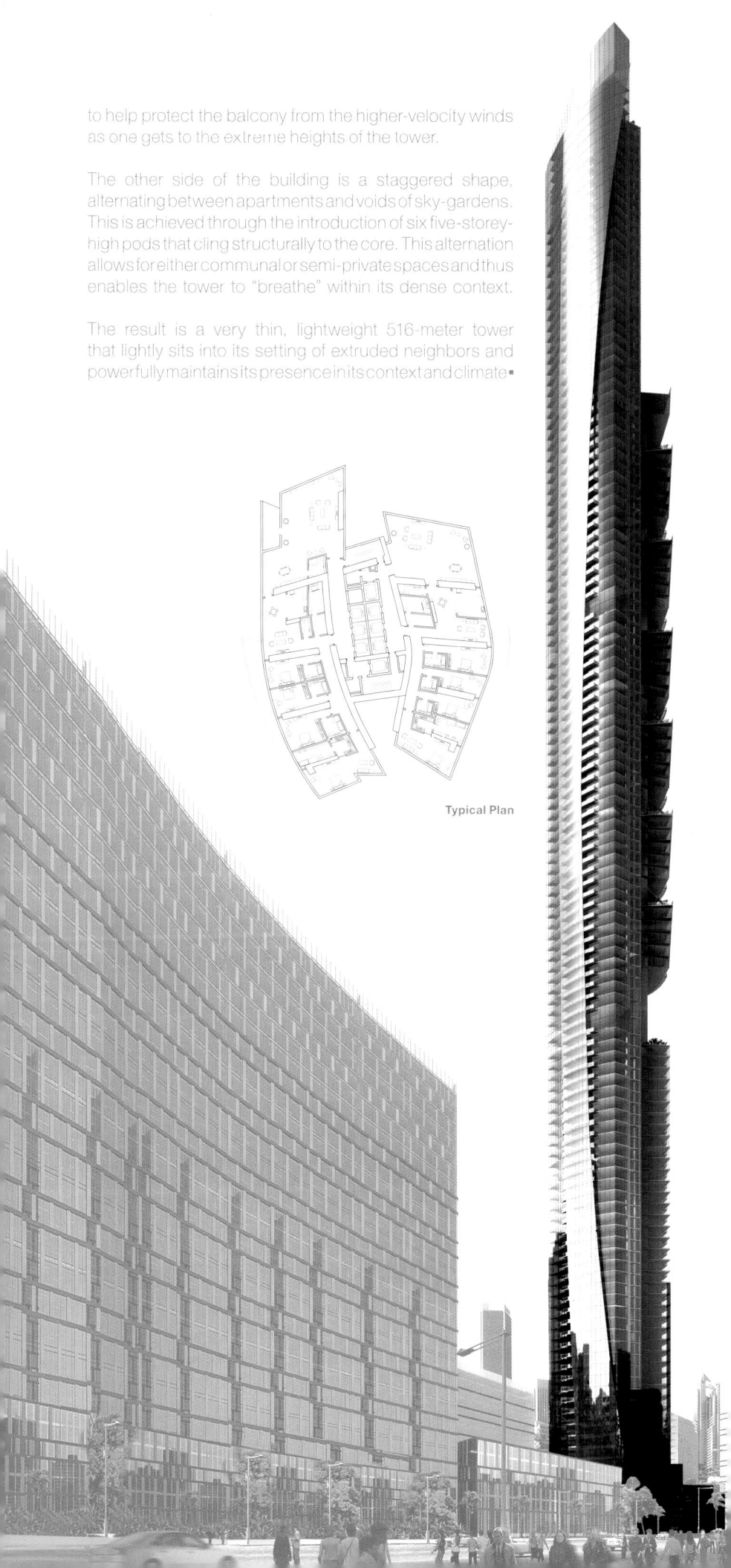

to help protect the balcony from the higher-velocity winds as one gets to the extreme heights of the tower.

The other side of the building is a staggered shape, alternating between apartments and voids of sky-gardens. This is achieved through the introduction of six five-storey-high pods that cling structurally to the core. This alternation allows for either communal or semi-private spaces and thus enables the tower to "breathe" within its dense context.

The result is a very thin, lightweight 516-meter tower that lightly sits into its setting of extruded neighbors and powerfully maintains its presence in its context and climate.

**Typical Plan**

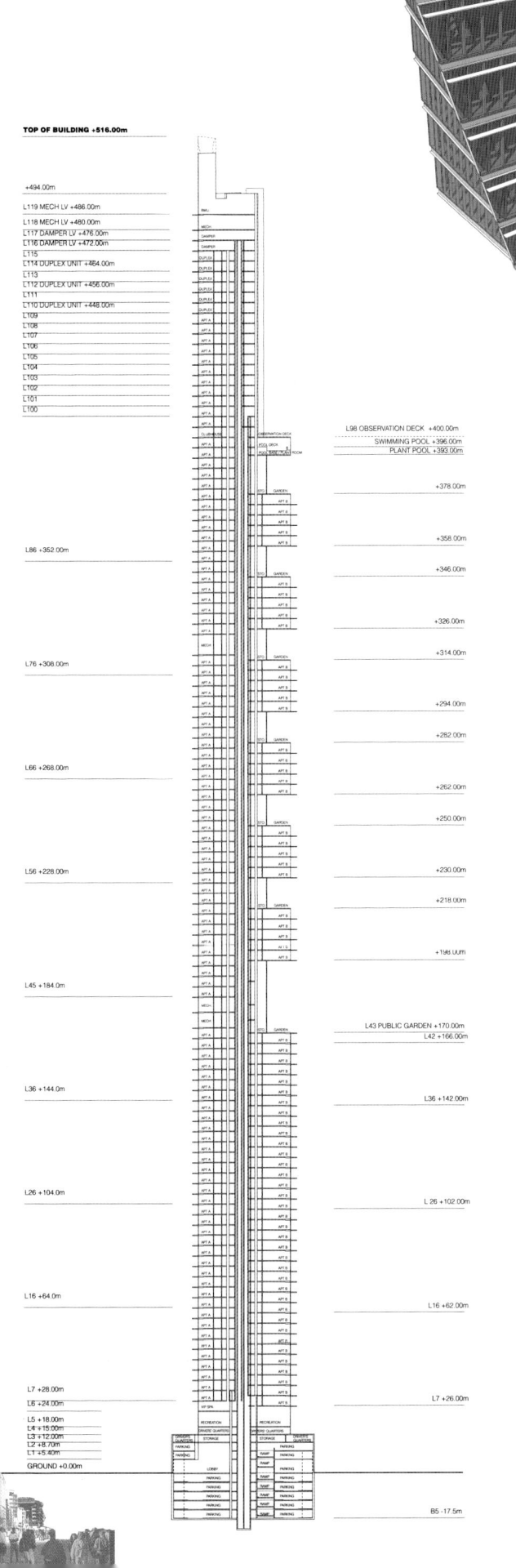

**TOP OF BUILDING +516.00m**

+494.00m

L119 MECH LV +486.00m

L118 MECH LV +480.00m
L117 DAMPER LV +476.00m
L116 DAMPER LV +472.00m
L115
L114 DUPLEX UNIT +464.00m
L113
L112 DUPLEX UNIT +456.00m
L111
L110 DUPLEX UNIT +448.00m
L109
L108
L107
L106
L105
L104
L103
L102
L101
L100

L86 +352.00m

L76 +308.00m

L66 +268.00m

L56 +228.00m

L45 +184.0m

L36 +144.0m

L26 +104.0m

L16 +64.0m

L7 +28.00m
L6 +24.00m
L5 +18.00m
L4 +15.00m
L3 +12.00m
L2 +8.70m
L1 +5.40m
GROUND +0.00m

L98 OBSERVATION DECK +400.00m
SWIMMING POOL +396.00m
PLANT POOL +393.00m

+378.00m

+358.00m

+346.00m

+326.00m

+314.00m

+294.00m

+282.00m

+262.00m

+250.00m

+230.00m

+218.00m

+198.00m

L43 PUBLIC GARDEN +170.00m
L42 +166.00m

L36 +142.00m

L 26 +102.00m

L16 +62.00m

L7 +26.00m

B5 -17.5m

Pod Detail

# Asia **Gateway Complex**

Utilizing the importance of a symbolic connection found in Chinese calligraphy, this project became a character defined by its role within a large master development of an Asian capital city. The project functions as a "gateway" both into the city as well as into its development. The Chinese character for "door" was one that played symbolically into its role as well as allowing for the correct mix of programmatic components. Serendipitously, in this instance, the relationship to the specific character was not realized until the presentation to the client, even though a relationship to calligraphy was a guiding force of the design.

The two towers bend toward each other at their midsections. The taller one, at 282 meters, reduces in size toward the top, decreasing the floor-plate from an efficient size for high-end residential to an efficient size for hotel-run service apartments. The other tower, with slightly larger floor plates for the office components, then turns horizontally for the top seven floors to house a "low-rise" hotel in the sky—200 meters.

Program **Mixed Use** Site Area **60,267 sqm**
Floor Area **195,803 sqm** Building Height **282 m**

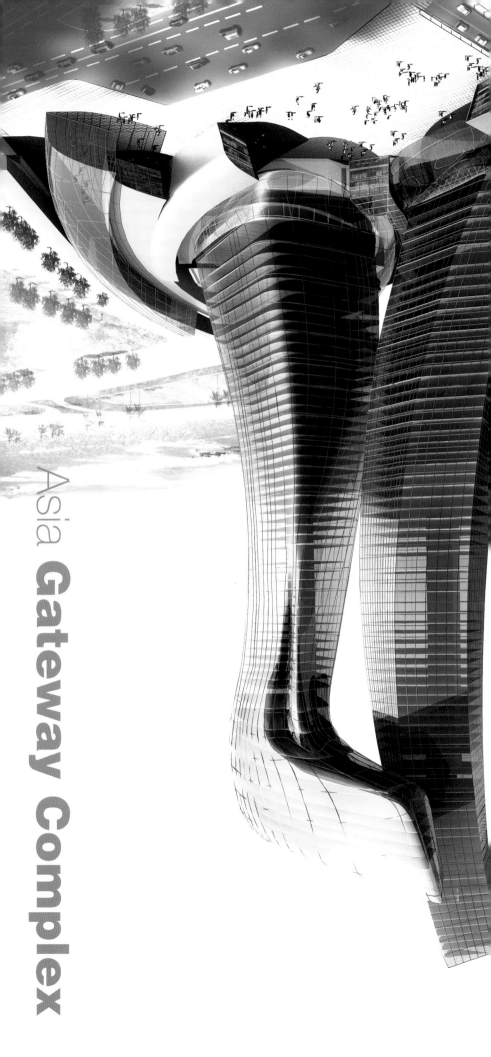

Asia **Gateway Complex**

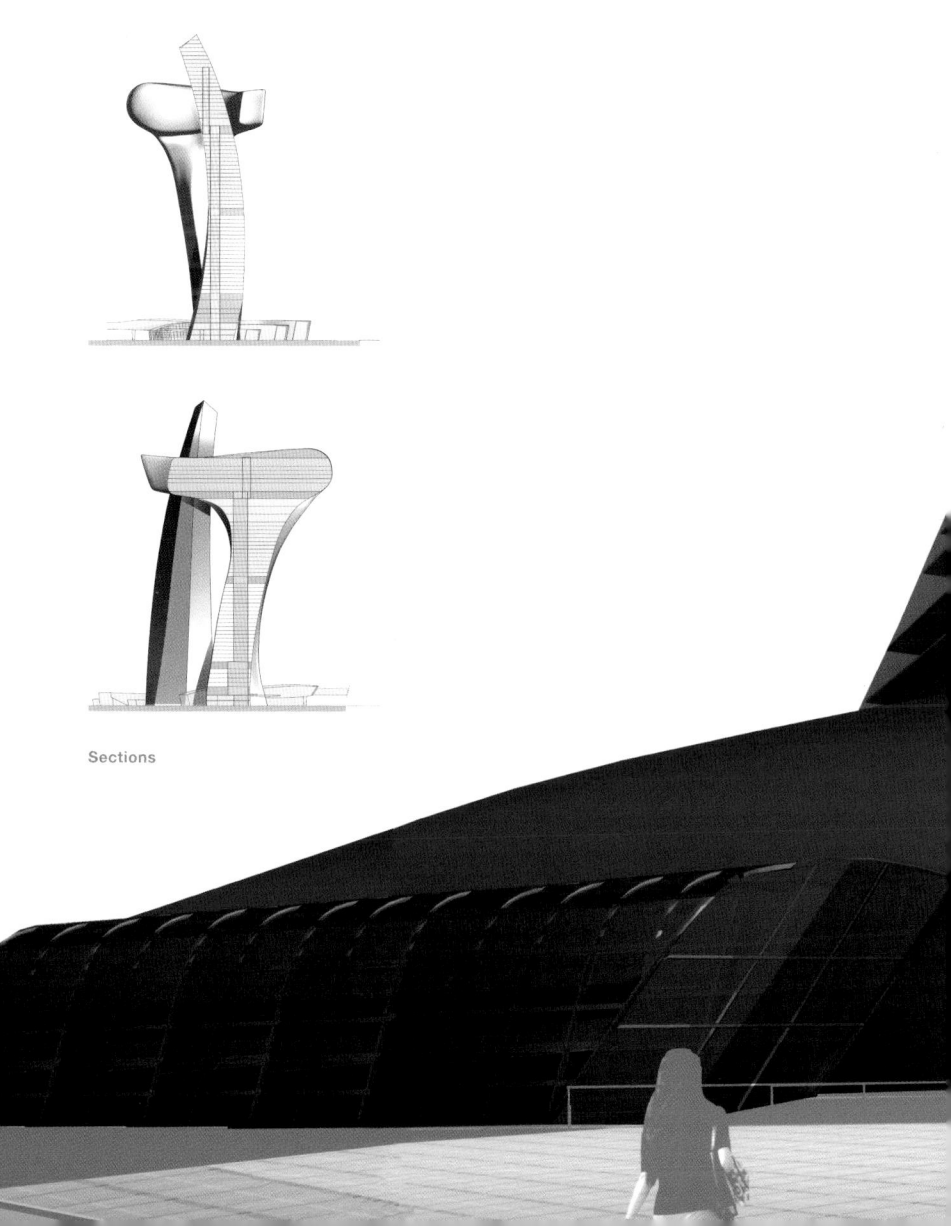

The figure "seven" building slightly overlaps the other tower on its cantilevered end to allow for a discreet connection between the two towers. This connection allows for a flow between the hotel and its service-apartment wing. The two towers intertwine subtly with each other but always maintain the image of a "gateway" from all sides and even from above. This flowing calligraphy formalizes into a true three-dimensional door seen from any direction ▪

Sections

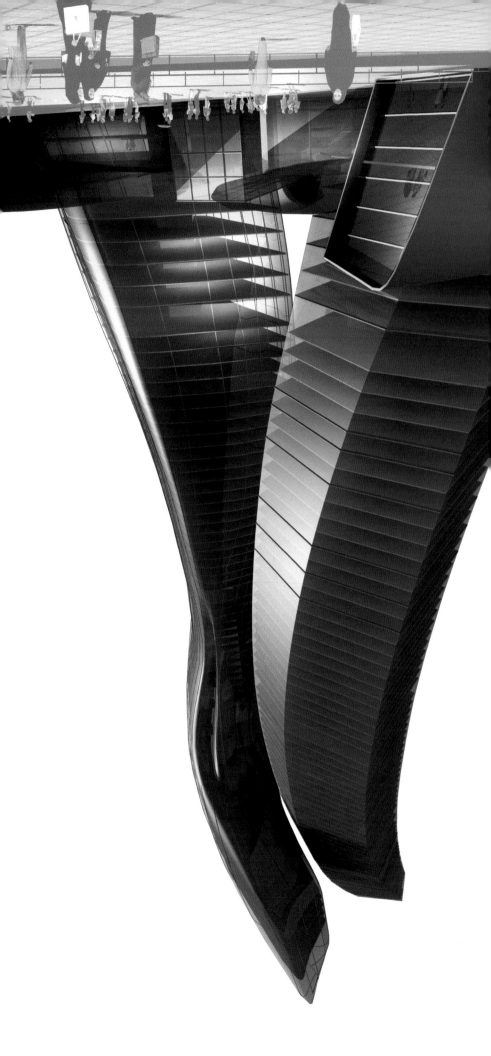

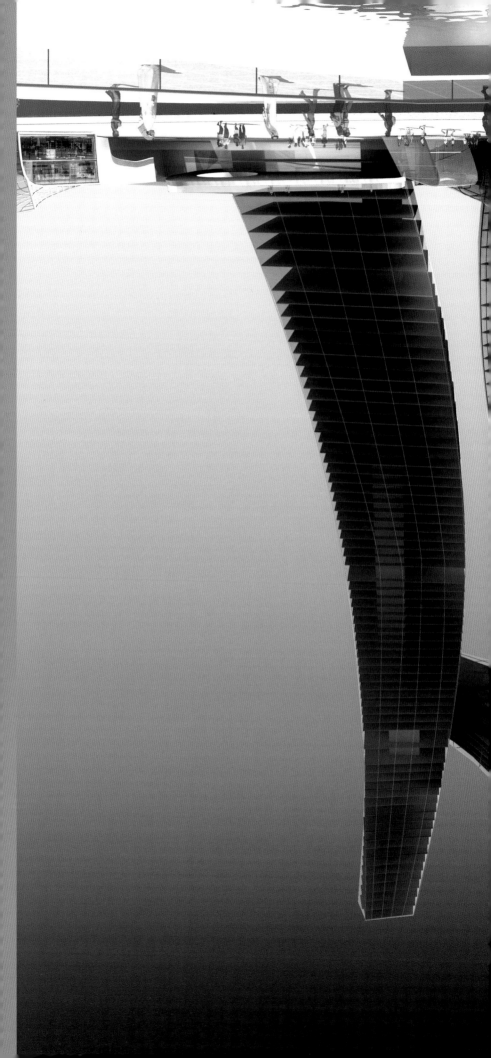

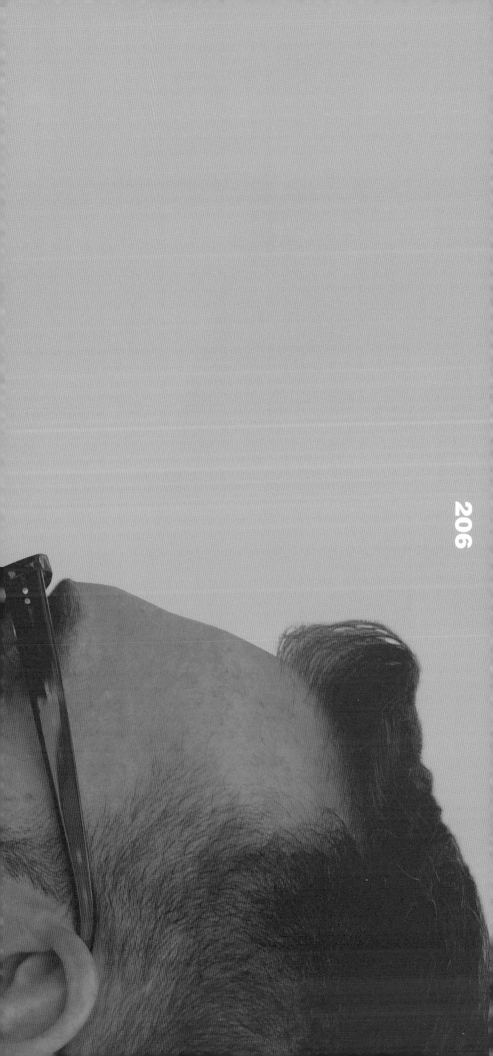

206

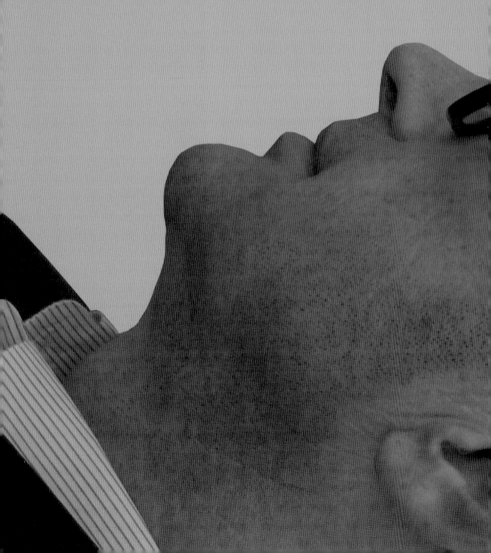

# Interview with **Michael Speaks**

Interview with
**Michael Speaks**

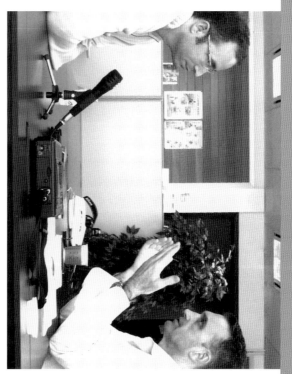

Interview: Feb. 05 2007

## Introduction:

At the invitation of developers, municipal officials, and sheikh, the great architects of the world are now gathering in China, India, and the United Arab Emirates in search of once-in-a-lifetime-commissions and the opportunity to build designs that otherwise would remain only in their imaginations. While the litany of famous architects answering the call is familiar to even the most casual observer, some of the most striking buildings being designed on these frontiers of global modernization are by relative newcomers not often associated with high design.

One such newcomer is commercial giant Aedas, whose star architect Andrew Bromberg has designed some of the most elegant and formally innovative projects slated for construction there or anywhere. With 11 buildings either under construction or in the works and several others awaiting final decision by clients or juries (including the crossed Legs towers designed originally for a competition in Abu Dhabi, and the otherworldly design for a performance venue in Dubai) Bromberg has become one of the most prolific and sought-after designers in China, India, and the United Arab Emirates.

Bromberg's beguiling pair of Dancing Towers, for example, soon to be under construction in Abu Dhabi, strike a formal pose so bold and yet so accommodating that their shape remained resolute through several

complete redesigns, including one that obliged Bromberg to switch the program requirements from one tower to the other. Likewise, the exquisitely turned sculptural profiles of Bromberg's design for Empire Tower in Abu Dhabi, the Boulevard Towers and U-Bora Towers in Dubai, and the North Star residential and commercial towers in Beijing, each conceal with their formal charms the enormous scale and robust massing required of projects with such demanding and varied programs. All are either under construction or slated for construction sometime in the next year. These and other tower projects designed by Bromberg, such as Pentominium Towers and Ocean Heights One—both also soon to be under construction in Dubai—reveal the hand of an extraordinarily talented designer able to thrive in one of the most uncompromising building markets in the world.

In the interview below, conducted with Bromberg in the Hong Kong offices of Aedas in January 2007, he describes how this came to be. While it is perhaps best simply to read the interview, I would like to point out a few threads in the conversation that reveal, more specifically, Bromberg's considerable design talents and why they are so well suited to the pace and scale of development in China and the UAE. Perhaps the most obvious thing to note is that Bromberg has a wonderfully organic design sensibility that, despite the scale of the project at hand, allows him to design for the context. This is especially evident in projects such as his residential urban plan for Xian, where he sought to weave

existing urban elements such as ammunition bunkers and rail lines into an urban design that is ordered yet flowing and free. Surprisingly, Bromberg's approach to the design of the Pentominium Tower, one of the tallest residential buildings in the world, was also guided by his insistence on the importance of context, even though that context was several hundred meters in the air. It is also apparent that Bromberg is able to size up the design challenge very quickly and bring to the table a powerful sculptural form or image that is adaptable but that nonetheless retains its original design intention and often its precise or exact shape. This is his real genius! But this intuitive ability has clearly been sharpened and honed through design competitions and through responding to the demands of clients who insist on innovative designs robust enough to thrive in ever-changing market and developmental conditions. In this way, Bromberg's considerable design talents—evident even in his university thesis project—are uniquely suited to the challenges that come with designing and building in China and in the UAE.

It is also apparent, meeting with his team at Aedas—which functions more like a small design atelier than a division of a large commercial firm—that Bromberg is a natural leader with the confidence of a Pritzker-Prize winner (perhaps someday he will be!) who understands the importance of seeking new design challenges. This is certainly

Michael Speaks: Aedas is a very large firm, one of the largest in the world, and it is still growing. How important is design in such a large firm?

Andrew Bromberg: In a very short time, Aedas has become one of the largest commercial offices in the world and is now beginning to focus on design and on how design adds value to the larger equation. While our chairman here in Hong Kong, Keith Griffiths, has managed to create a very successful commercial office, he obviously has great interest and expertise in design. That, in fact, is why I was brought into the firm—because he and the directors had faith in design and in what I might be able to do for them. That faith has given me a great deal of freedom—not only creative freedom, which, of course, is very important, but freedom to find clients who value design and who value the passion we bring to each project.

MS: It must also be comforting for clients to know that there is a solid firm able to get the job done standing behind the design.

AB: Absolutely. That certainly makes us a very strong competitor. I feel more confident with so many of our projects now slated for construction, knowing that there are 500+ people sitting with me here in the Hong Kong office who have made their reputation by executing, by getting big complex projects built.

one of his great strengths and is surely one of the reasons that he and his team have done so well in markets that, as Bromberg notes in the interview, are more inclined to select on the merit of the design than on reputation. On the strength of their selection as finalists in the urban planning competition for the West Kowloon Cultural District in Hong Kong, Bromberg and his team are now being invited to join competitions in Europe against some of Europe's most highly regarded architects. Indeed, as Bromberg begins to compete in venues and markets that put more stock in reputation and portfolios, and as his own reputation and portfolio grow, one can only believe that he will meet with the same kind of success in those places where he has already found it.

Interview: Feb. 05 2007

MS: You have several projects now under construction in China, but early on it seems you were winning lots of competitions that were not going forward?

AB: When I first came to Hong Kong, I did a lot of large-scale design competitions in China, many of which we won. But it was frustrating because for political reasons, and sometimes for reasons we did not understand, many of the competitions we won did not go forward. It was hard to get clients to sign up. We nonetheless learned a lot about the process in China from these competitions. We were invited, along with Steven Holl and LAB Studios, to compete for a master-plan design for a residential development in Xian, the site of a former ammunitions storage facility. We did a beautiful project, and even though we won in Beijing at the national level, when it went to the local government office in Xian they thought the design was over the top, and so the project was awarded to a local office. The client felt that our design was clearly the best, but in the end local politics decided the outcome. We were also invited, along with SOM and Arquitectonica to enter a competition to design a media center in Foshan, which we also won. And even though we were not able to go forward with the project, the competition was a turning point for me and for my team because it was our first opportunity to compete against big players. The Chinese are very brand name-conscious and so to win head to head on the basis of design rather than brand or reputation was very important for us.

MS: How did you get involved in the Middle East, especially in the Emirates?

AB: I had been discussing the recent developments in Dubai with David Roberts, another Director here at Aedas, and thought I might have a better chance of getting clients to sign up if I went after projects there. David introduced me to DAMAC, one of the leading developers in Dubai. We did not know it at the time, but they were running a competition for the design of their own headquarters and they invited us to join—with the provision that our proposal be available for them to review in less than a week. That was on Sunday. When I returned to Hong Kong Monday night, I was exhausted and so started the project in earnest on Tuesday morning. That is when I realized that in order to get renderings in time to be back in Dubai on Thursday evening, I needed to come up with a design in three hours or less. The team pushed really hard and we were able to get everything done in time to get back to Dubai on Thursday night. When I presented on Friday morning, they liked our scheme but thought it was not quite right. They gave me another week to revise the design. We took the opportunity and won the competition. That was our first project in Dubai and it is now under construction. Soon after that we began to be invited to compete in a number of other competitions.

the image—they need to see what it will look like. We were invited to participate in another competition for a residential tower in Dubai, which we won and which is now under construction. The project is called Ocean Heights One. Anyway, when we won the competition they wanted to add 10 additional floors to compensate for the loss of floor space our design had cost them. And they needed the renderings the next day. We got them the renderings, and a week later they were selling the units. Bear in mind this is an 82-storey tower, and they began selling units before it was even engineered. When we started to go back through the project, we realized that if we were able to move the sheer wall one-half meter we could solve a lot of design problems. But since the client had already sold all the lower units, we could not change anything. We learned that when you do a competition in this kind of market, you'd better get it right the first time.

MS: Would you say that the UAE present a more speculative market than China?

AB: Yes, in China you need to take the clients through the process so that they can sign off on every step. That way, when they see the final result, there are no surprises. I had an experience when presenting our Ziwei Mall proposal in Xi'an that taught me a very

MS: Had you designed large towers before you went to Dubai the first time?

AB: No, it's quite interesting. I knew that I did not have a tower portfolio. So at one point when we were considering going to Dubai, I had a discussion with our chairman, Keith Griffiths, about taking a few months and designing several towers of different heights with different programs so that I would have some examples to put in the brochure, even if they were just fictional. As it turns out, that discussion and that concern became a moot point six months later because I was designing several 300+ meter towers for real clients, that would be built.

MS: You are leading a very young and energetic team of designers that seems especially attuned to the frenetic pace of development in this part of the world. Does your experience with competitions give you an advantage in speculative markets like China and the UAE?

AB: I have a great team. And yes, I think we have become used to a pace that has allowed us to move from a design idea to what the client wants to see very quickly. In China they want to see the process, while in the Middle East, where the market is more speculative and where they pre-sell everything, they need to see

important lesson. I really wanted to make a strong statement with the design, and even though the proposal was not that aggressive, when I finished presenting there was silence in the room for about 15 minutes. No one said a word. They only started to smile and to warm up after I went through the entire process with them. It was clear that the design had started them at first—or at least the big moves I made—but when I explained the reasons for doing so, they were satisfied. So when I presented our next project, the North Star mixed-use development in Beijing near the site of the Olympics, I took a completely different approach. I went through the entire design process and built up the proposal step by step to show that there was no other scheme that could possibly work for them. They loved it! We won the competition and it is now under construction.

MS: And how does that process differ from what happens in the UAE?

AB: When we tried to do that kind of presentation in the Middle East, it failed miserably. We did a master-planning project for a site in Abu Dhabi, near the airport, and we spent several weeks working out all the proportions, the areas, and the road networks—880 hectares. The only thing we did not have were renderings to show them what it could look like. They were exasperated with us, because that is precisely what they wanted to see. I was amazed

but it taught me something. Our clients are developers, so the project must be viable—they pay attention to the plans and the efficiencies. But because everyone is in a race to get their projects sold before the development window closes—and they all expec t it to—there is frenzy and a balancing act between speed to market and quality. Everyone wants to have something fresh and unique, and the image is really important to convey design originality.

MS: You are now competing with some of the most recognizable names in the design world, including, among others, Pritzker-Prize winners. How does that feel?

AB: Great. I am enjoying that. Because Aedas is such a new player, it has allowed me to become one of the design faces of the company, especially in emerging markets such as China and the Middle East, where we have done especially well. It is exciting to compete in these markets, because even though clients, especially in China, can be influenced by name brands, for the most part they are more concerned about the merits of the design and the project in front of them than in past reputation or portfolios. Ironically, as our reputation has grown for strong design, we have begun to be invited to participate in competitions,

for this client—I started the design on the plane ride home to Hong Kong from Dubai. In the middle of the flight, when everyone was sleeping, I shredded my drink coaster trying to put together some shapes that might help me better understand the project. And, after a while, I came up with something that became the initial idea for the design. This was really a difficult project for me, personally, because once I had the design it was hard to figure out how to represent it two-dimensionally. It is a very organic form, and the time constraints made it very hard to come up with the right way to model it. Luckily, in the end we pulled it off. We still do not know what will happen with this project—but it was a lot of fun.

MS: One of the most striking and seemingly controversial projects that you have designed is the crossing towers, which you call the Legs. Can you say something about their design and if they will be built?

AB: The project was a competition entry designed initially for a client we were already doing a project for in Abu Dhabi and who really wanted something original. Many of the young sheikhs in Abu Dhabi felt that Dubai was getting too much attention, and so there was a hunger for projects that would grab everyone's attention and put Abu Dhabi on the map. We had been designing a lot of sculptural

which makes me a bit uneasy because the expectations are very different. We have been short-listed, for example, along with Coop Himmelblau and Herzog & de Meuron for a concert hall in Spain. If it were simply an open-design competition on the merits of the design alone, I know we could compete and stand a good chance to win. But it might be an interview competition, and if that is the case, I am not sure if I will be able to convince the jury to choose us over offices with established reputations and with portfolios of civic projects including concert halls.

MS: Can you say something about the design for the performing-arts center in the Middle East, one of the more exotic designs you have produced to date?

AB: With this project I pushed the design boat out as far as it would go. After I sent him the first images, I called the client to see if he had received them, and he asked what planet I was calling from. We had three weeks to come up with something more exciting than the project submitted to the client by a recent Pritzker-Prize winner, who had already been working on the design for a few months. Now that is a challenge! We were already doing some projects for the client, so they knew we could push the limit. With only three weeks—anc we were already driving hard on two other designs

towers, and I wanted to take on an issue that we had not yet taken on before, one that might give us more flexibility. And that was the constraint posed by the core and how it limited floor plans. I decided to take on the core problem by employing an exoskeleton structure that would free up the floors. I designed two towers that formed two crossing legs whose fish-net stockings served as the structural system. The tower legs were to be serviced by express elevators and joined by sky-bridges. It is one of our most ambitious and formally exotic designs, but it is completely feasible. Everything we proposed is possible. I thought I had read the situation correctly, but in the end it was just too much for them. However, there is another client interested in the design, so I am hopeful.

MS: You have designed a number of really beautiful towers in the UAE that are either in construction or are slated for construction in the near future. Can you say something about the design process of a few of these, perhaps beginning with the Trident Towers, one of the tallest towers you have designed, and if built today, the tallest building in the world?

AB: Our approach to the design of Pentominium Towers was not to look at it as an object, but rather, to view it as a contextual problem. We wanted to design it so that it could breathe. That might sound strange, but Dubai, especially the area of Dubai where this

project will be built, poses an interesting and unique contextual problem—so many towers are being built so close together so quickly that even several hundred meters in the air, there is a feeling of constriction and claustrophobia. That is not a problem you want to have with multi-million dollar apartments. From the beginning the tower was to be quite tall—320 meters. But the client wanted very large luxury apartments—only two units per floor—each around 600 square meters. Ultimately they wanted 170 units. The living room itself is four to five times the size of a two-bedroom apartment in Hong Kong. In order to accomplish this, I recommended that the units be designed with a floor-to-floor height very near a commercial volume, at 3.8 meters. At the time we were very busy, and while I cannot believe it now, I tried to turn down the project. We just had too many other things we were working on. The client made a trip to Hong Kong, and during our meeting they agreed with us about the size of the volumes. In fact, they had recalculated everything and now wanted to take the building up to around 360 meters. When you find a client like that—one that listens to your advice and is able to be as responsive with the brief as you are to the design—you have something special. We decided then to take it on.

MS: And how did it go from 360 meters to more than 500 meters, which would be its height if built today?

with only a little encouragement on my part—488, I reminded him is a good number for the Chinese because it brings wealth—the tower ended up at 618 meters. And it did not hurt that by going to 618 meters, it would overtop an I.M. Pei tower being developed by one of his friends, which was 484 meters. The last time I visited the client, we thought we would get the final go-ahead, but because of some other technical issues, he needed to take it up eight more stories. When we did this we all realized Pentominium was now 516 meters tall, eight meters taller than Taipei 101, currently the tallest building in the world. And that is where it is now. By the time it is completed, Pentominium will not be the tallest tower in the world—some will be over 1,000 meters. But those towers are mixed-use and Trident is residential, which means it could for some time be the tallest residential tower in the world.

MS: You have also designed a pair of very elegant towers, the Dancing Towers, which will soon be under construction in Abu Dhabi. Like many of the projects in the UAE you have designed, they seemed to demand not only formal but also design-process innovation.

AB: Our approach to this project was a very pure, sculptural one that went against traditional developer logic. The site was quite small and

AB: Once we decided to take on the project, we started to look at the site and were shocked by the proximity of all the other towers—some more than 300 meters tall. On the site immediately next to ours was planned a 380 meter tower that would have obscured the views of our tower on approach. Only 20 meters separated the two towers. It was within this context that we started to shape Trident towers. We designed vertical gardens that clung to the side of the building like pods; these created both visual and literal space between the towers. But once we made these moves, we needed to add height to the building to get the right number of units. We drew it up and realized that we now had a tower of 418 meters. The client was completely supportive. We did the renderings and went out to Dubai to show the client. They loved them but thought the top of the tower was not significant enough. So we made the top a little more sloped, and the tower rose to 618 meters.

MS: The pace of the growth of the tower is almost unimaginable.

AB: Yes, and after it grew to 428 meters, something clicked with the client and he began to read everything he could get his hands on that dealt with tall buildings. He continued to change the brief, and

normally would accommodate a single building. The surrounding buildings were relatively small, and I did not think it appropriate to drop the kind of huge building on the site that the brief called for. When the client, who is a very prominent figure in the UAE, saw our scheme, he picked up on what we had already nicknamed the two towers when he said, "They look as though they are dancing." "Yes," we said, "these are the "Dancing Towers." The only problem they had with our initial proposal was with the curtain wall, which they were afraid would be too expensive. We finally convinced them that it was financially viable, and we got the commission.

MS: And they decided to go with two towers?

AB: They decided to do an apartment building in the tall tower and a boutique hotel in the smaller one. Everything went well until the client hired a hotel consultant who convinced them to reverse the towers and put a large business hotel in the tall tower and the apartments in the small tower. Then the client decided to get rid of the hotel altogether and turn the large tower into office spaces and the small tower into furnished apartments. This entailed huge changes in parking and in floor-to-floor heights, but most significantly it entailed a huge change in the core, and consequently, with the number and type of lifts. We had to change the core from the center to the side in the office building. Ultimately, the structural system had to be

redesigned and was changed from concrete to steel. And with all this the shape of the towers stayed the same—a requirement that the client insisted on from the beginning. It was like a crazy thesis project: design two organically formed buildings and see how many different programs you can make work inside them. We have now completely redesigned the entire project three times in 14 months and are going to tender with it next week. What is amazing to me is that we went through all these contortions and ended up with a really nice design in less time than the same project designed once would have taken in the US.

MS: How do the demands of such projects make working here in Hong Kong different from working in the US?

AB: I have friends at a number of corporate offices that I see from time to time. In Dubai last month I was showing a few of them a mock-up version of this book on my projects, and one of them said, "You know, it would be great if one of these could get built." He was mildly shocked when I told him that, in fact, 11 of the projects would be built. The environment I am working in here in Hong Kong is extremely fluid and fast-paced, and I must admit it has become somewhat addictive. I cannot imagine this pace back in the US or in Europe.

working on it for some time now, but working on so many large-scale projects at one time makes it easy to lose perspective on just how massive they are and on the kind of impact they will have on the city. It is very strange, but before I visited the site, I had begun to think of North Star as one of our smaller projects.

MS: What effect does working on projects of this scale and at such a pace have on your design sensibility?

AB: Once you become acclimated to the pace here, it opens up a kind of creativity that I could never have experienced in a firm in the US. The design freedom Aedas has given me has led to opportunities that have in turn led to greater levels of creativity for me and also for my team. It is also a matter of finding new forms of creativity in efficiency and flexibility. Through the necessity of being forced to be nimble and responsive to changing conditions, we have developed a process and way of working that allows us to compete in this part of the world. I am not sure how long this will all continue, but for now I am thrilled to be here in Hong Kong, right in the middle of such incredible change in the Middle East and in Asia. It is an addiction I am happy to live with for as long as it lasts.

MS: It seems it is not just a matter of speed though, but also a matter of scale?

AB: Yes, that is certainly true. The West Kowloon Cultural District competition we did here in Hong Kong, for example, is a project whose scale and impact on the city is unimaginable in the US or in Europe. In the end our proposal, like that of Norman Foster's, contained almost 2.5-million square feet of cultural venues and a 40-hectare park, 55 percent of which was to be covered with an urban canopy. For political reasons this project is now on hold, but for some time it captivated all of Hong Kong. I was recently confronted with this same issue when visiting some of our projects in China that are now under construction. I was up in Beijing visiting the construction site for North Star and was completely overwhelmed by the size of the site excavations. I designed it and have been

**Biography**

**MICHAEL SPEAKS** (Ph.D., Duke University) is a Los Angeles-based educator and design-strategy consultant. He has published and lectured internationally on contemporary art, architecture, urban design, and scenario planning. Former Director of the Graduate Program and Founding Director of the Metropolitan Research and Design Post Graduate Program at the Southern California Institute of Architecture in Los Angeles. Speaks has also taught in the graphic design department at the Yale School of Art, and in the architecture programs at Harvard University, Columbia University, The University of Michigan, The Berlage Institute, UCLA, and the TU Delft. Speaks is founding editor of the cultural journal *Polygraph* and former editor at *A+y* in New York, and is currently a contributing editor for *Architectural Record*.

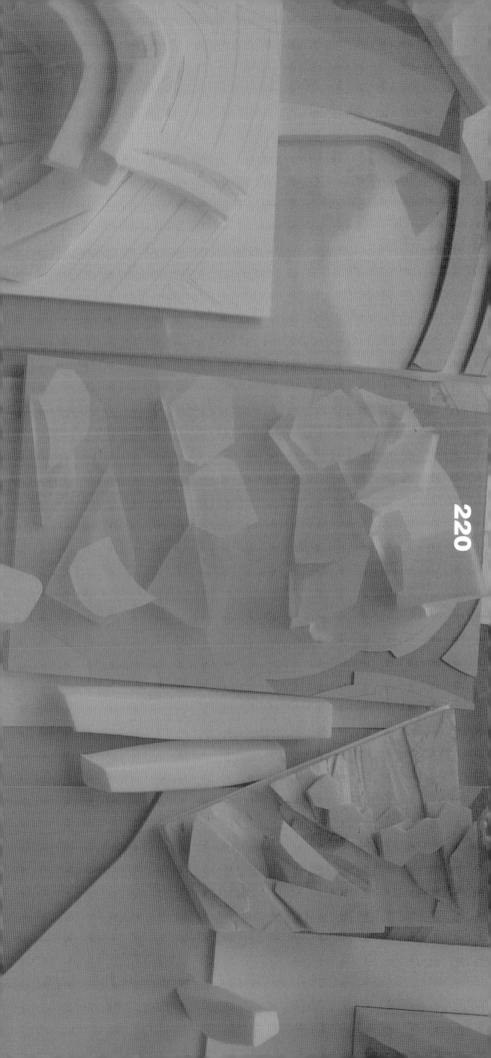

# Design Process

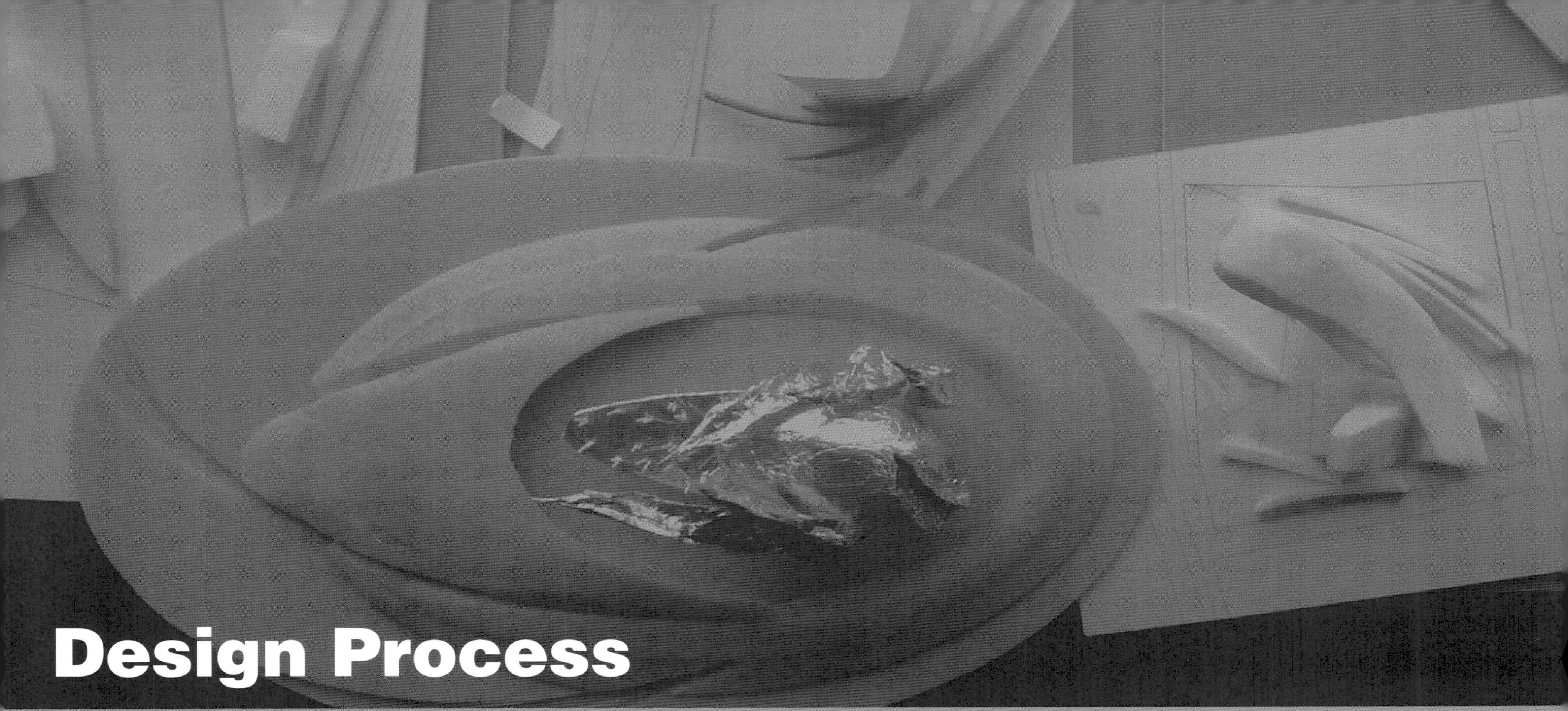

construction

digital process

analog process

schematic design

# Process

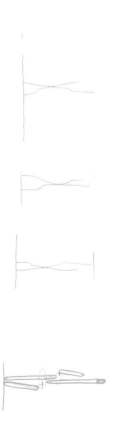

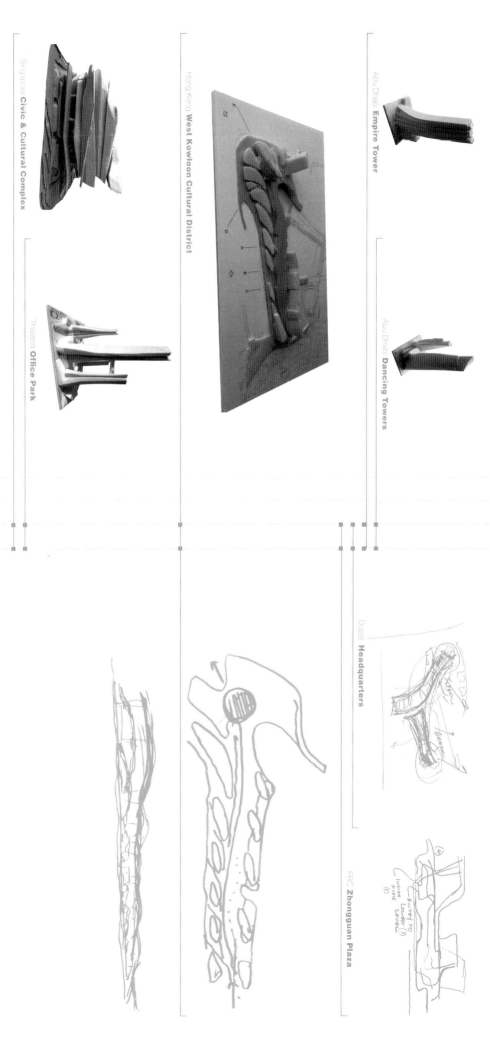

Singapore **Civic & Cultural Complex**

Hong Kong **West Kowloon Cultural District**

Abu Dhabi **Empire Tower**

Abu Dhabi **Dancing Towers**

Thailand **Office Park**

Dubai **Headquarters**

PRC **Zhongguan Plaza**

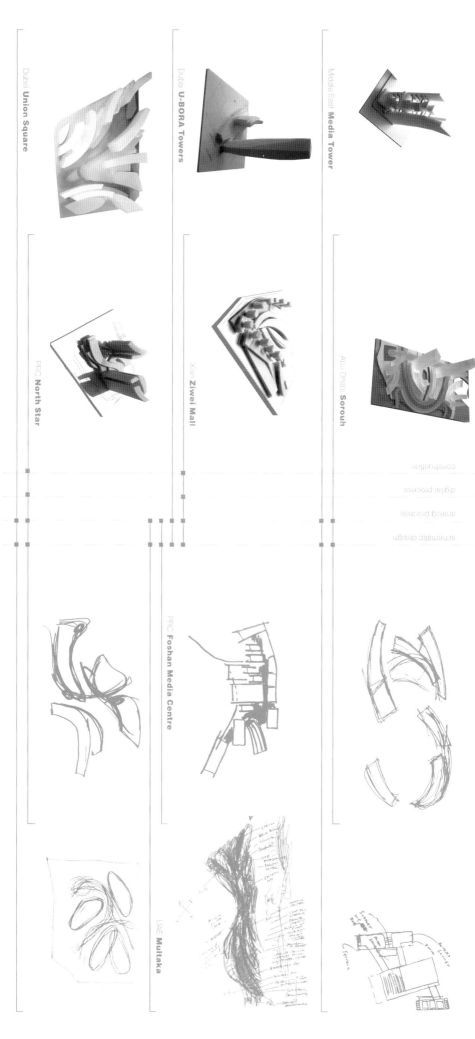

Middle East **Media Tower**

Abu Dhabi **Sorouh**

Dubai **U-BORA Towers**

Xi'an **Ziwei Mall**

Dubai **Union Square**

PRC **North Star**

PRC **Foshan Media Centre**

UAE **Multaka**

construction

digital process

analog process

schematic design

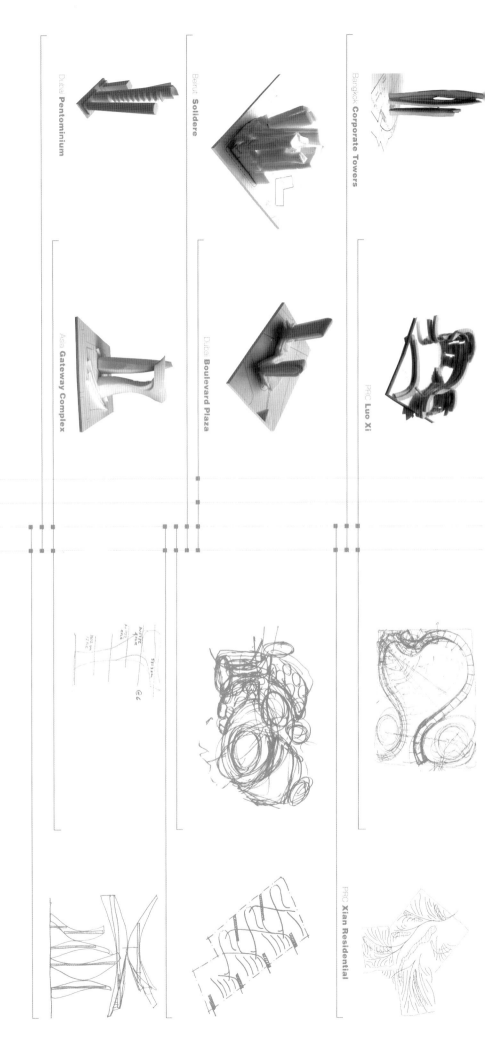

Bangkok **Corporate Towers**

Beirut **Solidere**

Dubai **Pentominium**

PRC **Luo Xi**

Dubai **Boulevard Plaza**

Asia **Gateway Complex**

PRC **Xian Residential**

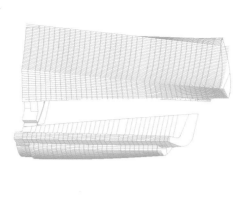

construction

digital process

analog process

schematic design

## Abu Dhabi **Dancing Towers**

Dancing Towers is a project with intersecting, curved geometries. The challenge in this project was documenting the individual two-dimensional floor plans in relation to the overall curvilinear form. The primary task of the parametric model was to represent the rationalized geometries and, therefore, form a centralized database of two-dimensional floor plates for documentation. With the parametric model, a 3-D plot (i.e., a physical model) was produced to visualize the building form before construction and to remove any discrepancies in the smoothness of the form.

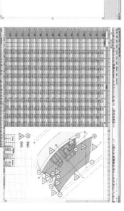

Plans - Structural Plan - T1-01.jpg  Plans - Structural Plan - T1-02.jpg  Plans - Structural Plan - T1-03.jpg  Plans - Structural Plan - T1-04.jpg  Plans - Structural Plan - T1-05.jpg  Plans - Structural Plan - T1-06.jpg  Plans - Structural Plan - T1-07.jpg  Plans - Structural Plan - T1-08.jpg

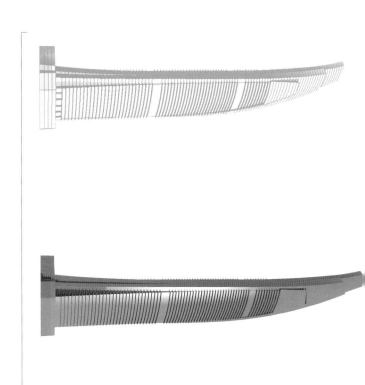

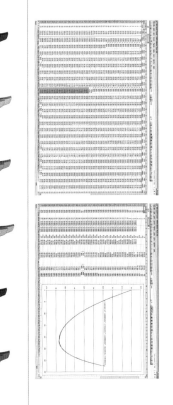

## Dubai **Ocean Heights Two**

Like the other projects, Ocean Heights Two was developed using parametric programming. However, during the design development, the client asked for options to the overall building height to optimize the floor area. Due to the sophisticated geometry of the form, the changes in building height could not be simply done by removing the floors. The geometry had to be worked out to suit each option. With the parametric model, the options were worked out quickly to present the feasibility of each option. Overall, 14 options were produced quickly as to provide a clear picture of the changes to the building proportions and geometry.

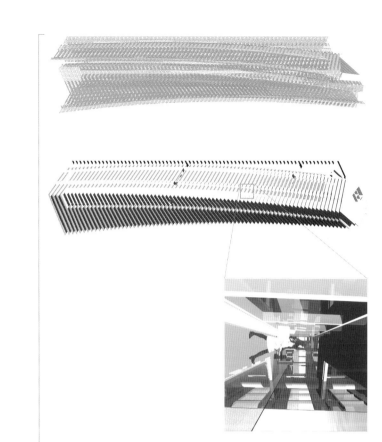

construction

digital process

analog process

schematic design

## Dubai **Ocean Heights One**

With Ocean Heights One, the façade geometry became an issue of feasibility when it came to the façade's panelization. This required that the mullions and panels could not be set out from simple elevation drawings. Therefore, the façade was calculated by numerical method and presented in a parametric model. Two-dimensional drawings were produced from the model to show the internal design of the façade and to prove the feasibility of the curtain-wall system for this twisting building.

With the parametric model, a schedule of the panels was produced showing dimensions and quantity of individual panels. These dimensions showed that the deviations from panel to panel and twisting of each individual panel were within acceptable limits. This eased the design team's concern for the practicality and cost-efficiency of the design.

## Abu Dhabi **Empire Tower**

Unlike the other projects, Empire Tower is relatively modular in plan. However, when these individual modular plans were vertically stacked along a curved profile, the overall geometry and form of the building became complicated. Modeling the plans and building form in parametric programming became a working process for drawing production.

The designers felt that the first parametric model did not have the presence of the original study model when it came to the view from the street front. In response, several options were created to study the building as its modular units tapered towards the roof.

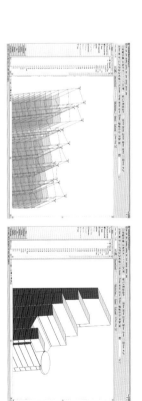

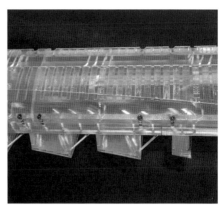

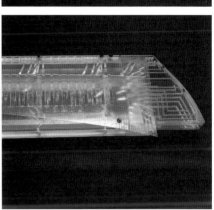

## Dubai **Pentominium**

The structural design of tall buildings in the Gulf region is normally governed by wind loading. As buildings grow taller and more slender they become more susceptible to cross-wind dynamic response, also known as vortex shedding. This can lead to both large loads and uncomfortable accelerations (swaying) for the building occupants. The irregular vertical profiles of Pentominium, however, work to break up the formation of the regular vortices needed to generate large cross-wind responses. Due to the architectural form, Pentominium experiences unprecedentedly low loads and accelerations for a building of its height and slenderness.

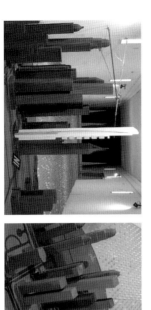
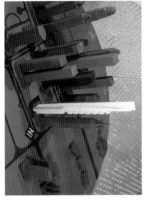
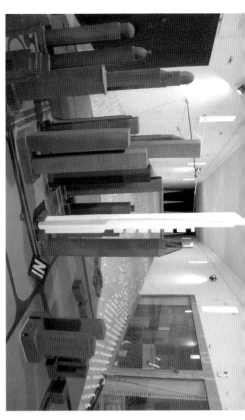

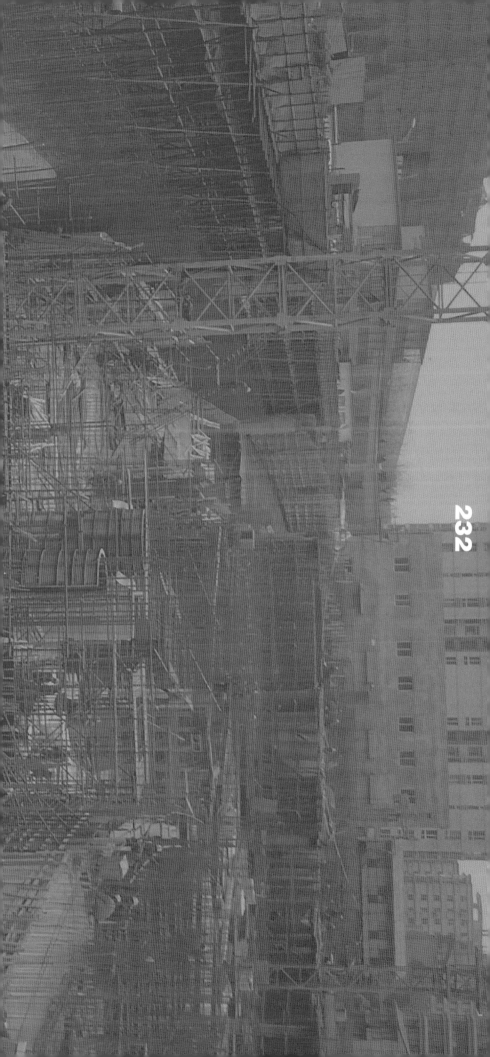

232

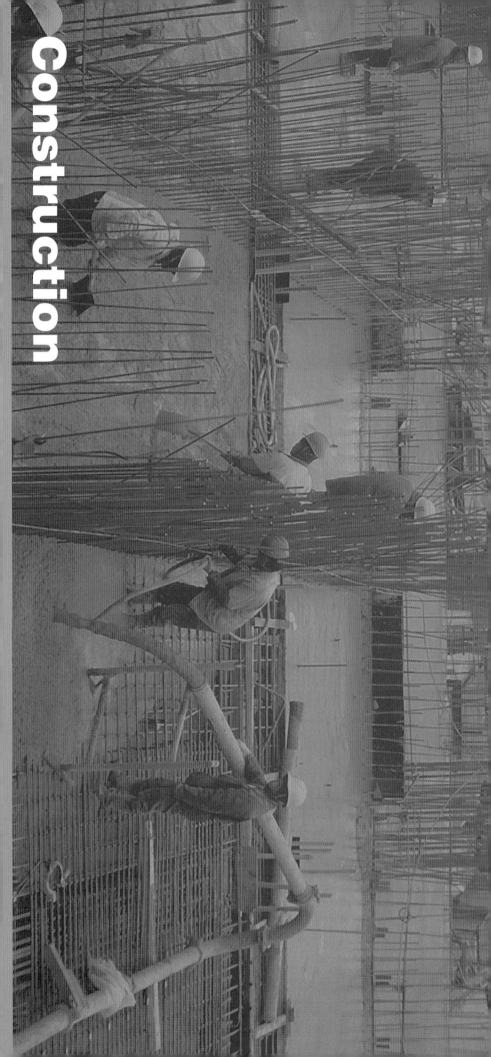

Construction

## Construction

Completion Date: 2009
Site Area **4,180 sqm**
Floor Area **44,235 sqm**
Building Height **160 m**

Abu Dhabi **Dancing Towers**

## Dubai **Ocean Heights One**

Completion Date: 2009
Site Area **3,746 sqm**
Floor Area **858,665 sqm**
Building Height **304 m**

PRC **Crowne Plaza Hotel**

Completion Date: 2009
Site Area **9,904 sqm**
Floor Area **84,237 sqm**
Building Height **97 m**

Dubai **U-BORA Towers**

Completion Date: 2009
Site Area **19,883 sqm**
Floor Area **119,298 sqm**
Building Height **263 m**

Completion Date: 2009
Site Area **17,200 sqm**
Floor Area **60,927 sqm**
Building Height **174 m**

Dubai **Boulevard Plaza**

PRC **North Star**

Completion Date: 2008
Site Area **2,525 sqm**
Floor Area **161,780 sqm**
Building Height **107 m**

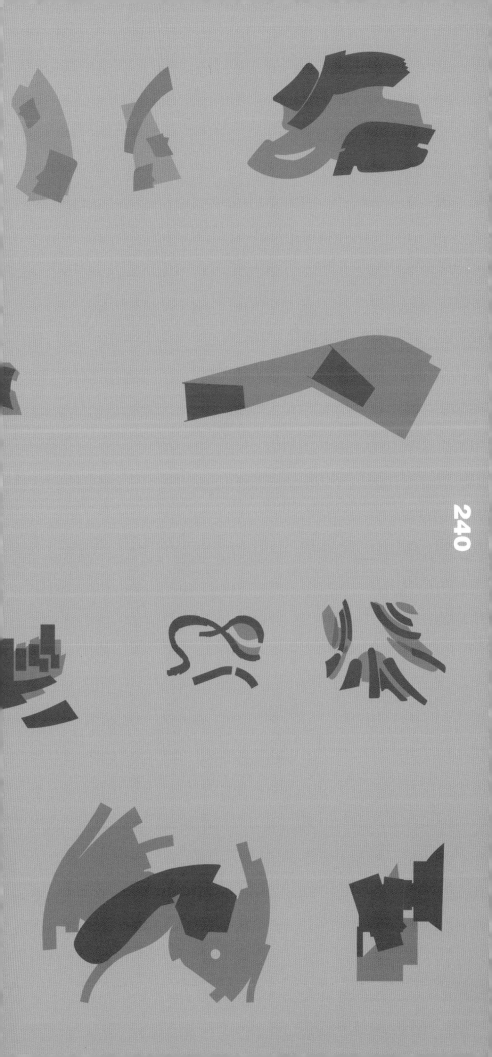

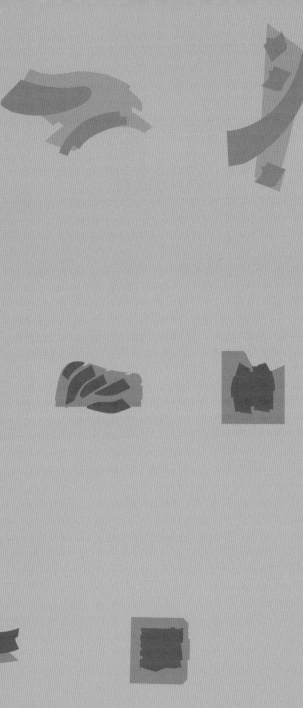

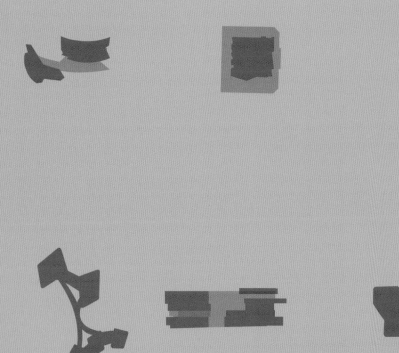

## Chronology

### Selected Work Previous To Aedas

**1990** Denver International Airport Terminal **With** CW Fentress / HMA **Client** Denver International Airport

**1991** Boulder Public Library **With** Midyette / Seieroe **Client** Boulder City Municipality

**2000** Reebok World Headquarters **With** NBBJ **Client** Reebok

**2003** Mann Theatre **With** NBBJ **Client** Mann Theatre

**2003** Seattle-Tacoma International Airport South Terminal **With** NBBJ **Client** Seattle International Airport

### Aedas Projects 2003-2007

**2003** Beijing International Plaza

**2003** San Lin Project

**2003** Oriental Silicon Valley Master Planning

**2004** Chinese University College of Technology Chapel

**2004** Szechuan Financial Corporation

**2004** Luo Xi Residential

**2004** Sunshine 100 Residential Development

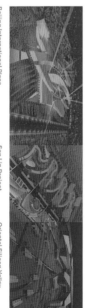

**Beijing International Plaza**
PRC

**San Lin Project**
PRC

**Oriental Silicon Valley**
PRC

CU Chapel

Szechuan

Luo Xi

Sunshine Residential

**2004** HKIA Exhibition Center
**2004** The Landmark
**2004** Government Headquarters
**2004** Zhongguan International Plaza
**2004** Dong Zhi Men Mixed-Use Development

**2004** Foshan Media Centre
**2004** Xian Ziwei Mall
**2004** HKU Space

**2005** Sheth Headquarters
**2005** West Kowloon Cultural District
**2005** North Star

**2005** Multaka Master Plan
**2005** Union Square
**2005** Grand Marco Polo Hotel & Residential

**Multaka**
Abu Dhabi

**Union Square**
Dubai

**HKIA Exhibition Centre**
Hong Kong

**Landmark**
Hong Kong

**Government HQ**
Hong Kong

**Zhongguan**
PRC

**Dong Zhi Men**
PRC

**Foshan Media Centre**
PRC

**Xian Ziwei Mall**
PRC

**HKU Space**
Hong Kong

**Sheth Headquarters**
India

**West Kowloon Cultural District**
Hong Kong

**North Star**
PRC

**Grand Marco Polo Hotel & Residential**
PRC

U-BORA Towers
Dubai

Jebel Hafeet Resort
Abu Dhabi

Boulevard Plaza
Dubai

Ocean H. Two
Dubai

Dancing Towers
Abu Dhabi

Ocean Heights One
Dubai

Solidere
Beirut

Headquarters
Dubai

Crowne Plaza Hotel
PRC

Sorouh
Abu Dhabi

Xian Residential
PRC

Atlas Mills
India

The Legs
Middle East

**More to Come**

**132**
Dubai **Union Square**

**186**
PRC **Luo Xi**

Scale

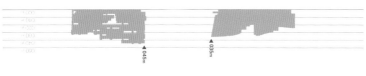

▲045m   ▲035m

Corporate Towers
Bangkok

Office Park
Thailand

Civic & Cultural Com.
Singapore

Corp. Towers 2
Asia

Gateway Complex
Asia

**148**
Singapore **Civic & Cultural Complex**

**070**
PRC **Zhongguan Plaza**

▲060m

▲079m

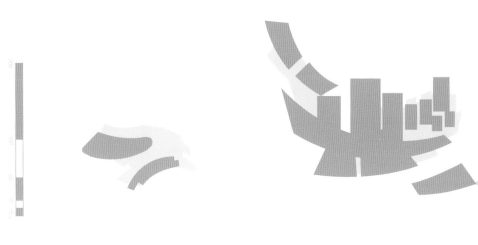

120
PRC **Crowne Plaza Hotel**

138
PRC **Foshan Media Centre**

▲ 0.97m

▲ 0.82m

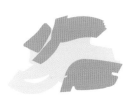

**140**
PRC **North Star**

**180**
Beirut **Solidere**

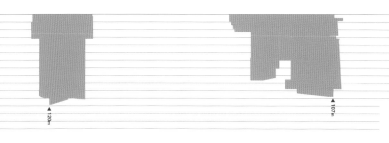

▲120m

▲107m

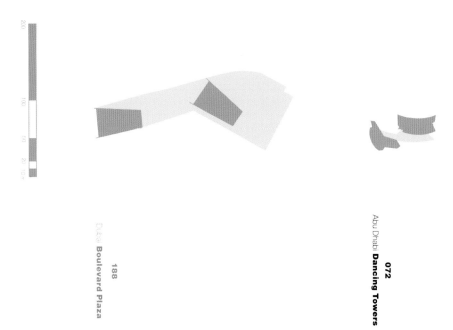

072
Abu Dhabi **Dancing Towers**

188
Dubai **Boulevard Plaza**

▲173m

▲160m

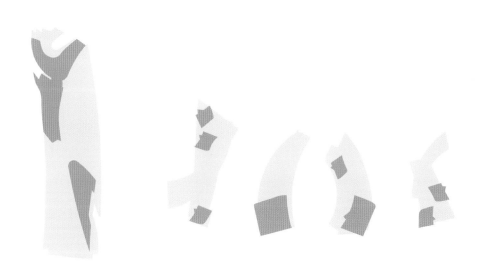

**054**
Headquarters
Dubai

**126**
Sorouh
Abu Dhabi

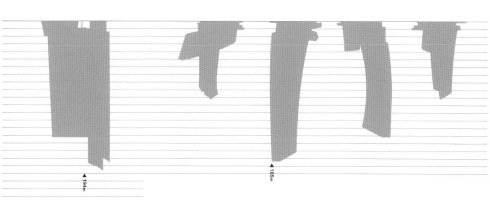

▲194m

▲185m

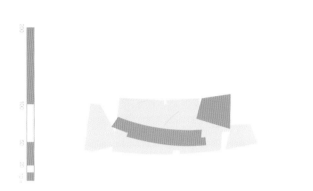

## 064
Abu Dhabi **Empire Tower**

## 112
Dubai **U-BORA Towers**

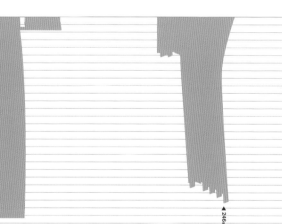

▲ 246m

▲ 263m

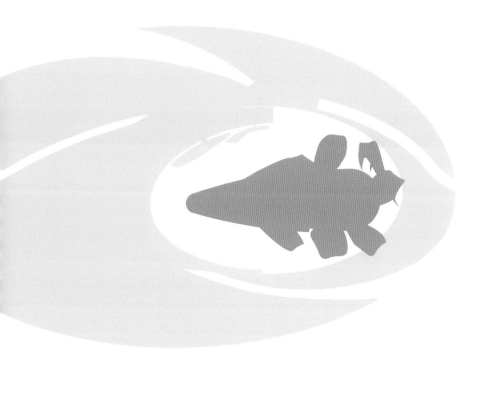

▲ 284m

200
Asia **Gateway Complex**

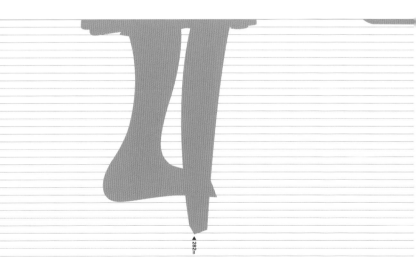

▲282m

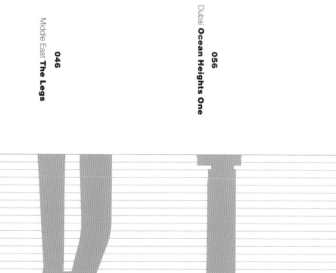

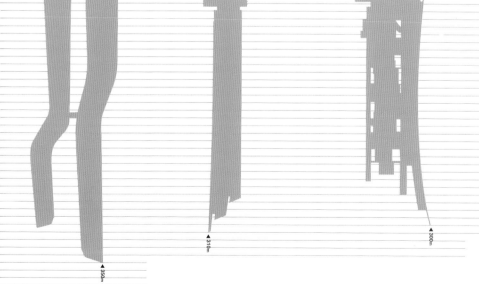

**100**
Middle East **Media Tower**

**056**
Dubai **Ocean Heights One**

**046**
Middle East **The Legs**

▲300m

▲310m

▲350m

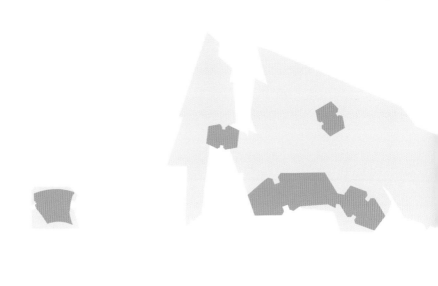

**066**
Dubai **Ocean Heights Two**

**118**
Thailand **Office Park**

▲420m

▲409m

256

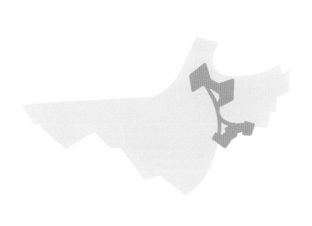

172
Bangkok **Corporate Towers**

196
Dubai **Pentominium**

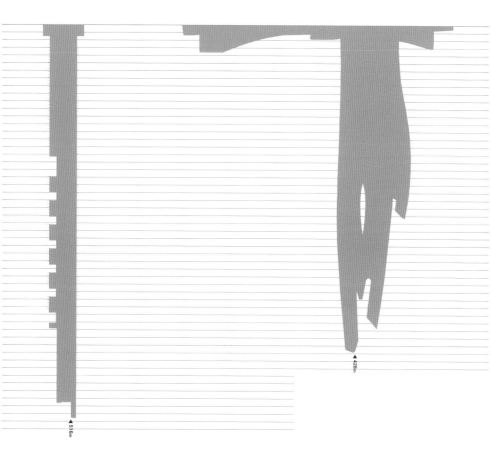

▲428m

▲516m

Abu Dhabi **Jebel Hafeet Resort**

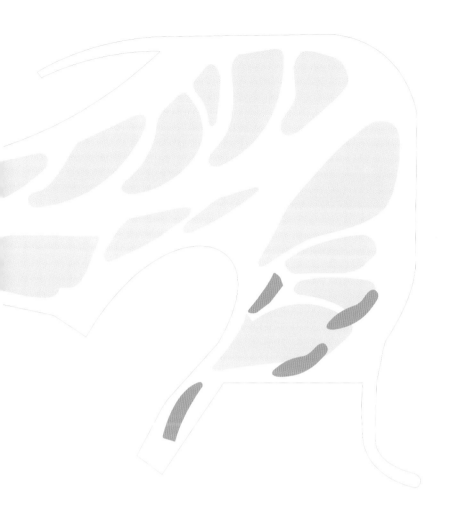

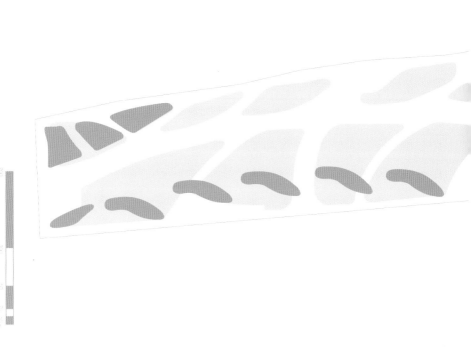

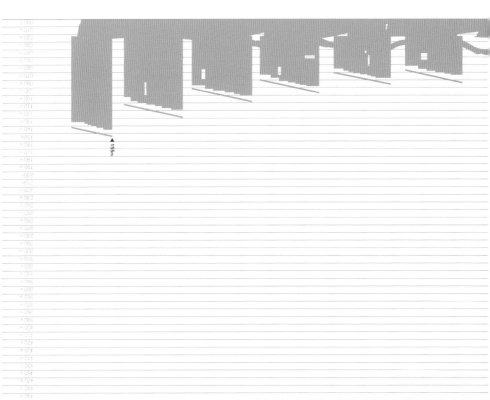

▲ 155m

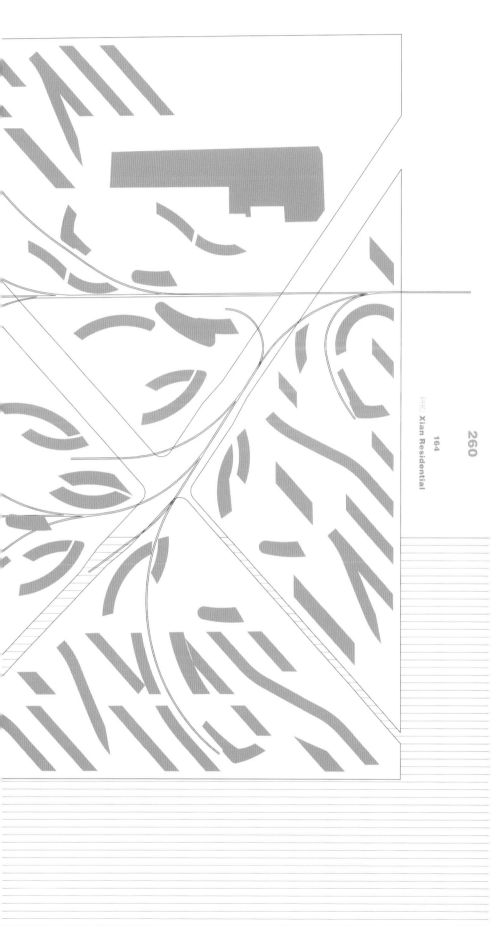

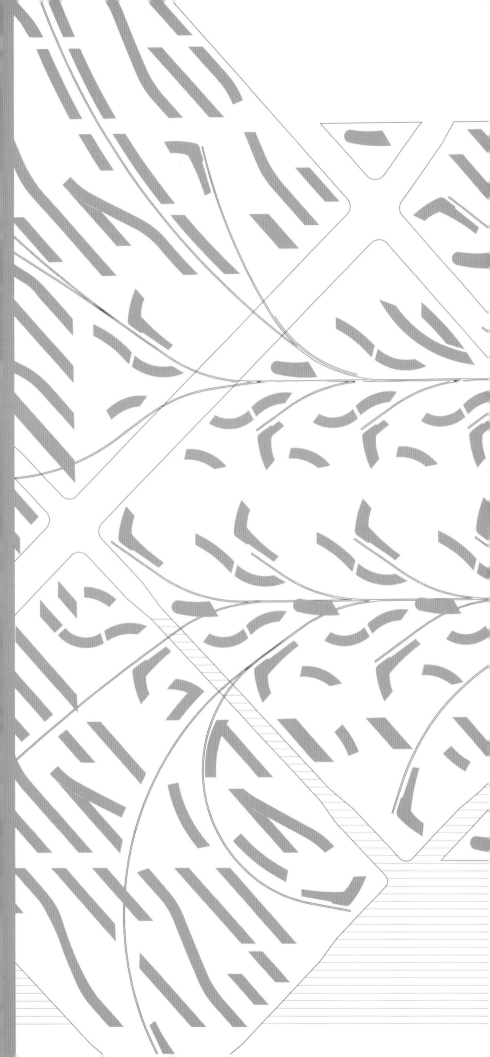

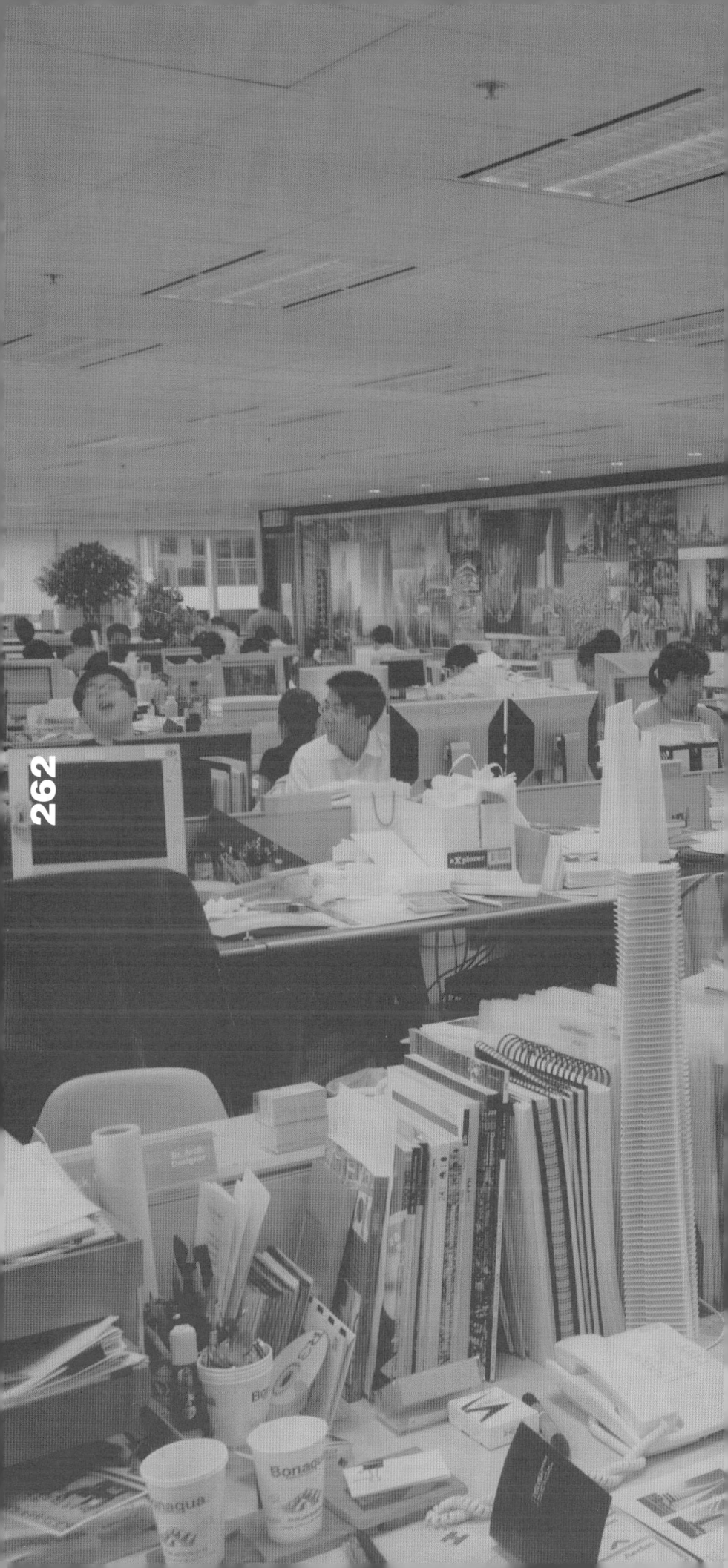

262

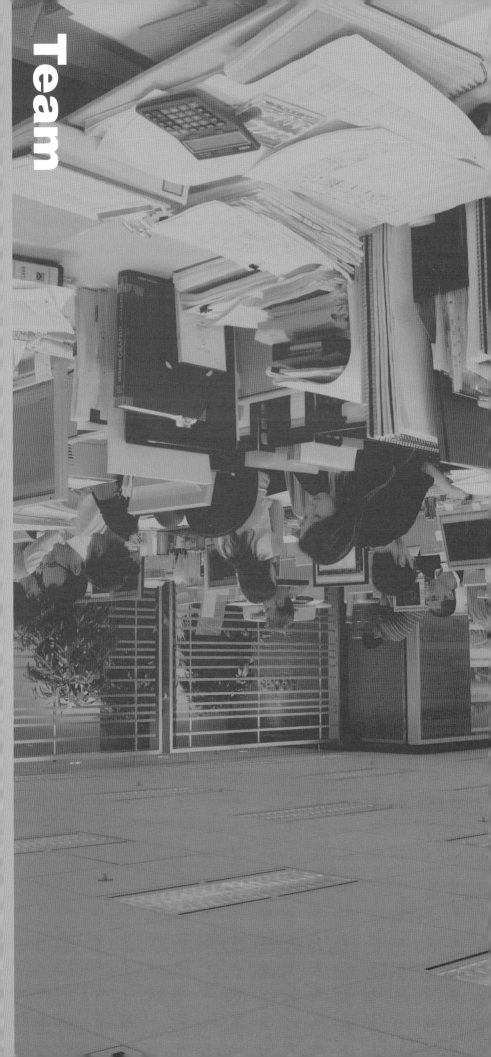

Team

<cent;border>
</cent;border>

# Andrew Bromberg

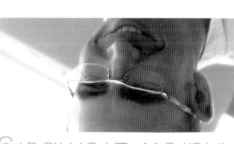

Biography

Bachelor's in Environmental Design
**University of Colorado**
**Arizona State University**
**(Special Honors)**

Master's in Architecture
**Southern California Institute of Architecture**
**University of Washington**

Awards

**2007 - 40 Under 40, Perspective Magazine**
Andrew Bromberg

**2006 - Cityscape Architectural Review, Design Commendation for Sport & Leisure**
Jebel Hafeet

**2006 - MIPIM Architectural Review, Commendation For Master Planned Communities**
West Kowloon Culture District

**2006 - Arabian Property Award, Best Architecture Award**
Ocean Heights Two

**2006 - Arabian Property Award, Best Development Award**
Oceanscape

**2005 - Bentley International Award, Best Architecture**
Ocean Heights

**2004 - Cityscape Architectural Review, Commendation For Master Planning**
West Kowloon Culture District

**2004 - Cityscape Architectural Review, Commendation For Residential Projects**
Luo Xi

**2001 - American Society of Landscape Architects, Merit Award, Ohio Chapter**
Reebok World Headquarters

**2000 - American Institute of Architects Seattle, Merit Award**
Reebok World Headquarters

**2000 - Chicago Athenaeum American Architect Awards**
Reebok World Headquarters

**1999 - National Association of Industrial and Office Properties: Office of the Year**
Adobe NW Headquarters

**1995 - American Institute of Architects Seattle Honor Award: Conceptual Work**
Four Houses and a Bluff, Selection Juror - Steven Holl

Andrew Bromberg, the lead designer for Aedas in Asia, is recognized for his ability to conceptualize and realize complex and sensual designs for a wide range of projects. Bromberg has over 15 years of professional experience, with the last six of them being in Hong Kong. Using invited competitions as a way of exploring and exposing new ideas, Bromberg has compiled an impressive body of work in a considerably short period of time. With many projects under construction or in the works, Andrew Bromberg has become one of the most prolific and sought-after designers in China, India, and the United Arab Emirates.

Before coming to work in Asia's emerging economies, he was a designer for more established North American offices. He currently resides in Hong Kong but rarely can be found there, as he is constantly on the go to find new opportunities. ▪

1993 - Rice University Fellowship, by Lars Lerup, Dean

1989 - American Institute of Architects Colorado Anniversary Fellowship

1988 - Dana Giffen Soper Memorial Fellowship

# Competitions

| | | |
|---|---|---|
| 1st Prize Civic Cultural Complex, Singapore | 2007 |
| 1st Prize U-BORA Towers Complex, Dubai | 2006 |
| 1st Prize Oceanscape Shams, Abu Dhabi | 2006 |
| 1st Prize Solidere Development Block 20, Beirut, Lebanon | 2006 |
| 1st Prize Ocean Heights Two, Dubai | 2005 |
| 1st Prize Grand Marco Polo Hotel, Beijing | 2005 |
| 1st Prize The Legs, Middle East | 2005 |
| 1st Prize Jebel Hafeet Hotel, Al Ain, UAE | 2005 |
| 1st Prize Khaldeya Mixed (Dancing Tower), Abu Dhabi | 2005 |
| 2nd Prize Dong Zhi Men Mixed-Use Development, Beijing | 2005 |
| 2nd Prize Xian Residential Development, Xian | 2005 |
| 1st Prize Ocean Heights Residential Tower, Dubai | 2004 |

Publications

New Architecture in the Middle East, Dancing Towers, The Legs, Ocean Heights Two, Apr 2008

Architecture in the Emirates, Dancing Towers & Pentominium, Oct 2007

Future World Skyline, The Legs, U-Bora, Aug 2007

Perspective, "40 under 40" - Andrew Bromberg, Jul 2007

MGS Architecture, Empire Tower, Jun/Jul 2007

Die Welt, Pentominium, Jun 18, 2007

Architecture Plus, Emaar Towers, May 2007

Ottagano, Dancing Towers, May 2007

World Architecture News.com, Pentominium, May 18, 2007

Mark, Empire Tower & The Legs, Apr/May 2007

MGS Architecture, U-Bora, Apr/May 2007

Sustain Magazine, The Legs, Mar 1, 2007

Interior + Design Magazine Moscow, The Legs, Mar 2007

Hinge Magazine, Ocean Heights One, Feb 2007

The Big Project, U-Bora, Issue 2, 2007

Elle Décor Russia, The Legs, Feb 2007

Word Architecture News.com, U-Bora, Feb 26, 2007

Ediliportale.com, Emaar Towers, Feb 26, 2007

Ediliportale.com, Dancing Towers, Feb 19, 2007

Archiportale.com, Dancing Towers, Feb 16, 2007

Archiportale.com, Emaar Towers, Feb 13, 2007

Word Architecture News.com, Empire Tower, Feb 6, 2007

Tall Buildings, Ocean Heights One, Jan 30, 2007

| | |
|---|---|
| **1st Prize** Sunshine 100, Residential Development, Chongqing | 2004 |
| **1st Prize** Damac Headquarters, Dubai | 2004 |
| **Shortlisted** West Kowloon Cultural District, Hong Kong | 2003 |
| **1st Prize** North Star Mixed-Use Development, Beijing | 2003 |
| **1st Prize** Foshan Media Center, Foshan | 2003 |
| **2nd Prize** Luo Xi Residential Development, Guangzhou | 2003 |
| **1st Prize** Goldfield San Lin Residential, Shanghai | 2003 |
| **1st Prize** Zhongguan International Plaza, Beijing | 2003 |
| **1st Prize** Workers Daily, Beijing | 2003 |
| **1st Prize** Szechuan Financial Corporation, Chengdu | 2002 |
| **1st Prize** Beijing International Plaza, Beijing | 2002 |
| **Shortlisted** Hong Kong Tamer Government Headquarters, Hong Kong | 2002 |
| **1st Prize** Chinese Overseas Bank Headquarters, Taipei | 2001 |

**Archiportale.com,** The Legs, Jan 22, 2007

**BD World Architecture,** The Legs, Jan 2007

**World Architecture News.com,** Ocean Heights One, Emaar Towers, Jacel Hafeet, Jan 2007

**Cityscape Dubai Magazine,** "Aedas Building Distinctive Skyline" Dec 2006

**Costa - Urola,** "Bromberg visits Zarautz Y Salberdin", Dec 2006

**South China Morning Post,** U-Bora, Sept 20, 2006

**Gulf News,** Ocean Heights Two, Oct 31, 2006

**Construir Magazine,** Dancing Towers, Nov 30, 2006

**South China Morning Post,** "Hong Kong Architects Reach For The Sky In Dubai", Aug 7, 2006

**Construction Week,** "Legs project akimbo as client rethinks designs", Jun 24, 2006

**Property Weekly,** "South Korean Developer Sees Great Promise in Dubai", Jun 14, 2006

**Hinge Magazine,** The Legs, Mar 13, 2006

**Tall Buildings: Europe, the Middle East and Africa,** Ocean Heights One, 2006

**101 of the World's Tallest Buildings,** Ocean Heights One, 2006

**The Architects' Journal,** "Zaha and Aedas Think Along Similar Lines in Middle East", Jun 28, 2006

**Perspective,** North Star, May 2006

**Architecture @ 07 BCI Asia,** North Star, Mar 2006

**Perspective,** Ocean Heights One & Two, Apr 2006

**Architectural Record,** "South Terminal Expansion Project – Seattle Washington", Oct 2005

**Architecture China,** Ocean Heights One, May 25, 2005

**architecture+,** Ocean Heights One, May 19, 2005

**The Sunday Times,** Ocean Heights One, Apr 10, 2005

**Construction Week,** Ocean Heights One, Jan 29, 2005

**BD World Architecture,** "Top 200 Architecture Firms", Jan 2005

**BD World Architecture,** DAMAC Headquarters, Jan 2005

**The Standard,** "5,000 Luxury Flats For Cultural Hub", Nov 16, 2004

**Capital CEO,** "West Kowloon", Jul 2004

**Architectural Record,** "Reebok's New World Headquarters", 2002

**Architecture,** Reebok World Headquarters, Sept 2000

**Seattle Times,** "Art Spaces - Davidson Gallery", 1996

**Retrospect,** "A Prototypical House For Exhibition", 1994

**Architecture,** Denver International Airport, Aug 1994

**Architecture,** Boulder Public Library, Oct 1992

Just as his designs attract the attention of many, Andrew as a designer has drawn an international pool of design talent to work alongside him. The team is comprised of designers from North America, Europe and Asia. Many of who trained in selective schools or have honed their skills through practice in the design capitals of the world. With this collective ability and aptitude, the Aedas design team is responsible for bringing to life Andrew's visions, to a complete and comprehensive design level. ∎

Team

Andrew Bromberg
Ada Leung
Andy Lai
Andy Lu
Alex Dabringhausen
Albert Yu
Anthony Fok
Bahar Afshar
Benjamin Lee
Boran Agoston
Bosco Chu
Candy Chan
David Chan
David Fung

Judy Chan
Julie Valette
Karen Fung
Karen Pang
Karl Poon
Karma Barfungpa
Kevin Kasparek
Kyle Hyde
Leo Lau
Lyla Wu
Maffrine Ong
Martin Lai
Matthew Shao
Max Ng

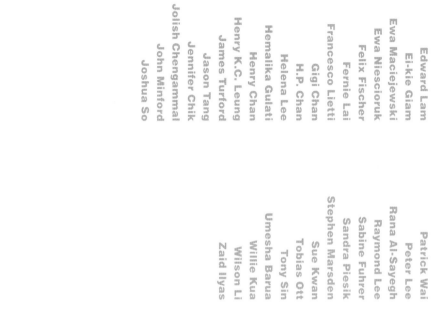

Derek McEneaney
Diarmaid Brophy
Edward Lam
Ei-kie Giam
Ewa Maciejewski
Ewa Niescioruk
Felix Fischer
Fernie Lai
Francesco Lietti
Gigi Chan
H.P. Chan
Helena Lee
Hemalika Gulati
Henry Chan
Henry K.C. Leung
James Turford
Jason Tang
Jennifer Chik
Joiish Chengammal
John Minford
Joshua So

May Leung
Mirco Pieroni
Patrick Wai
Peter Lee
Rana Al-Sayegh
Raymond Lee
Sabine Fuhrer
Sandra Piesik
Stephen Marsden
Sue Kwan
Tobias Ott
Tony Sin
Umesha Barua
Willie Kua
Wilson Li
Zaid Ilyas

# Aedas

Europe
U.K.
Warsaw
Moscow
Bahrain
Dubai
Mumbai
Almaty
Beijing
Chengdu
Macau
Shenzhen
Shanghai
Singapore
Hong Kong
**Asia**

**Americas**
New York
Washington D.C.
San Paulo

Currently the fourth largest architectural practice in the world, Aedas employs over 1,900 staff in 26 offices in the leading cities of London, Hong Kong, and New York, and in the rapidly growing economies of China, Southeast Asia, India, Kazakhstan, the United Arab Emirates, Russia, Poland, and Brazil. The global force offers a wealth of experience and expertise in Architecture, Interior Design, Urban Design, Landscape, and Graphic Design across a diverse range of market sectors.

In Europe, Aedas is driven by a growing complement of 680 staff throughout Britain in London and 10 other offices in the country, and a further 30 staff in Warsaw and Moscow. They have designed some of the largest and most important commercial and residential schemes in numerous regional cities in Britain. The practice also has a long history of producing notable successes on public finance initiative school projects, as well as a solid presence in healthcare, pharmaceutical, and bio-pharmaceutical industries. In Central and Eastern Europe, Aedas projects range from apartment blocks to major waterside residential developments, business parks, and hotels.

In Asia, Aedas employs over 890 staff and is now the largest architectural practice in Hong Kong, with offices also in Singapore, Beijing, Shanghai, Chengdu, Shenzhen, Macau, Mumbai, and Dubai.

Aedas is well known for its master planning and cutting-edge, high-density mixed commercial designs, particularly in China: notably, R&F City, with a GFA of 1.3 million sq m, in Beijing; HKr Properties' Fortune Plaza in Beijing; Hutchison Whampoa Properties' Mixed-Use Development, with a GFA of 2.4 million sq m, in Chengdu; and International Cruise Terminal in Xiamen.

Aedas brought this large-scale mixed-use expertise to the United Arab Emirates in 2004 and since then has carried out over 1.8 million sq m of adventurous designs in Dubai and Abu Dhabi. A selection of their diverse portfolio includes U-BORA Tower Mixed-Use Development in Business Bay, Dubai; Emaar Commercial Towers near Eurj, Dubai; Dubai TV Station; DAMAC Ocean Heights Residential Towers at Dubai Marina; and Dancing Towers Mixed-Commercial Complex in Abu Dhabi.

Aedas has a substantial track record of creating Asia's key transportation network, including 24 rail stations and 6 depots throughout Asia, 11 buildings at the HK International Airport, and 6 seaport terminals for the world's busiest container port in HK. Aedas has also migrated their rail expertise to the UAE for an enormous contract consisting of 43 rail stations and 2 depots.

Aedas has successfully transformed all of HongKong Land's retail portfolio in Central HK into the world's premier shopping precinct, and has vastly expanded the shopping and dining experience at the HK International Airport.

Aedas' retail expertise has opened huge opportunities for the practice to work on cultural, leisure, and entertainment projects. Key projects include several massive casino and resort integrated developments for Venetian Macau, West Kowloon Cultural Development, the Ngong Ping cable car journey to the world's biggest Buddha statue, and the redevelopment of Ocean Park.

In America, Aedas employs over 120 staff in New York; Washington, DC; and Sao Paulo. The practice is among the USA's leading architectural design firms, known for innovative solutions to complex design challenges. In North America, the firm is one of the premier designers of academic facilities and civic projects. The practice is currently serving as Design Architect for the World Trade Center Memorial Museum and as Associate Architect for the World Trade Center Memorial. In South America, Aedas has additional expertise in the design of commercial research and manufacturing facilities.

The rationale behind Aedas' globalization is to maximize the diversity each Aedas office offers. Under the Aedas brand, they have successfully transformed into a global force, providing a wealth of experience and expertise across a vast range of market sectors, including commercial, education, healthcare, hotels, museums, pharmaceuticals, residential, resorts and casinos, retail, and transportation. The value of sharing resources and exchanging ideas is evident in the collaboration of their offices for a major Mixed-Use Development in London, the Dubai Light Rail Network, and more recently the UK Cross Rail.

Contact

**Petchey Academy**
London, UK

**Sunny Bay Station**
Hong Kong, PRC

**MOMA Celeste Bartos**
**Film Preservation Center**
Hamlin, USA

**West Tower**
Liverpool, UK

**Fortune Plaza Phase 1**
Beijing, PRC

**Valeo Thermal Systems**
Detroit, USA

## Aedas

employs over 1,900 staff
allocated in 26 offices
across 4 continents

**EUROPE**

**London, UK**
T +44 (0)20 7837 9789
london@aedas.com

**Birmingham, UK**
T +44 (0)121 456 1591
birmingham@aedas.com

**Bristol, UK**
T +44 (0)117 929 9146
bristol@aedas.com

**Edinburgh, UK**
T +44 (0)131 226 7280
edinburgh@aedas.com

**Glasgow, UK**
T +44 (0)141 225 0655
glasgow@aedas.com

**Huddersfield, UK**
T +44 (0)1484 537 411
huddersfield@aedas.com

**Leeds, UK**
T +44 (0)113 385 8787
leeds@aedas.com

**Liverpool, UK**
T +44 (0)151 702 7000
liverpool@aedas.com

**Manchester, UK**
T +44 (0)161 828 7900
manchester@aedas.com

**Shrewsbury, UK**
T +44 (0)1743 283 000
shrewsbury@aedas.com

**Warsaw, Poland**
T +48 22 389 8500
warsaw@aedas.com

**Moscow, Russia**
T +44 7901 516 943
moscow@aedas.com

**ASIA**

**Hong Kong, PRC**
T +852 2861 1728
hongkong@aedas.com

**Beijing, PRC**
T +86 10 65862020
beijing@aedas.com

**Chengdu, PRC**
T +86 28 85190441
chengdu@aedas.com

**Macau, PRC**
T +853 755530
macau@aedas.com

**Shanghai, PRC**
T +86 21 61379200
shanghai@aedas.com

**Shenzhen, PRC**
T +86 755 82077385
shenzhen@aedas.com

**Singapore**
T +65 6734 4733
singapore@aedas.com

**Bahrain**
T +973 1721 8777
bahrain@aedas.com

**Dubai, UAE**
T +9714 3557233
dubai@aedas.com

**Almaty, Kazakhstan**
T +7 (810)3272 7334433
almaty@aedas.com

**Mumbai, India**
T +91 98 67751066
mumbai@aedas.com

**AMERICAS**

**New York, USA**
T +1 212 633 4700
newyork@aedas.com

**Washington DC, USA**
T +1 202 449 1190
washington@aedas.com

**Sao Paulo, Brazil**
T +55 11 3085 0655
saopaulo@aedas.com

**aedas.com**

# Acknowledgements

Special Thanks to:

Clients:

Bando E&C Ltd
Canela Brown
Capitaland
Capital Investment
China Overseas
City of Foshan
Damac Properties
Emaar
Empire Holdings
Gulf Development
North Star
Nameson Group
Rock Productions
Sama-Dubai
Sorouh
Sino-Land
Trident International Holding
Yin Xin Development

Construction Consultants:

Adrian L. Norman Ltd.
ALT Cladding Inc.
Anthony Hunt Engineers
Artec Consultants Inc.
Arup Engineers
AWA- Abhay Wadhwa Associates
BMT Fluid Mechanics Ltd.
Bo Steiber Lighting Design
Brewer Smith & Brewer Gulf
CCP Wind Engineering
De Leeuw Middle East
ECG: Engineering Consultant Group
EDAW
Fast Forward BIM Consulting Ltd.

Foresight
Form and Structure
Gallagher and Associates
(Façade Consultant for North Star) German
Group Consult International
GMS Consultants Pty Ltd.
Hanscomb
HBA: Hirsch Bedner Associates
Hyder Consulting Engineers
IBA: Ian Banham & Associates
IMG Artist
James Cubitt & Partners Consultants
(LDI for North Star)
Maunsell Engineering
Max Fordham Partnership
Meinhardt Engineering
MMC (Museum Management Consultants, Inc.)
Mott Connell Ltd.
Point of Design
Semaan & Soberman
Whitby and Bird Engineers
WSP Group

**Visual Consultants:**

Crystal Beijing
King 3-d models
Kerun Ip, the photographer
RJ models
Szrzepan Urbanowicz, Illustrator

**Andrew Bromberg Would Like to Thank:**

Everyone at Aedas, The Aedas Board, Jeffrey Ludlow, Francis Leung,
Joyce Lam, Judy Law and Especially Andrew's Team-The Force Behind.

Special thanks to all of our contributors: Larry Rouch,
Rodolphe el-Khoury and Michael Speaks.

# Production

**ORO** editions

Publishers of Architecture, Art, and Design
Gordon Goff & Oscar Riera Ojeda – Publishers
West Coast: PO Box 150338, San Rafael, CA 94915
East Coast: 143 South Second Street, Ste. 208,
Philadelphia, PA 19106
www.oroeditions.com
info@oroeditions.com

ISBN:
0-9774672-8-7
978-0-9774672-8-0

**Editing:**
Jeffrey Ludlow (jeffreylsaenz@yahoo.com)

**Graphic Design**
Jeffrey Ludlow (jeffreylsaenz@yahoo.com) with assistance from
Oscar Riera Ojeda (oscar@oroeditions.com)

**Project Coordination:**
Oscar Riera Ojeda

**Copy Editing:**
Nirmala Nataraj (nirmala@nirmalanataraj.com)

**Distribution**

In North America:
D.A.P.
Distributed Art Publishers,Inc.
155 Sixth Avenue, Second Floor
New York, NY 10013, USA

In Europe:
Art Books International
The Blackfriars Foundry, Unit 200
156 Blackfriars Road
SE1 8EN, United Kingdom

In Asia:
Page One Publishing Private Ltd.
20 Kaki Bukit View
Kaki Bukit Techpark II
Singapore 415967

**Project Assistance:**
Catherine Chan (catherine.chan@aedas.com), Joyce Lam (joyce.
lam@aedas.com), Judy Law (judy.law@aedas.com).

**Photo Research:**
Jeffrey Ludlow (Jeffrey.lsaenz@yahoo.com).

**Foreign Editions Sales:**
Gordon Goff (gordon@oroeditions.com).

**Production:**
Oscar Riera Ojeda, Gordon Goff.

**Color Separation and Printing:** ORO *editions* HK.
**Covers:** New-G Matt Art Paper 170 gsm.
**End Paper Sheet:** 150 Impressions Parchment.
**Text Paper:** New-G Matt Art Paper 170 gsm.

Cover Image: Middle East The Legs, pg. 052

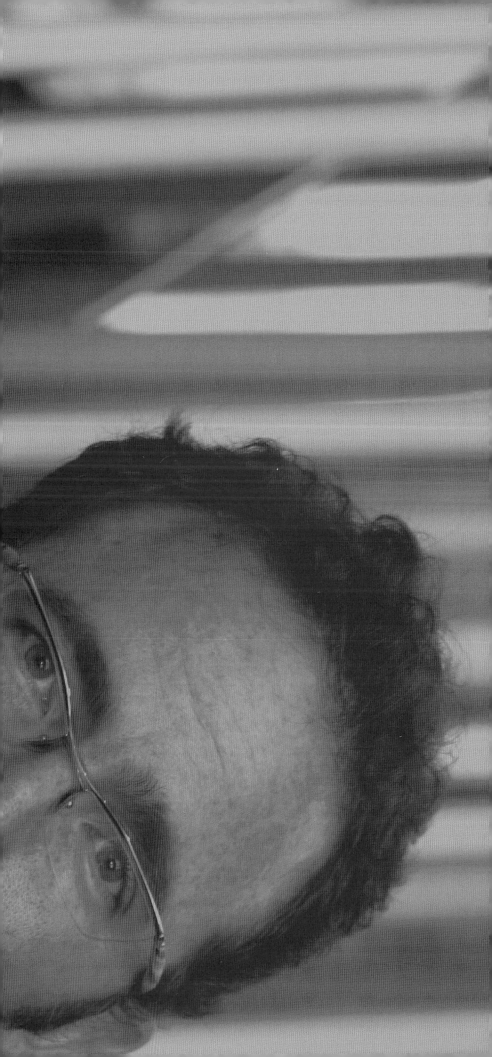

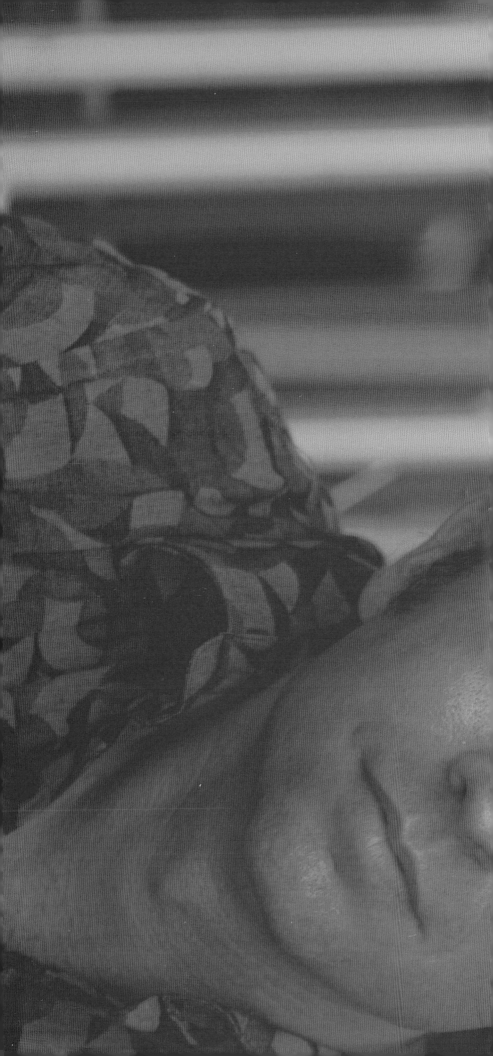

CW00956995